SUNY series on Sport, Culture, and Social Relations
CL Cole and Michael A. Messner, editors

Out of Play

Out of Play

Critical Essays on Gender and Sport

Michael A. Messner

Foreword by Raewyn Connell

State University of New York Press

Cover illustration courtesy of Kayann Legg/iStock.photo.com

Published by
State University of New York Press, Albany

For information, contact State University of New York Press, Albany, NY
www.sunypress.edu

Production by Kelli Williams
Marketing by Anne M. Valentine

Library of Congress Cataloging-in-Publication Data

Messner, Michael A.
Out of play : critical essays on gender and sport / Michael A. Messner;
foreword by Raewyn Connell.
    p. cm. — (SUNY series in sport, culture, and social relations)
    Includes bibliographical references and index.
    ISBN 978-0-7914-7171-5 (hardcover : alk. paper)
    ISBN 978-0-7914-7172-2 (pbk. : alk. paper)
    1. Sports—Social aspects. 2. Sex role. 3. Masculinity in sports. 4. Sex
discrimination in sports. 5. Athletes in mass media. 6. Television and sports.
I. Title

GV706.5M46 2007
306.4'83—dc22

2006101101

10 9 8 7 6 5 4 3 2 1

For Pierrette

Contents

Foreword

I t's not often that one author makes fundamental contributions to the understanding of three major problems that are usually thought about separately. Yet that's what Michael Messner has done in this book. It is a splendid collection of pathbreaking, profound, and passionate research.

The first problem is the nature of masculinity. Messner's early essays on this issue came as something of a bombshell. There wasn't even a proper research field of "men's studies" at the time, though the idea had occurred to a few people. There was a good deal of pop psychology in the man-as-mammoth-hunter vein, and a vague discussion of problems about the even vaguer "male role," but there was very little actual research.

Messner practically created the genre of precise, sophisticated life-history research on the construction of masculinity. His pioneering study of the lives of professional athletes, as we see in "Masculinities and Athletic Careers," negated the idea of a "natural" masculinity. These men *work* at making their masculinity, often suffering serious physical damage to do so. Equally important, they don't do it alone. The kind of masculinity they display isn't just an individual character trait; it's embedded in the institution they work in. For instance, the competitiveness they display is inherent in the fierce selection pressures that youngsters face as they move from local amateur sport to professional leagues. The violence that many of them display is structured into the body-contact sports, in Messner's memorable phrase, "When Bodies Are Weapons."

Messner has continued to do important work on the construction of gender, as we see in the charming essay on children and their images. We also see it in the subtle discussion of constructions of masculinity in beer advertising, and in the much blunter account of "televised sports manhood" in the editorial content of sports programming. The contrast between these two cases is extremely interesting, and suggests some of the tensions in representations of manhood that rely, as both advertising and sports commentary do, on public fantasies about gender.

Messner's thinking thus leads to a second major problem, the nature of modern sport and its relationship to other institutions, particularly the media.

Over many years, his research has illuminated sport as an institutional system and as a political arena. No one could doubt that he is one of the leading contemporary sociologists of sport.

I value his persistent concern with popular participation in sport. This issue is very much against the grain of our mainstream understanding of sport, focusing as we do on stars, heroic performances, and records. But who gets to play? And who is seen to play? Messner's research over a fifteen-year period, a kind of sociological audit of sports media, shows that there is a shattering mismatch between the rising mass participation in sport by girls and women and the almost complete failure of the U.S. mass media to report women's sport. Messner isn't content just to report this fact; he is concerned with the mechanisms behind it, and its political consequences. This concern equally comes through in the subtly observed essay on the media's "framing" of a story about a professional boxer, in which a moral fairytale about fall and redemption in relation to drugs completely eclipsed the story about the same man's bashing of his wife. Messner argues convincingly that the marginalizing of the issue of violence against women is an important lesson about how contemporary media work.

This leads to the third major problem, the nature of power, privilege, and exclusion in modern society. Here Messner is concerned with questions of social justice that have been central to modern social science and modern social movements. His focus is the "trilogy" of race, class, and gender. But he doesn't deal with them in a conventional way. Messner insists on the importance of "studying up," that is, focusing on the privileged, in any system of inequality. Therefore he discusses race in "White Men Misbehaving" as well as sexuality by focusing on heterosexual men as the bearers of privilege, disguised as "normality."

Messner is concerned with face-to-face, and body-to-body, interaction—negotiations in everyday life, embodied action in games, violence on the field, sexual and domestic violence. This gives his writing great power and immediacy. But he is also aware that in contemporary conditions, power and privilege are often, literally, mediated. So he is concerned with the sports/media/commercial "complex" in which corporate interests are deeply embedded. Messner's analysis of the role of "audience-building" in the strategies of this complex is particularly interesting as it depicts one of the mechanisms by which the inequalities of representation are produced.

Messner recognizes that power doesn't necessarily show its face plainly. Indeed it is often manifest more through what the media *don't* say (e.g., never mention domestic violence, don't show women's sport) than through what they do—though some of that is pretty obnoxious, too.

Messner is also aware that power often operates through symbolism. The earliest essay in this book, "Sports and Male Domination: The Female

Athlete as Contested Ideological Terrain," opens this discussion of gender symbolism and its politics. The professional athletes of Messner's life-history research were not, themselves, holders of great social power. Some had lost whatever money they had made, and some were suffering severely from the long-term damage to their bodies in professional sports. They served as *symbols* of power, more than holders of power. The same point applies to the recent study of the "televised sports manhood formula." As Messner and his co-authors note, this picture of power is actually a collective fiction, a strikingly narrow and archaic model of masculinity, whose appeal to an audience of men and boys is diagnostic of cultural problems. It tells us something about the uncertainties of masculine authority that have developed in the last generation—and not only in the United States. I have been reading this text in Australia, and I wince to see how accurately Messner's diagnosis matches the media representation of sports, and the patterns of sports professionals' lives, in my country as well. These issues are transnational.

I enjoy reading Messner's work, not only because it is first-class research, but also because it is extremely well written. There is precision about the facts, but there is also passion here, and a sustained desire to communicate. Messner really cares about his subject. He cares about the people he profiles, about gender equality and social justice. Hence, he moves from documenting inequalities and oppressive behaviors to thinking what to do about them. The essay "Scoring without Consent: Confronting Male Athletes' Sexual Violence" is a clear call to action, not contemplation. The same concern to redress injustice, and prevent injustice for the future, runs through the whole book.

This carries weight, in the world he is writing about, because Messner cares about sports, too. He knows their pleasures and benefits, for both children and adults. He is worried about the corruption of sport and the destruction of these benefits by commercial power, racial privilege and patriarchal dominance. He would like to see human physical recreation be participatory, nonsexist, nonviolent, and enjoyable. And why shouldn't it?

I salute a book that is rich in information, insight, and commitment. Sociology is often a grim subject, documenting oppression, marginalization, and the disappointment of hopes. Messner is the kind of intellectual who can face these realities, but can also come out the other side, to see the humane and democratic possibilities in human institutions such as sport. We need more like him.

Raewyn Connell
University of Sydney

Acknowledgments

I t's difficult to thank everyone who helped or inspired me over the course of the nearly two decades that these essays span. I do want to thank by name those who appear in this book as coauthors of particular chapters: Mark Stevens (chapter 7), William S. Solomon (chapter 8), Michele Dunbar and Darnell Hunt (chapter 9), Margaret Carlisle Duncan and Nicole Willms (chapter 10), and Jeff Montez de Oca (chapter 11). My collaborations with these valued colleagues, students, and former students deepened and broadened the value of these works, and their support and friendship enriched the experience of conducting research and writing.

I also want to thank CL Cole, with whom I have had the pleasure for many years of co-editing the SUNY Press series on Sport, Culture, and Social Relations that this book appears in. I also thank Nancy Ellegate, who has been a supportive and encouraging editor of this book, and of the series. Thanks to Nicole Willms for helping to compile the list of references. And thanks to the anonymous reviewers to whom SUNY sent the manuscript. I appreciate the support of all in making this "greatest hits" collection a reality.

In my writings, I frequently draw from my own life experiences—memories of my past as an athlete, questions that arise from past and current experiences as a sports spectator, or, more recently, observations I have had as a parent of boys who are playing in youth sports. I use these experiences in my writings as empirical examples, as analytic points of departure, and as emotional "hooks." I realize that using my own life experiences as "data" is a somewhat unconventional practice, perhaps even frowned upon in the social sciences. But I have consciously deployed this strategy in much of my writing for many years due to my engagement with feminism, which taught me the importance of connecting personal life to larger social issues. As a class-privileged, white, heterosexual man writing about gender, race, class, and sexual orientation issues, I think it's especially useful to put myself (strategically, I hope carefully, and only when useful) into my analysis—both as an exercise in self-reflexivity, and as a way to illuminate for readers how privilege works. This strategy never would have occurred to me, were it not for the groundwork laid by three-plus decades of feminism. I am indebted to the women's movement, and to feminist scholars who have substantially shifted the academic landscape in ways that have made the kind of work I do possible—including each and every essay in this book.

I dedicate this book to my USC sociology colleague, partner, lover, and wife Pierrette Hondagneu-Sotelo. To say that Pierrette doesn't care for sports is an understatement. It's a testament to her love for her sons that she has sat through as many soccer and baseball games as she has over the past dozen years. And it's a statement of her support for me that she has cheered me on, all along the way, as I conducted research and wrote the essays in this book. My respect for Pierrette's professional accomplishments, my appreciation for the love and work she devotes to our family, and my thanks for her support for my academic work just grows and grows.

Introduction

Gender and Sports

A couple of weeks ago, I went with my twelve-year-old son Sasha to watch a basketball game between USC (the university at which I teach) and Arizona State. Sasha and I were both enthralled with the action, and pleased that our team played well and won. And we were especially excited by the fact that after the game we got to meet the USC players, and had our souvenir basketballs signed by each of them. Sasha displays his autographed ball proudly on his bedroom dresser, next to his own baseball and soccer trophies; I have mine in my office. Tomorrow, we will bring two of Sasha's friends with us to watch the big USC–UCLA cross-town rivalry showdown. Sasha and I love the games, and we admire the players; indeed, we have season tickets and attend all of the home games. And there's nothing notable about this kind of fan connection to a team, except perhaps that it is USC's *women's* basketball program to which we are so attached.

Sasha is growing up in a world that has been substantially transformed by feminism. When I was a boy in the 1950s and early 1960s, sports seemed to be a world that belonged unambiguously to boys and men. My sisters didn't play; they cheered for the boys. And the few girls who were athletically inclined were often stigmatized for their interest in sport: maybe, it was whispered, they weren't real girls? These athletic girls offered little challenge to what seemed a natural equation between sports, men, and masculinity. Even if they had some athletic ability or interest, these girls were easily marginalized, since there were few, if any, opportunities for them to play organized sports anyway. Boys, it was thought, were naturally inclined to play sports, due to their inborn aggressiveness, muscularity, and competitiveness. Girls, it was believed, naturally lacked these traits and abilities. This was common knowledge.

1

Now, half a century later, this common knowledge has been seriously disrupted. We now have over three decades of scholarly research that shows how these beliefs in the essential differences between women and men were constructed through the routine operation of institutions, including organized sports. Boys' access to sports, coupled with girls' lack of access, literally shaped our bodies and thus our belief that men were naturally strong and athletic, while women were naturally frail and in need of protection—a belief that not-so-incidentally corresponded with the post–World War II pushing of women out of the labor force and into the cult of motherhood and homemaking. But feminism, coupled with large-scale shifts in national and global economies, undermined the structural basis of this postwar middle-class ideal of "the family" as a heterosexual couple with a breadwinning husband and a homemaking wife/mother. Since that time, we have witnessed an historic sea change in gender relations, and sport has been an important site of these changes.

Worldwide, women's sports participation began to grow dramatically in the early 1970s. In the United States, millions of girls now enthusiastically participate in youth soccer, softball, basketball, and other community sports. High school sports are no longer totally dominated by boys. In 1971, only 294,000 U.S. high school girls played interscholastic sports, compared with 3.7 million boys. By 2005, the participation gap had narrowed: 4.1 million boys and 2.9 million girls now play interscholastic sports. This trend is echoed in college sports participation rates. In 1972, the year Title IX was enacted, there were only a little over two women's athletics teams per school at the college level. By 2004, the number had risen to 8.32 teams per NCAA school. From 2000 to 2004, 631 new women's teams were added in U.S. universities. Women's participation rates in the Olympic Games have risen dramatically over the past three decades, and women's professional sports have also grown.

However, we have not yet achieved anything close to equality in sport. Girls have an expanding array of opportunities to play sports, but sometimes the coaching they receive is substandard, compared to the boys. Girls are channeled at an early age away from playing baseball to softball, a move that raises questions about whether "separate" forms of sport can really ever be "equal." In middle schools and high schools, girls still too often have substandard athletic facilities, and have to resort to legal action to push their schools to move toward fair and equal treatment for girls. Few U.S. colleges and universities are in compliance with Title IX, as funding for recruitment, scholarships, and ongoing support of women's athletics teams lags far behind that of men's teams. At the societal level, conservative politicians have continued to attempt to chip away at Title IX, supported in part by representatives of men's college sports who claim that "quota systems" used by colleges to move toward equity for women's sports have led to discrimination against men.

While this sluggish pace and contested movement toward fairness and equity for female participants in sport might be frustrating to some, the mainstream electronic media's continued silence surrounding women's sports is outright stunning. There are several minutes devoted to sports on every televised news broadcast. Yet only about 6% of that sports news time is devoted to coverage of women's sports. Cable television networks like ESPN and Fox Sports have emerged in recent years, as have radio talk shows devoted entirely to sports coverage. But a miniscule proportion of airtime (e.g., only about 2% of ESPN's popular sports highlights show *SportsCenter*) is devoted to coverage of women's sports. A sizable section of my daily newspaper is devoted to sports coverage. Yet rarely does a women's sports story appear before page 4 of the sports section, and most often that page 4 story will be short and without a photo. Sports imagery and talk are omnipresent, it seems. But in terms of the dominant cultural imagery of sports in the mass media, sports is still *men's sports.*

SPORTS AS A GENDER CONSTRUCTION SITE

In the past decade or so, the study of gender and sports has moved beyond the notion that masculinity and femininity are "sex roles" that people simply absorb during childhood and then bring to their sports experiences in the same ways that they might bring different-sized baseball bats or various kinds of soccer shoes. Instead, gender is seen as a multilayered social process that is not simply part of the personality structure of individuals, but also a fundamental aspect of everyday group interactions, institutions, and the cultural symbols that swirl around us. People are not passive dupes in gender systems; rather, we are active participants in creating gender. In the language of social theory, people exercise *agency* in the creation of everyday social life. Agency is often *reproductive:* when our actions are consistent with traditions and conventions of existing gender differences and hierarchies, we help to reproduce those existing relations. Sometimes, agency is *resistant;* when our actions disrupt existing gender differences or hierarchies, we contribute to changing existing gender relations. Often, reproductive and resistant agencies are simultaneously evident in contemporary sport. We see this paradoxical simultaneity operating every day: when a heavily muscled woman bodybuilder gets breast implants in order to appear strong *and* conventionally heterosexy; when coed community softball teams flourish, yet informal practices reinforce gender hierarchies (like men cutting in front of women teammates to catch fly balls); when women's college sports grows by leaps and bounds, but head coaching shifts from a primarily female profession to one dominated by men.

In short, sport is a "contested terrain," in which gender is being constructed in complex and often contradictory ways. In Part I of this book, I focus on sport as a contested "gender construction site." In the first chapter, I employ a micro-level approach to examining gender construction in children's sport. Through an examination of an interaction between four- and five-year-old boys' and girls' soccer teams, I explore how, even in this era of greater equity for girls and boys, sport still provides a context for reproductive agencies that reconstruct dichotomous views of girls and boys as binary opposite sex categories. In chapter 2, I examine sport in a broad historical and cultural frame, and argue that in the late twentieth century, the female athlete challenged patriarchal assumptions and became a contested symbol of gender meanings. The mere fact of women playing sports in great numbers challenges narrow and constraining definitions of femininity. But the question remains whether women's increased athleticism will be contained or ghettoized (as women's early twentieth-century surge in sports participation eventually was), or whether it will contribute to larger feminist social transformations. And a more radical question concerns whether the liberal quest for equal (but usually separate) opportunities for women in sport might leave men's sports largely intact and able to continue to reproduce hegemonic masculinity, replete with its traditions of violence, sexism, homophobia, and militarism.

SPORT AND THE MATRIX OF DOMINATION

A generation of scholarship has fully established that gender is omni-present, in all institutions and interactions. However, this is not to say that gender is always in all situations the most important dynamic. To the contrary, gender varies in salience from situation to situation. And this is because people have multiple identities, shaped not only by gender, but also by social class, sexual orientation, race and ethnicity, national origin, and other factors. Likewise, institutions are structured simultaneously by multiple systems of inequality. Race, social class, gender, and sexuality can be seen as semiautonomous systems of social inequality and difference, and they structure each other in complex and sometimes contradictory ways. So, for instance, though it is true that sports participation usually has a "masculinizing" effect on boys and men, are gay athletes masculinized in precisely the same ways as heterosexually identified boys? Does a sexualized image in a popular sports magazine of an African American woman athlete—say, tennis star Serena Williams— have the same meanings to readers as a sexualized image of blonde white tennis star Maria Sharapova?

Feminist scholars have deployed an array of concepts to attempt to understand the simultaneity of race, class, gender, and sexual orientation:

"intersectionality," and the "matrix of domination" seem the most accepted terms among sociologists. In Part II, I explore the ways that gender is constructed in sport, with an eye to how gender intersects with other systems of inequality. In chapter 3, based on a life-history study of male former athletes, I examine how men's different socioeconomic backgrounds structure their experiences in sport in ways that shape different masculinities. In chapter 4, I argue that black feminist thought offers us a fresh standpoint through which we can better understand the relationship between race and gender in contemporary sport. In chapter 5, based in part on a deconstruction of a story from my own high school sports experiences, I examine the ways that sport has tended to construct dominant forms of masculinity and femininity that are explicitly tied to heterosexuality. That heterosexuality is *actively constructed* in sport—just as dominant forms of race and gender are—illustrates the reproductive power of the institution. But we can also see the cracks and fissures in this matrix of domination in the rising existence of gay, lesbian, and queer sports. Sport is a contested terrain not only of gender relations, but also of racial, class, and sexual relations as well.

BODIES AND VIOLENCE

As girls and women become more integrated into mainstream sport, they reap more of the benefits of sports, such as social status, healthy exercise, bodily empowerment, self-confidence, and even (occasionally) money. But they also are increasingly facing some of the dangers and costs of athletic competition, such as pain and injury that might lead to permanent physical debility. In gymnastics, ice skating, or other individual sports in which very young girls participate at highly competitive levels, athletes face the dangers of eating disorders, amenorrhea (which is often accompanied by low bone density), and playing with painful injuries—all reinforced by sometimes abusive coaches. Women competing in track and field and other sports based on explosive strength are now faced with a decision to take anabolic steroids or other performance-enhancing drugs, in order to establish a competitive edge. Just as with men's sports, at the highest levels women's sports increasingly demonstrate an ironic paradox: the athlete is viewed as an icon of health, but the reality is that the high-level athlete's body is constructed through processes that are often very unhealthy.

While women athletes' bodies are increasingly treated instrumentally, as machines that are constructed for high-level performance, just as men's bodies are, what we see less of thus far in women's sports is the construction of athletic bodies as violent weapons to be used against other bodies. Men's sports—especially the "combat sports" of football, boxing, and ice hockey—tend to glorify and reward violence. Part III examines the meanings of violence in

men's sports. In chapter 6, I draw from life-history research with former athletes to reflect on how dominant modes of sport construct violence as "natural." Men are rewarded when they successfully objectify their own bodies as
weapons to be used against opponents, who are in turn objectified as legitimate objects of violence. In chapter 7, coauthor Mark Stevens and I examine
the dynamics of off-field violence perpetrated by male athletes—especially
sexual violence against women. We discuss how the culture of the athletic
team constructs sexist attitudes and fears that sometimes result in assaults
against women. And we draw from clinical work to discuss how the culture of
men's athletics can be changed to eliminate or reduce the rates of sexual
assault committed by athletes.

GENDERED IMAGERY

We are surrounded and inundated with images and talk about sports.
Conventional mass media (network television, radio, newspapers, and magazines) devote a huge amount of time to the coverage of sports. New media,
especially cable television and the Internet) provide an ever-widening
range of sports information that is targeted to specific demographic groups.
But what do these images and stories tell us about gender? The chapters in
Part IV are concerned with how gender is constructed in the dominant
sports media.

    In chapter 8, my colleague William Solomon and I employ the concept
of "news frames" to analyze the ways that the print media covered a story of a
famous athlete's admitted acts of violence against his wife. Chapter 9 is based
on a study that I conducted with colleagues Michele Dunbar and Darnell
Hunt of televised sports that boys watch. In analyzing an array of sports programs with their accompanying commercials, we concluded that together
these shows offer boys a reasonably coherent (and narrowly backwards) "formula" for what it means to be a man (and, by extension, what roles boys and
men might expect women to play). Chapter 10 reports on the latest installment of data from a longitudinal study of televised sports news and highlights
shows, conducted with my colleagues Margaret Carlisle Duncan and Nicole
Willms. We show how, from 1989, when we first gathered data for this study,
through our most recent study in 2004, the proportions of television news
time devoted to women's sports has remained almost identical, and very low.
Finally, chapter 11 is a study conducted with Jeffrey Montez de Oca of the
gender and sexual imagery in beer and liquor advertising in the televised
broadcast of the Super Bowl, and in the *Sports Illustrated* swimsuit issue.
These "mega sports media events," we argue, present their target audience of
young males with images of men as "losers" who can resuscitate their fragile

sense of manhood by consuming the right kinds of beer, while bonding with their male buddies and avoiding emotional commitment to women, who are best related to as sexual objects.

The chapters in this book were written between 1988 and 2006. Though some of the names of famous athletes from the earlier articles now might appear to be of historic rather than of current interest, it strikes me that the major themes cutting across this nearly two-decade time period are alive and well indeed. Girls' and women's sports participation continues to grow, yet women's sports advocates must continue to fight for more opportunities for girls, and continually expend energy to defend Title IX against periodic challenges by conservative leaders. The mass media continues its deafening silence around women's sports. In this morning's *Los Angeles Times,* I note that the only mention of women's sports is a short piece on page 6 on a WNBA game, and a brief note on page 2 that former gymnastics champion Nadia Comenici has given birth to a baby. Men's sports continues to grow, too, and continues to generate both excitement and problems. That same morning paper tells the story of yet another performance-enhancing drug use scandal in Major League Baseball. Within the past few weeks, a male athlete from my university's championship football team was arrested for an alleged rape, while three men from Duke University's lacrosse team are under indictment for an alleged sexual assault of a female exotic dancer who had been hired by members of the team. Meanwhile, several universities are investigating athletic teams (some of them men's teams, some of them women's teams) for engaging in sexually humiliating and sometimes dangerous hazing ceremonies.

The tremendous and enthusiastic growth of girls' and women's sports in the United States and in many other parts of the world is, I believe, here to stay. But it is still an open question just what kinds of roles women's sports will play in today's terrain of shifting social relations. Though I believe questions of simple numerical equity are important, it's equally important to critically analyze the underlying cultural values and organizing structures of sport. Too often when we think of gender and sport, we simply debate the question of what's a fair way to divide up the institutional pie. As many of the essays in this book suggest, I think we need simultaneously to ask about the ingredients of the pie, and come up with some new recipes—and that means critically analyzing the fundamental structure and values of *men's sports,* rather than uncritically taking it as a standard within which women should strive for equal opportunities. It's my hope that this book will make a contribution to this sort of radical rethinking of sport.

Part I

Sport as a Gender Construction Site

1

Barbie Girls versus Sea Monsters

Children Constructing Gender

Author's note: Some sociologists discover their best ideas right under their noses. I have found that being a "participant observer" in the everyday lives of my two sons has provided me with some of my most useful observations. This chapter is based not on a systematic research study, but rather on a serendipitous observation I made at the opening ceremony of my then six-year-old son Sasha's soccer season. When I saw a team of boys and team of girls having a brief and hilarious conflict over a huge Barbie doll, and observed the response of the kids' parents, it brought out the gender sociologist in me. The fact that most of the adults around me apparently found pleasure in interpreting this moment as evidence of natural differences between boys and girls led me to an examination of how the social context had shaped this moment, making this kind of highly gendered interaction between boys and girls possible. I used this moment of gender construction to explore the utility of a tri-level theoretical analysis. Most obvious to me initially was that an interactionist perspective was useful in describing how the children and the parents actively "do" or "perform" gender. But I also wanted to explore how institutional context (in this case, a sex-segregated youth sports league) and familiar cultural symbols (gendered team names and especially Barbie) create contexts that shape the possibilities of group interactions. Gender, this perspective suggests, is not simply something that individuals "have"—like the color of their eyes—rather, it is actively constructed by groups, within institutional and cultural contexts that are themselves organized by gender, and saturated with gender meanings.

In the past decade, studies of children and gender have moved toward greater levels of depth and sophistication (e.g., Jordan and Cowan 1995; McGuffy and Rich 1999; Thorne 1993). In her groundbreaking work on children and gender, Thorne (1993) argued that previous theoretical frameworks, although helpful, were limited: The top-down (adult-to-child) approach of socialization theories tended to ignore the extent to which children are active agents in the creation of their worlds—often in direct or partial opposition to values or "roles" to which adult teachers or parents are attempting to socialize them. Developmental theories also had their limits due to their tendency to ignore group and contextual factors while overemphasizing "the constitution and unfolding of *individuals* as boys or girls" (Thorne 1993, 4). In her study of grade-school children, Thorne demonstrated a dynamic approach that examined the ways in which children actively construct gender in specific social contexts of the classroom and the playground. Working from emergent theories of performativity, Thorne developed the concept of "gender play" to analyze the social processes through which children construct gender. Her level of analysis was not the individual but "*group life—* with social relations, the organization and meanings of social situations, the collective practices through which children and adults create and recreate gender in their daily interactions" (Thorne 1993, 4).

A key insight from Thorne's research is the extent to which gender varies in salience from situation to situation. Sometimes, children engage in "relaxed, cross sex play"; other times—for instance, on the playground during boys' ritual invasions of girls' spaces and games—gender boundaries between boys and girls are activated in ways that variously threaten or (more often) reinforce and clarify these boundaries. However, these varying moments of gender salience are not free-floating; they occur in social contexts such as schools, in which gender is formally and informally built into the division of labor, power structure, rules, and values (Connell 1987).

The purpose of this chapter is to use an observation of a highly salient gendered moment of group life among four- and five-year-old children as a point of departure for exploring the conditions under which gender boundaries become activated and enforced. I was privy to this moment as I observed my five-year-old son's first season (including weekly games and practices) in organized soccer. Unlike the long-term, systematic ethnographic studies of children conducted by Thorne (1993) or Adler and Adler (1998), this essay takes one moment as its point of departure. I do not present this moment as somehow "representative" of what happened throughout the season; instead, I examine this as an example of what Hochschild (1994, 4) calls "magnified moments," which are "episodes of heightened importance, either epiphanies, moments of intense glee or unusual insight, or moments in which things go intensely but meaningfully wrong. In either case, the moment stands out; it is metaphorically rich, unusually elaborate and often echoes [later]."A magnified moment in daily life offers a window into the social construction of reality. It presents researchers with an opportunity to excavate gendered meanings and processes through an analysis of institutional and cultural contexts. The single empirical observation that serves as the point of departure for this essay was made during a morning. Immediately after the event, I recorded my observations with detailed notes. I later slightly revised the notes after developing the photographs that I took at the event.

I will first describe the observation—an incident that occurred as a boys' four- and five-year-old soccer team waited next to a girls' four-and five-year-old soccer team for the beginning of the community's American Youth Soccer League (AYSO) season's opening ceremony. I will then examine this moment using three levels of analysis.

1. *The interactional level:* How do children "do gender," and what are the contributions and limits of theories of performativity in understanding these interactions?
2. *The level of structural context:* How does the gender regime, particularly the larger organizational level of formal sex segregation of AYSO, and the concrete, momentary situation of the opening ceremony provide a context that variously constrains and enables the children's interactions?
3. *The level of cultural symbol:* How does the children's shared immersion in popular culture (and their differently gendered locations in this immersion) provide symbolic resources for the creation, in this situation, of apparently categorical differences between the boys and the girls?

Although I will discuss these three levels of analysis separately, I hope to demonstrate that interaction, structural context, and culture are simultaneous and mutually intertwined processes, none of which supersedes the others.

BARBIE GIRLS VERSUS SEA MONSTERS

It is a warm, sunny Saturday morning. Summer is coming to a close, and schools will soon reopen. As in many communities, this time of year in this small, middle- and professional-class suburb of Los Angeles is marked by the beginning of another soccer season. This morning, 156 teams, with approximately 1,850 players ranging from four to seventeen years old, along with another 2,000 to 3,000 parents, siblings, friends, and community dignitaries have gathered at the local high school football and track facility for the annual AYSO opening ceremonies. Parents and children wander around the perimeter of the track to find the assigned station for their respective teams. The coaches muster their teams and chat with parents. Eventually, each team will march around the track, behind their new team banner, as they are announced over the loudspeaker system and applauded by the crowd. For now, though, and for the next forty-five minutes to an hour, the kids, coaches, and parents must stand, mill around, talk, and kill time as they await the beginning of the ceremony.

The Sea Monsters is a team of four- and five-year-old boys. Later this day, they will play their first-ever soccer game. A few of the boys already know each other from preschool, but most are still getting acquainted. They are wearing their new uniforms for the first time. Like other teams, they were assigned team colors—in this case, green and blue—and asked to choose their team name at their first team meeting, which occurred a week ago. Although they preferred "Blue Sharks," they found that the name was already taken by another team and settled on "Sea Monsters." A grandmother of one of the boys created the spiffy team banner, which was awarded a prize this morning. As they wait for the ceremony to begin, the boys inspect and then proudly pose for pictures in front of their new award-winning team banner. The parents stand a few feet away—some taking pictures, some just watching. The parents are also getting to know each other, and the common currency of topics is just how darned cute our kids look, and will they start these ceremonies soon before another boy has to be escorted to the bathroom?

Queued up one group away from the Sea Monsters is a team of four- and five-year-old girls in green and white uniforms. They, too, will play their first game later today, but, for now, they are awaiting the beginning of the opening ceremony. They have chosen the name "Barbie Girls," and they also have a spiffy new team banner. But the girls are pretty much ignoring their banner, for they have created another, more powerful symbol around which to rally. In fact, they are the only team among the 156 marching today with a team float—a red Radio Flyer wagon base, on which sits a Sony boom box playing music, and a three-foot-plus-tall Barbie doll on a rotating pedestal. Barbie is dressed in the team colors—indeed, she sports a custom-made green-and-white cheerleader-style outfit, with the Barbie Girls' names written on the skirt. Her normally all-blonde hair has been streaked with Barbie Girl green and features a green bow, with white polka dots. Several of the girls on the team also have supplemented their uniforms with green bows in their hair.

The volume on the boom box nudges up and four or five girls begin to sing a Barbie song. Barbie is now slowly rotating on her pedestal, and as the girls sing more gleefully and more loudly, some of them begin to hold hands and walk around the float, in sync with Barbie's rotation. Other same-aged girls from other teams are drawn to the celebration and, eventually, perhaps a dozen girls are singing the Barbie song. The girls are intensely focused on Barbie, on the music, and on their mutual pleasure.

As the Sea Monsters mill around their banner, some of them begin to notice, and then begin to watch and listen as the Barbie Girls rally around their float. At first, the boys are watching as individuals, seemingly unaware of each other's shared interest. Some of them stand with arms at their sides, slack-jawed, as though passively watching a television show. I notice slight smiles on a couple of their faces, as though they are drawn to the Barbie Girls' celebratory fun. Then, with side glances, some of the boys begin to notice each other's attention on the Barbie Girls. Their faces begin to show signs of distaste. One of them yells out, "NO BARBIE!" Suddenly, they all begin to move—jumping up and down, nudging and bumping one other—and join into a group chant: "NO BARBIE! NO BARBIE! NO BARBIE!" They now appear to be every bit as gleeful as the girls, as they laugh, yell, and chant against the Barbie Girls.

The parents watch the whole scene with rapt attention. Smiles light up the faces of the adults, as our glances sweep back and forth, from the sweetly celebrating Barbie Girls to the aggressively protesting Sea Monsters. "They are so different!" exclaims one smiling mother approvingly. A male coach offers a more in-depth analysis: "When I was in college," he says, "I took these classes from professors who showed us research that showed that boys and girls are the same. I believed it, until I had my own kids and saw how different they are." "Yeah," another dad responds, "Just look at them! They are so different!"

The girls, meanwhile, show no evidence that they hear, see, or are even aware of the presence of the boys who are now so loudly proclaiming their opposition to the Barbie Girls' songs and totem. They continue to sing, dance, laugh, and rally around the Barbie for a few more minutes, before they are called to reassemble in their groups for the beginning of the parade.

After the parade, the teams reassemble on the infield of the track but now in a less organized manner. The Sea Monsters once again find themselves in the general vicinity of the Barbie Girls and take up the "NO BARBIE!" chant again. Perhaps put out by the lack of response to their chant, they begin to dash, in twos and threes, invading the girls' space, and yelling menacingly. With this, the Barbie Girls have little choice but to recognize the presence of the boys—some look puzzled and shrink back, some engage the boys and chase them off. The chasing seems only to incite more excitement among the boys. Finally, parents intervene and defuse the situation, leading their children off to their cars, homes, and eventually to their soccer games.

THE PERFORMANCE OF GENDER

In the past decade, especially since the publication of Judith Butler's highly influential *Gender Trouble* (1990), it has become increasingly fashionable among academic feminists to think of gender not as some "thing" that one "has" (or not) but rather as situationally constructed through the performances of active agents. The idea of gender as performance analytically foregrounds the agency of individuals in the construction of gender, thus highlighting the situational fluidity of gender: here, conservative and reproductive, there, transgressive and disruptive. Surely, the Barbie Girls versus Sea Monsters scene described above can be fruitfully analyzed as a moment of crosscutting and mutually constitutive gender performances: The girls—at least at first glance—appear to be performing (for each other?) a conventional four- to five-year-old version of emphasized femininity. At least on the surface, there appears to be nothing terribly transgressive here. They are just "being girls," together. The boys initially are unwittingly constituted as an audience for the girls' performance but quickly begin to perform (for each other?—for the girls, too?) a masculinity that constructs itself in opposition to Barbie, and to the girls, as not feminine. They aggressively confront—first through loud verbal chanting, eventually through bodily invasions—the girls' ritual space of emphasized femininity, apparently with the intention of disrupting its upsetting influence. The adults are simultaneously constituted as an adoring audience for their children's performances and as parents who perform for each other by sharing and mutually affirming their experience-based narratives concerning the natural differences between boys and girls.

In this scene, we see children performing gender in ways that constitute themselves as two separate, opposed groups (boys vs. girls) and parents performing gender in ways that give the stamp of adult approval to the children's performances of difference, while constructing their own ideological narrative that naturalizes this categorical difference. In other words, the parents do not seem to read the children's performances of gender as social constructions of gender. Instead, they interpret them as the inevitable unfolding of natural, internal differences between the sexes. That this moment occurred when it did and where it did is explicable, but not entirely with a theory of performativity. As Walters (1999, 250) argues,

> The performance of gender is never a simple voluntary act.... Theories of gender as play and performance need to be intimately and systematically connected with the power of gender (really, the power of male power) to constrain, control, violate, and configure. Too often, mere lip service is given to the specific historical, social, and political configurations that make certain conditions possible and others constrained.

Indeed, feminist sociologists operating from the traditions of symbolic interactionism and/or Goffmanian dramaturgical analysis have anticipated the recent interest in looking at gender as a dynamic performance. As early as 1978, Kessler and McKenna developed a sophisticated analysis of gender as an everyday, practical accomplishment of people's interactions. Nearly a decade later, West and Zimmerman (1987) argued that in people's everyday interactions, they were "doing gender" and, in so doing, they were constructing masculine dominance and feminine deference. As these ideas have been taken up in sociology, their tendencies toward a celebration of the "freedom" of agents to transgress and reshape the fluid boundaries of gender have been put into play with theories of social structure (e.g., Lorber 1994; Risman 1998). In these accounts, gender is viewed as enacted or created through everyday interactions, but crucially, as Walters suggested above, within "specific historical, social, and political configurations" that constrain or enable certain interactions.

The parents' response to the Barbie Girls versus Sea Monsters performance suggests one of the main limits and dangers of theories of performativity. Lacking an analysis of structural and cultural context, performances of gender can all too easily be interpreted as free agents' acting out the inevitable surface manifestations of a natural inner essence of sex difference. An examination of structural and cultural contexts, though, reveals that there was nothing inevitable about the girls' choice of Barbie as their totem, or in the boys' response to it.

THE STRUCTURE OF GENDER

In the entire subsequent season of weekly games and practices, I never once saw adults point to a moment in which boy and girl soccer players were doing the *same* thing and exclaim to each other, "Look at them! They are *so similar!*" The actual similarity of the boys and the girls, evidenced by nearly all of the kids' routine actions throughout a soccer season—playing the game, crying over a skinned knee, scrambling enthusiastically for their snacks after the games, spacing out on a bird or a flower instead of listening to the coach at practice—is a key to understanding the salience of the Barbie Girls versus Sea Monsters moment for gender relations. In the face of a multitude of moments that speak to similarity, it was this anomalous Barbie Girls versus Sea Monsters moment—where the boundaries of gender were so clearly enacted—that the adults seized to affirm their commitment to difference. It is the kind of moment—to use Lorber's (1994, 37) phrase—where "believing is seeing," where we selectively "see" aspects of social reality that tell us a truth that we prefer to believe, such as the belief in categorical sex difference. No matter that our eyes do not see evidence of this truth most of the rest of the time.

In fact, it was not so easy for adults to actually "see" the empirical reality of sex similarity in everyday observations of soccer throughout the season.

That is due to one overdetermining factor: an institutional context that is characterized by informally structured sex segregation among the parent coaches and team managers, and by formally structured sex segregation among the children. The structural analysis developed here is indebted to Acker's (1990) observation that organizations, even while appearing "gender neutral," tend to reflect, re-create, and naturalize a hierarchical ordering of gender. Following Connell's (1987, 98–99) method of structural analysis, I will examine the "gender regime"—that is, the current "state of play of sexual politics"—within the local AYSO organization by conducting a "structural inventory" of the formal and informal sexual divisions of labor and power.

Adult Divisions of Labor and Power

There was a clear—although not absolute—sexual division of labor and power among the adult volunteers in the AYSO organization. The Board of Directors consisted of twenty-one men and nine women, with the top two positions—commissioner and assistant commissioner—held by men. Among the league's head coaches, 133 were men and twenty-three women. The division among the league's assistant coaches was similarly skewed. Each team also had a team manager who was responsible for organizing snacks, making reminder calls about games and practices, organizing team parties and the end-of-the-year present for the coach. The vast majority of team managers were women. A common slippage in the language of coaches and parents revealed the ideological assumptions underlying this position: I often noticed people describe a team manager as the "team mom." In short, as Table 1.1 shows, the vast majority of the time, the formal authority of the head coach and assistant coach was in the hands of a man, while the backup, support role of team manager was in the hands of a woman.

Table 1.1

Adult Volunteers as Coaches and Team Managers, by Sex
(N = 156 teams)

	Head Coaches	Assistant Coaches	Team Managers
Women	15%	21%	86%
Men	85%	79%	14%

These data illustrate Connell's (1987, 97) assertion that sexual divisions of labor are interwoven with, and mutually supportive of, divisions of power and authority among women and men. They also suggest how people's choices to volunteer for certain positions are shaped and constrained by previous institutional practices. There is no formal AYSO rule that men must be the leaders, women the supportive followers. And there are, after all, *some* women coaches and *some* men team managers. So, it may appear that the division of labor among adult volunteers simply manifests an accumulation of individual choices and preferences. When analyzed structurally, though, individual men's apparently free choices to volunteer disproportionately for coaching jobs, alongside individual women's apparently free choices to volunteer disproportionately for team manager jobs, can be seen as a logical collective result of the ways that the institutional structure of sport has differentially constrained and enabled women's and men's previous options and experiences (Messner 1992). Since boys and men have had far more opportunities to play organized sports and thus to gain skills and knowledge, it subsequently appears rational for adult men to serve in positions of knowledgeable authority, with women serving in a support capacity (Boyle and McKay 1995). Structure—in this case, the historically constituted division of labor and power in sport—constrains current practice. In turn, structure becomes an object of practice, as the choices and actions of today's parents re-create divisions of labor and power similar to those that they experienced in their youth.

THE CHILDREN: FORMAL SEX SEGREGATION

As adult authority patterns are informally structured along gendered lines, the children's leagues are formally segregated by AYSO along lines of age and sex. In each age-group, there are separate boys' and girls' leagues. The AYSO in this community included eighty-seven boys' teams and sixty-nine girls' teams. Although the four- to five-year-old boys often played their games on a field that was contiguous with games being played by four-to five-year-old girls, there was never a formal opportunity for cross-sex play. Thus, both the girls' and the boys' teams could conceivably proceed through an entire season of games and practices in entirely homosocial contexts. In the all-male contexts that I observed throughout the season, gender never appeared to be overtly salient among the children, coaches, or parents. It is against this backdrop that I might suggest a working hypothesis about structure and the variable salience of gender: The formal sex segregation of children does not, in and of itself, make gender overtly salient. In fact, when children are absolutely segregated, with no opportunity for cross-sex interactions, gender may appear to disappear as an overtly salient organizing principle. However, when formally sex-segregated children are placed into immediately contiguous locations, such as during the opening ceremony, highly charged gendered interactions between the groups (including invasions and other kinds of border work) become more possible.

Although it might appear to some that formal sex segregation in children's sports is a natural fact, it has not always been so for the youngest age-groups in AYSO. As recently as 1995, when my older son signed up to play as a five year old, I had been told that he would play in a coed league. But when he arrived to his first practice and I saw that he was on an all-boys team, I was told by the coach that AYSO had decided this year to begin sex segregating all age-groups, because "during half-times and practices, the boys and girls tend to separate into separate groups. So the league thought it would be better for team unity if we split the boys and girls into separate leagues." I suggested to some coaches that a similar dynamic among racial ethnic groups (say, Latino kids and white kids clustering as separate groups during halftimes) would not similarly result in a decision to create racially segregated leagues. That this comment appeared to fall on deaf ears illustrates the extent to which many adults' belief in the need for sex segregation—at least in the context of sport—is grounded in a mutually agreed-upon notion of boys' and girls' "separate worlds," perhaps based in ideologies of natural sex difference.

The gender regime of AYSO, then, is structured by formal and informal sexual divisions of labor and power. This social structure sets ranges, limits, and possibilities for the children's and parents' interactions and performances of gender, but it does not determine them. Put another way, the formal and informal gender regime of AYSO made the Barbie Girls versus Sea Monsters moment possible, but it did not make it inevitable. It was the agency of the children and the parents within that structure that made the moment happen. But why did this moment take on the symbolic forms that it did? How and why do the girls, boys, and parents construct and derive meanings from this moment, and how can we interpret these meanings? These questions are best grappled within in the realm of cultural analysis.

THE CULTURE OF GENDER

The difference between what is "structural" and what is "cultural" is not clear-cut. For instance, the AYSO assignment of team colors and choice of team names (cultural symbols) seem to follow logically from, and in turn reinforce, the sex segregation of the leagues (social structure). These cultural symbols such as team colors, uniforms, songs, team names, and banners often carried encoded gendered meanings that were then available to be taken up by the children in ways that constructed (or potentially contested) gender divisions and boundaries.

TEAM NAMES

Each team was issued two team colors. It is notable that across the various age-groups, several girls' teams were issued pink uniforms—a color commonly recognized as encoding feminine meanings—while no boys' teams were issued pink uniforms. Children, in consultation with their coaches, were asked to choose their own team names and were encouraged to use their assigned team colors as cues to theme of the team name (e.g., among the boys, the "Red Flashes," the "Green Pythons," and the blue-and-green "Sea Monsters"). When I analyzed the team names of the 156 teams by age-group and by sex, three categories emerged:

1. *Sweet names*: These are cutesy team names that communicate small stature, cuteness, and/or vulnerability. These kinds of names would most likely be widely read as encoded with feminine meanings (e.g., "Blue Butterflies," "Beanie Babes," "Sunflowers," "Pink Flamingos," and "Barbie Girls").

2. *Neutral or paradoxical names*: Neutral names are team names that carry no obvious gendered meaning (e.g., "Blue and Green Lizards," "Team Flubber," "Galaxy," "Blue Ice"). Paradoxical names are girls' team names that carry mixed (simultaneously vulnerable *and* powerful) messages (e.g., "Pink Panthers," "Flower Power," "Little Tigers").

3. *Power names*: These are team names that invoke images of unambiguous strength, aggression, and raw power (e.g., "Shooting Stars," "Killer Whales," "Shark Attack," "Raptor Attack," and "Sea Monsters").

As Table 1.2 illustrates, across all age-groups of boys, there was only one team name coded as a sweet name—"The Smurfs," in the ten- to eleven-year-old league. Across all age categories, the boys were far more likely to choose a power name than anything else, and this was nowhere more true than in the youngest age-groups, where thirty-five of forty (87%) of boys' teams in the four-to-five and six-to seven age-groups took on power names. A different pattern appears in the girls' team name choices, especially among the youngest girls. Only two of the twelve four- to five-year-old girls' teams chose power names, while five chose sweet names and five chose neutral/paradoxical names. At age six to seven, the numbers begin to tip toward the boys' numbers but still remain different, with half of the girls' teams now choosing power names. In the middle and older girls' groups, the sweet names all but disappear, with power names dominating, but still a higher proportion of neutral/paradoxical names than among boys in those age-groups.

	4-5	6-7	8-13	14-17	Total
Table 1.2					
Team Names, by Age Groups and Sex					
Girls					
Sweet names	5 (42%)	3 (17%)	2 (7%)	0 (0%)	10 (15%)
Neutral paradoxical	5 (42%)	6 (33%)	7 (25%)	5 (45%)	23 (32%)
Power names	2 (17%)	9 (50%)	19 (68%)	6 (55%)	36 (52%)
Boys					
Sweet names	0 (0%)	0 (0%)	1 (4%)	0 (0%)	1 (1%)
Neutral paradoxical	1 (7%)	4 (15%)	4 (12%)	4 (31%)	13 (15%)
Power names	13 (93%)	22 (85%)	29 (85%)	9 (69%)	73 (82%)

BARBIE NARRATIVE VERSUS WARRIOR NARRATIVE

How do we make sense of the obviously powerful spark that Barbie provided in the opening ceremony scene described earlier? Barbie is likely one of the most immediately identifiable symbols of femininity in the world. More conservatively oriented parents tend to happily buy Barbie dolls for their daughters, while perhaps deflecting their sons' interest in Barbie toward more sex-appropriate "action toys." Feminist parents, on the other hand, have often expressed open contempt—or at least uncomfortable ambivalence—toward Barbie. This is because both conservative and feminist parents see dominant cultural meanings of emphasized femininity as condensed in Barbie and assume that these meanings will be imitated by their daughters. Recent developments in cultural studies, though, should warn us against simplistic readings of Barbie as simply conveying hegemonic messages about gender to unwitting children (Attfield 1996; Seiter 1995). In addition to critically analyzing the cultural values (or "preferred meanings") that may be encoded in Barbie or other children's toys, feminist scholars of cultural studies point to the necessity of examining "reception, pleasure, and agency," and especially "the fullness of reception contexts" (Walters 1999, 246). The

Barbie Girls versus Sea Monsters moment can be analyzed as a "reception context," in which differently situated boys, girls, and parents variously used Barbie to construct pleasurable intergroup bonds, as well as boundaries between groups.

Barbie is plastic both in form and in terms of cultural meanings children and adults create around her (Rogers 1999). It is not that there are not hegemonic meanings encoded in Barbie: Since its introduction in 1959, Mattel has been successful in selling millions of this doll that "was recognized as a model of ideal teenhood" (Rand 1998, 383) and "an icon—perhaps *the* icon—of true white womanhood and femininity" (DuCille 1994, 50). However, Rand (1998) argues that "we condescend to children when we analyze Barbie's content and then presume that it passes untransformed into their minds, where, dwelling beneath the control of consciousness or counterargument, it generates self-image, feelings, and other ideological constructs." In fact, people who are situated differently (by age, gender, sexual orientation, social class, race/ethnicity, and national origin) tend to consume and construct meanings around Barbie variously. For instance, some adult women (including many feminists) tell retrospective stories of having rejected (or even mutilated) their Barbies in favor of boys' toys, and some adult lesbians tell stories of transforming Barbie "into an object of dyke desire" (Rand 1998, 386).

Mattel, in fact, clearly strategizes its marketing of Barbie not around the imposition of a singular notion of what a girl or woman should be but around "hegemonic discourse strategies" that attempt to incorporate consumers' range of possible interpretations and criticisms of the limits of Barbie. For instance, the recent marketing of "multicultural Barbie" features dolls with different skin colors and culturally coded wardrobes (DuCille 1994). This strategy broadens the Barbie market, deflects potential criticism of racism, but still "does not boot blond, white Barbie from center stage" (Rand 1998, 391). Similarly, Mattel's marketing of Barbie (since the 1970s) as a career woman raises issues concerning the feminist critique of Barbie's supposedly negative effect on girls. When the AAUW recently criticized Barbie, adult collectors defended Barbie, asserting that "Barbie, in fact, is a wonderful role model for women. She has been a veterinarian, an astronaut, and a soldier—and even before real women had a chance to enter such occupations" (Spigel 2001). And when the magazine *Barbie Bazaar* ran a cover photo of its new "Gulf War Barbie," it served "as a reminder of Mattel's marketing slogan: 'We Girls Can Do Anything'" (Spigel 2001). The following year, Mattel unveiled its "Presidential Candidate Barbie" with the statement: "It is time for a woman president, and Barbie had the credentials for the job." Spigel observes that these liberal feminist messages of empowerment for girls run—apparently unambiguously—alongside a continued unspoken understanding that Barbie must be beautiful, with an ultraskinny waist and long, thin legs that taper to feet that appear deformed so that they may fit (only?) into high heels. "Mattel does not mind equating beauty with intellect. In fact, so long as the 11$\frac{1}{2}$ inch Barbie body remains intact, Mattel is willing to accessorize her with a number of fashionable perspectives—including feminism itself" (Spigel 2001).

It is this apparently paradoxical encoding of the all-too-familiar oppressive bodily requirements of feminine beauty alongside the career woman role modeling and empowering message that "we girls can do anything" that may inform how and why the Barbie Girls appropriated Barbie as their team symbol. Emphasized femininity—Connell's (1987) term for the current form of femininity that articulates with hegemonic masculinity—as many Second Wave feminists have experienced and criticized it, has been characterized by girls' and women's embodiments of oppressive conceptions of feminine beauty that symbolize and reify a thoroughly disempowered stance *vis-à-vis* men. To many Second Wave feminists, Barbie seemed to symbolize all that was oppressive about this femininity—the bodily self-surveillance, accompanying eating disorders, slavery to the dictates of the fashion industry, and compulsory heterosexuality. But Rogers (1999, 14) suggests that rather than representing an unambiguous image of emphasized femininity, perhaps Barbie represents a more paradoxical image of "emphatic femininity" that

> takes feminine appearances and demeanor to unsustainable extremes. Nothing about Barbie ever looks masculine, even when she is on the police force.... Consistently, Barbie manages impressions so as to come across as a proper feminine creature even when she crosses boundaries usually dividing women from men. Barbie the firefighter is in no danger, then, of being seen as "one of the boys." Kids know that; parents and teachers know that; Mattel designers know that too.

Recent Third Wave feminist theory sheds light on the different sensibilities of younger generations of girls and women concerning their willingness to display and play with this apparently paradoxical relationship between bodily experience (including "feminine" displays) and public empowerment. In Third Wave feminist texts, displays of feminine physical attractiveness and empowerment are not viewed as mutually exclusive or necessarily opposed realities, but as lived (if often paradoxical) aspects of the same reality (Heywood and Drake 1997). This embracing of the paradoxes of post–Second Wave femininity is manifested in many punk, or Riot Grrrl, subcultures (Klein 1997) and in popular culture in the resounding late 1990s success of the Spice Girls' mantra of "Girl Power." This generational expression of "girl power" may today be part of "the pleasures of girl culture that Barbie stands for" (Spigel 2001). Indeed, as the Barbie

Girls rallied around Barbie, their obvious pleasure did not appear to be based on a celebration of quiet passivity (as feminist parents might fear). Rather, it was a statement that they—the Barbie Girls—were here in this public space. They were not silenced by the boys' oppositional chanting. To the contrary, they ignored the boys, who seemed irrelevant to their celebration. And, when the boys later physically invaded their space, some of the girls responded by chasing the boys off. In short, when I pay attention to what the girls *did* (rather than imposing on the situation what I *think* Barbie "should" mean to the girls), I see a public moment of celebratory "girl power."

And this may give us better basis from which to analyze the boys' oppositional response. First, the boys may have been responding to the threat of displacement they may have felt while viewing the girls' moment of celebratory girl power. Second, the boys may simultaneously have been responding to the fears of feminine pollution that Barbie had come to symbolize to them. But why might Barbie symbolize feminine pollution to little boys? A brief example from my older son is instructive. When he was about three, following a fun day of play with the five-year-old girl next door, he enthusiastically asked me to buy him a Barbie like hers. He was gleeful when I took him to the store and bought him one. When we arrived home, his feet had barely hit the pavement getting out of the car before an eight-year-old neighbor boy laughed at and ridiculed him: "A *Barbie?* Don't you know that Barbie is a *girl's toy?*" No amount of parental intervention could counter this devastating peer-induced injunction against boys playing with Barbie. My son's pleasurable desire for Barbie appeared almost overnight to transform itself into shame and rejection. The doll ended up at the bottom of a heap of toys in the closet, and my son soon became infatuated, along with other boys in his preschool, with Ninja Turtles and Power Rangers.

Research indicates that there is widespread agreement as to which toys are appropriate for one sex and polluting, dangerous, or inappropriate for the other sex. When Campenni (1999) asked adults to rate the gender appropriateness of children's toys, the toys considered most appropriate to girls were those pertaining to domestic tasks, beauty enhancement, or childrearing. Of the 206 toys rated, Barbie was rated second only to Makeup Kit as a female-only toy. Toys considered most appropriate to boys were those pertaining to sports gear (football gear was the most masculine-rated toy, while boxing gloves were third),vehicles, action figures (G.I. Joe was rated second only to football gear), and other war-related toys. This research on parents' gender stereotyping of toys reflects similar findings in research on children's toy preferences (Bradbard 1985; Robinson and Morris 1986). Children tend to avoid cross-sex toys, with boys' avoidance of feminine-coded toys appearing to be stronger than girls' avoidance of masculine-coded toys (Etaugh and Liss

1992). Moreover, preschool-age boys who perceive their fathers to be opposed to cross-gender-typed play are more likely than girls or other boys to think that it is "bad" for boys to play with toys that are labeled as "for girls" (Raag and Rackliff 1998).

By kindergarten, most boys appear to have learned—either through experiences similar to my son's, where other boys police the boundaries of gender-appropriate play and fantasy and/or by watching the clearly gendered messages of television advertising—that Barbie dolls are not appropriate toys for boys (Rogers 1999, 30). To avoid ridicule, they learn to hide their desire for Barbie, either through denial and oppositional/pollution discourse and/or through sublimation of their desire for Barbie into play with male-appropriate "action figures" (Pope et al. 1999). In their study of a kindergarten classroom, Jordan and Cowan (1995, 728) identified "warrior narratives... that assume that violence is legitimate and justified when it occurs within a struggle between good and evil" to be the most commonly agreed-upon currency for boys' fantasy play. They observe that the boys seem commonly to adapt story lines that they have seen on television. Popular culture—film, video, computer games, television, and comic books—provides boys with aseemingly endless stream of Good Guys versus Bad Guys characters and stories—from cowboy movies, Superman and Spiderman to Ninja Turtles, Star Wars, and Pokemon—that are available for the boys to appropriate as the raw materials for the construction of their own warrior play.

In the kindergarten that Jordan and Cowan studied, the boys initially attempted to import their warrior narratives into the domestic setting of the "Doll Corner." Teachers eventually drove the boys' warrior play outdoors, while the Doll Corner was used by the girls for the "appropriate" domestic play for which it was originally intended. Jordan and Cowan argue that kindergarten teachers' outlawing of boys' warrior narratives inside the classroom contributed to boys' defining schools as a feminine environment, to which they responded with a resistant, underground continuation of masculine warrior play. Eventually though, boys who acquiesce and successfully sublimate warrior play into fantasy or sport are more successful in constructing what Connell (1989, 291) calls "a masculinity organized around themes of rationality and responsibility [that is] closely connected with the 'certification' function of the upper levels of the education system and to a key form of masculinity among professionals."

In contrast to the "rational/professional" masculinity constructed in schools, the institution of sport historically constructs hegemonic masculinity as *bodily superiority* over femininity and nonathletic masculinities (Messner 1992). Here, warrior narratives are allowed to publicly thrive—indeed, are openly celebrated (witness, for instance, the commentary of a televised NFL

[National Football League] football game or especially the spectacle of tele-vised professional wrestling). Preschool boys and kindergartners seem already to know this, easily adopting aggressively competitive team names and an us-versus-them attitude. By contrast, many of the youngest girls appear to take two or three years in organized soccer before they adopt, or partially accom-modate themselves to, aggressively competitive discourse, indicated by the ten-year-old girls' shifting away from the use of sweet names toward more power names. In short, where the gender regime of preschool and grade school may be experienced as an environment in which mostly women lead-ers enforce rules that are hostile to masculine fantasy play and physicality, the gender regime of sport is experienced as a place where masculine styles and values of physicality, aggression, and competition are enforced and cele-brated by mostly male coaches.

A cultural analysis suggests that the boys' and the girls' previous immer-sion in differently gendered cultural experiences shaped the likelihood that they would derive and construct different meanings from Barbie—the girls through pleasurable and symbolically empowering identification with "girl power" narratives; the boys through oppositional fears of feminine pollution (and fears of displacement by girl power?) and with aggressively verbal, and eventually physical, invasions of the girls' ritual space. The boys' collective response thus constituted them differently, *as boys*, in opposition to the girls' constitution of themselves *as girls*. An individual girl or boy, in this moment, who may have felt an inclination to dissent from the dominant feelings of the group (say, the Latina Barbie Girl who, her mother later told me, did not want the group to be identified with Barbie, or a boy whose immediate inner response to the Barbie Girls' joyful celebration might be to join in) is most likely silenced into complicity in this powerful moment of border work.

What meanings did this highly gendered moment carry for the boys' and girls' teams in the ensuing soccer season? Although I did not observe the Barbie Girls after the opening ceremony, I did continue to observe the Sea Monsters' weekly practices and games. During the boys' ensuing season, gender never reached this "magnified" level of salience again—indeed, gender was rarely raised verbally or performed overtly by the boys. On two occasions, though, I observed the coach jokingly chiding the boys during practice that "if you don't watch out, I'm going to get the Barbie Girls here to play against you!" This warning was followed by gleeful screams of agony and fear, and nervous hopping around and hugging by some of the boys. Normally, though, in this sex-segregated, all-male context, if boundaries were invoked, they were not boundaries between boys and girls but boundaries between the Sea Monsters and other boys' teams, or sometimes age bound-aries between the Sea Monsters and a small group of dads and older brothers who would engage them in a mock scrimmage during practice. But it was also evident that when the coach was having trouble getting the boys to act together, as a group, his strategic and humorous invocation of the dreaded Barbie Girls once again served symbolically to affirm their group status. They were a team. They were the boys.

CONCLUSION

The overarching goal of this essay has been to take one empirical observation from everyday life and demonstrate how a multilevel (interactionist, structural, cultural) analysis might reveal various layers of meaning that give insight into the everyday social construction of gender. This essay builds on observations made by Thorne (1993) concerning ways to approach sociological analyses of children's worlds. The most fruitful approach is not to ask why boys and girls are so different but rather to ask how and under what conditions boys and girls constitute themselves as separate, oppositional groups. Sociologists need not debate whether gender is "there"—clearly, gender is always already there, built as it is into the structures, situations, culture, and consciousness of children and adults. The key issue is under what conditions gender is activated as a salient organizing principle in social life and under what conditions it may be less salient. These are important questions, especially since the social organization of categorical gender difference has always been so clearly tied to gender hierarchy (Acker 1990; Lorber 1994). In the Barbie Girls versus Sea Monsters moment, the performance of gendered boundaries and the construction of boys' and girls' groups as categorically different occurred in the context of a situation systematically structured by sex segregation, sparked by the imposing presence of a shared cultural symbol that is saturated with gendered meanings, and actively supported and applauded by adults who basked in the pleasure of difference, reaffirmed.

I have suggested that a useful approach to the study of such "how" and "under what conditions" questions is to employ multiple levels of analysis. At the most general level, this project supports the following working propositions.

Interactionist theoretical frameworks that emphasize the ways that social agents "perform" or "do" gender are most useful in describing how groups of people actively create (or at times disrupt) the boundaries that delineate seemingly categorical differences between male persons and female persons. In this case, we saw how the children and the parents interactively performed gender in a way that constructed an apparently natural boundary between the two separate worlds of the girls and the boys.

Structural theoretical frameworks that emphasize the ways that gender is built into institutions through hierarchical sexual divisions of labor are most useful in explaining under what conditions social agents mobilize variously to disrupt or to affirm gender differences and inequalities. In this case, we saw how the sexual division of labor among parent volunteers (grounded in their own histories in the gender regime of sport), the formal sex segregation of the children's leagues, and the structured context of the opening ceremony created conditions for possible interactions between girls' teams and boys' teams.

Cultural theoretical perspectives that examine how popular symbols that are injected into circulation by the culture industry are variously taken up by differently situated people are most useful in analyzing how the meanings of cultural symbols, in a given institutional context, might trigger or be taken up by social agents and used as resources to reproduce, disrupt, or contest binary conceptions of sex difference and gendered relations of power. In this case, we saw how a girls' team appropriated a large Barbie around which to construct a pleasurable and empowering sense of group identity and how the boys' team responded with aggressive denunciations of Barbie and invasions.

Utilizing any one of the above theoretical perspectives by itself will lead to a limited, even distorted, analysis of the social construction of gender. Together, they can illuminate the complex, multileveled architecture of the social construction of gender in everyday life. For heuristic reasons, I have falsely separated structure, interaction, and culture. In fact, we need to explore their constant interrelationships, continuities, and contradictions. For instance, we cannot understand the boys' aggressive denunciations and invasions of the girls' space and the eventual clarification of categorical boundaries between the girls and the boys without first understanding how these boys and girls have already internalized four or five years of "gendering" experiences that have shaped their interactional tendencies and how they are already immersed in a culture of gendered symbols, including Barbie and sports media imagery. Although "only" preschoolers, they are already skilled in collectively taking up symbols from popular culture as resources to be used in their own group dynamics—building individual and group identities, sharing the pleasures of play, clarifying boundaries between in-group and out-group members, and constructing hierarchies in their worlds.

Furthermore, we cannot understand the reason that the girls first chose "Barbie Girls" as their team name without first understanding the fact that a particular institutional structure of AYSO soccer preexisted the girls' entrée into the league. The informal sexual division of labor among adults, and the formal sex segregation of children's teams, is a preexisting gender regime that constrains and enables the ways that the children enact gender relations and construct identities. One concrete manifestation of this constraining nature of sex segregated teams is the choice of team names. It is reasonable to speculate that if the four- and five-year-old children were still sex integrated, as in the pre-1995 era, no team would have chosen "Barbie Girls" as its team name, with Barbie as its symbol. In other words, the formal sex segregation created the conditions under which the girls were enabled—perhaps encouraged—to choose a "sweet" team name that is widely read as encoding feminine meanings. The eventual interactions between the boys and the girls were made possible—although by no means fully determined—by the structure of the gender regime and by the cultural resources that the children variously drew on.

On the other hand, the gendered division of labor in youth soccer is not seamless, static, or immune to resistance. One of the few woman head coaches, a very active athlete in her own right, told me that she is "challenging the sexism" in AYSO by becoming the head of her son's league. As post–Title IX women increasingly become mothers and as media images of competent, heroic female athletes become more a part of the cultural landscape for children, the gender regimes of children's sports may be increasingly challenged (Dworkin and Messner 1999). Put another way, the dramatically shifting opportunity structure and cultural imagery of post–Title IX sports have created opportunities for new kinds of interactions, which will inevitably challenge and further shift institutional structures. Social structures simultaneously constrain and enable, while agency is simultaneously reproductive and resistant.

2

Sports and Male Domination

The Female Athlete as Contested Ideological Terrain

Author's note: In the mid-1980s, when I began to study sport, I wondered what the emergence of women's athleticism meant for the larger field of gender relations. Were muscular and athletic women a sign of the inevitable and unstoppable progress of feminist social transformation?—or, conversely, was the rise of female athleticism being contained and marginalized in ways that neutralized the feminist impulse of women's sports, thus reinforcing historical notions of the "natural superiority" of men's bodies? At this time, much of the research on gender and sport in the United States was descriptive, and utilized a "sex roles" perspective that was not well suited to asking these kinds of questions about institutional forces, cultural meanings, and historical change. Meanwhile a few scholars from Canada (e.g., Richard Gruneau) and the UK (e.g., Jennifer Hargreaves, Paul Willis) had begun to adapt Gramscian theories to develop more sophisticated historical analyses of sport. The mid-1980s were also a time during which a literature on the critical study of masculinities was emerging. In this 1988 essay, I drew from these developments to reflect on sport as a "contested terrain" of gender meanings. My concern here was in looking at sport through a "reflexive historical framework" that foregrounded the relationship between structure and agency, thus illustrating the ways that sport can be examined as a cultural site in which gender meanings are constructed in often paradoxical ways. My focus on contested meanings of athletic women's bodies (especially those of women body builders), and of the ways that the mass media frame women athletes in contradictory ways, anticipated a good deal of my subsequent work.

W omen's quest for equality in society has had its counterpart in the sports world. Since the 1972 passage of Title IX, women in the United States have had a legal basis from which to push for greater equity in high school and college athletics. Although equality is still a distant goal in terms of funding, programs, facilities, and media coverage of women's sports, substantial gains have been made by female athletes in the past ten to fifteen years, indicated by increasing numerical participation as well as by expanding peer and self-acceptance of female athleticism (Hogan 1982; Sabo 1985; Woodward 1985). A number of commentators have pointed out that the degree of difference between male and female athletic performance—the "muscle gap"—has closed considerably in recent years as female athletes have gained greater access to coaching and training facilities (Crittenden 1979; Dyer 1983; Ferris 1978).

However, optimistic predictions that women's movement into sport signals an imminent demise of inequalities between the sexes are premature. As Willis (1982, 120) argues, what matters most is not simply how and why the gap between male and female athletic performance is created, enlarged, or constricted; what is of more fundamental concern is "the manner in which this gap is understood and taken into the popular consciousness of our society." This essay is thus concerned with exploring the historical and ideological meaning of organized sports for the politics of gender relations. After outlining a theory for building a historically grounded understanding of sport, culture, and ideology, I will demonstrate how and why organized sports have come to serve as a primary institutional means for bolstering a challenged and faltering ideology of male superiority in the twentieth century.

It will be argued that women's movement into sport represents a genuine quest by women for equality, control of their own bodies, and self-definition, and as such it represents a challenge to the ideological basis of male domination. Yet it will also be demonstrated that this quest for equality is not without contradictions and ambiguities. The social meanings surrounding the physiological differences between the sexes in the male-defined institution of organized sports and the framing of the female athlete by the sports media threaten to subvert any counterhegemonic potential posed by women athletes. In short, the female athlete—and her body—has become a contested ideological terrain.

SPORT, CULTURE, AND IDEOLOGY

Most theoretical work on sport has fallen into either of two traps: an idealist notion of sport as a realm of freedom divorced from material and historical constraints, or a materialist analysis that posits sport as a cultural mechanism through which the dominant classes control the unwitting masses. Marxists have correctly criticized idealists and functionalists for failing to understand how sport tends to reflect capitalist relations, thus serving to promote and ideologically legitimize competition, meritocracy, consumerism, militarism, and instrumental rationality, while at the same time providing spectators with escape and compensatory mechanisms for an alienated existence (Brohm 1978; Hoch 1972). But Marxist structuralists, with their view of sport as a superstructural expression of ideological control by the capitalist class, have themselves fallen into a simplistic and nondialectical functionalism (Gruneau 1983; Hargreaves 1982). Within the deterministic Marxian framework, there is no room for viewing people (athletes, spectators) as anything other than passive objects who are duped into meeting the needs of capitalism.

Neo-Marxists of the 1980s have argued for the necessity of placing an analysis of sport within a more reflexive framework, wherein culture is seen as relatively autonomous from the economy and human subjectivity occurs within historical and structural limits and constraints. This theory puts people back at the center stage of history without falling into an idealistic voluntarism that ignores the importance of historically formed structural conditions, class inequalities, and unequal power relations. Further, it allows for the existence of critical thought, resistance to dominant ideologies, and change. Within a reflexive historical framework, we can begin to understand how sport (and culture in general) is a dynamic social space where dominant (class, ethnic, etc.) ideologies are perpetuated as well as challenged and contested.

Recent critics have called for a recasting of this reflexive theory to include gender as a centrally important process rather than as a simple effect of class dynamics (Critcher 1986; McKay 1986). Indeed, sport as an arena of ideological battles over gender relations has been given short shrift throughout the sociology of sport literature. This is due in part to the marginalization of feminist theory within sociology as a discipline (Stacey and Thorne 1985) and within sport sociology in particular (Birrell 1984; Hall 1984). When gender has been examined by sport sociologists, it has usually been within the framework of a sex role paradigm that concerns itself largely with the effects of sport participation on an individual's sex role identity, values, and so on (Lever 1976; Sabo and Runfola 1980; Schafer 1975). "Although social-psychological examinations of the sport-gender relationship are important, the sex role paradigm often used by these studies too often ignores the extent to which our conceptions of masculinity and femininity— the content of either the male or female sex role—is relational, that is, the product of gender relations which are historically and socially conditioned.... The sex role paradigm also minimizes the extent to which gender relations are based on power.

Not only do men as a group exert power over women as a group, but the his-torically derived definitions of masculinity and femininity reproduce those power relations" (Kimmel 1986, 520–521).

The twentieth century has seen two periods of crisis for masculinity—each marked by drastic changes in work and family and accompanied by significant feminist movements (Kimmel 1987). The first crisis of masculin-ity stretched from the turn of the century into the 1920s, and the second from the post–World War II years to the present. I will argue here, using a historical/relational conception of gender within a reflexive theory of sport, culture, and ideology, that during these two periods of crisis for masculinity, organized sport has been a crucial arena of struggle over basic social con-ceptions of masculinity and femininity, and as such has become a funda-mental arena of ideological contest in terms of power relations between men and women.

CRISES OF MASCULINITY AND THE RISE OF ORGANIZED SPORTS

Reynaud (1981, 9) has stated that "the ABC of any patriarchal ideology is precisely to present that division [between the sexes] as being of biological, natural, or divine essence." And, as Clarke and Clarke (1982, 63) have argued, because sport "appears as a sphere of activity outside society, and par-ticularly as it appears to involve natural, physical skills and capacities, [it] presents these ideological images *as if they were natural.*" Thus, organized sport is clearly a potentially powerful cultural arena for the perpetuation of the ideology of male superiority and dominance. Yet, it has not always been of such importance.

The First Crisis of Masculinity: 1890s through the 1920s

Sport historians have pointed out that the rapid expansion of organized sport after the turn of the century into widespread "recreation for the masses" rep-resented a cultural means of integrating immigrants and a growing industrial working class into an expanding capitalist order where work was becoming rationalized and leisure time was expanding (Brohm 1978; Goldman 1983/1984; Gruneau 1983; Rigauer 1981). However, few scholars of sport have examined how this expanding industrial capitalist order was interacting with a relatively autonomous system of gender stratification, and this severely limits their ability to understand the cultural meaning of organized sport. In fact, industrial capitalism both bolstered and undermined traditional forms of male domination.

The creation of separate (public/domestic) and unequal spheres of life for men and women created a new basis for male power and privilege (Hartmann 1976; Zaretsky 1973). But in an era of wage labor and increasingly concentrated ownership of productive property, fewer males owned their own businesses and farms or controlled their own labor. The breadwinner role was a more shaky foundation upon which to base male privilege than was the patriarchal legacy of property-ownership passed on from father to son (Tolson 1977). These changes in work and family, along with the rise of female-dominated public schools, urbanization, and the closing of the frontier all led to widespread fears of "social feminization" and a turn-of-the-century crisis of masculinity. Many men compensated with a defensive insecurity that manifested itself in increased preoccupation with physicality and toughness (Wilkenson 1984), warfare (Filene 1975), and even the creation of new organizations such as the Boy Scouts of America as a separate cultural sphere of life where "true manliness" could be instilled in boys by men (Hantover 1978). Within this context, organized sports became increasingly important as a "primary masculinity-validating experience" (Dubbert 1979, 164). Sport was a male-created homosocial cultural sphere that provided men with psychological separation from the perceived feminization of society while also providing dramatic symbolic proof of the "natural superiority" of men over women.

This era was also characterized by an active and visible feminist movement, which eventually focused itself on the achievement of female suffrage. These feminists challenged entrenched Victorian assumptions and prescriptions concerning femininity, and this was reflected in a first wave of athletic feminism that blossomed in the 1920s, mostly in women's colleges (Twin 1979). Whereas sports participation for young males tended to confirm masculinity, female athleticism was viewed as conflicting with the conventional ethos of femininity, thus leading to virulent opposition to women's growing athleticism (Lefkowitz-Horowitz 1986). A survey of physical education instructors in 1923 indicated that 93% were opposed to intercollegiate play for women (Smith 1970). And the Women's Division of the National Amateur Athletic Foundation, led by Mrs. Herbert Hoover, opposed women's participation in the 1928 Olympics (Lefkowitz-Horowitz 1986). Those involved in women's athletics responded to this opposition defensively (and perhaps out of a different feminine aesthetic or morality) with the establishment of an anticompetitive "feminine philosophy of sport" (Beck 1980). This philosophy was at once responsible for the continued survival of women's athletics, as it was successfully marginalized and thus easily "ghettoized" and ignored, and it also ensured that, for the time being, the image of the female athlete would not become a major threat to the hegemonic ideology of male athleticism, virility, strength, and power.

The breakdown of Victorianism in the 1920s had a contradictory effect on the social deployment and uses of women's bodies. On the one hand, the female body became "a marketable item, used to sell numerous products and services" (Twin 1979, xxix). This obviously reflected women's social subordination, but, ironically,

> The commercialization of women's bodies provided a cultural opening for competitive athletics, as industry and ambitious individuals used women to sell sports. Leo Seltzer included women in his 1935 invention, roller derby, "with one eye to beauty and the other on gate receipts," according to one writer. While women's physical marketability profited industry, it also allowed females to do more with their bodies than before. (Twin 1979, xxix)

Despite its limits, the first wave of athletic feminism, even in its more commercialized manifestations, did provide an initial challenge to men's creation of sport as an uncontested arena of ideological legitimation for male dominance. In forcing an acknowledgment of women's physicality, albeit in a limited way, this first wave of female athletes laid the groundwork for more fundamental challenges. While some cracks had clearly appeared in the patriarchal edifice, it would not be until the 1970s that female athletes would present a more basic challenge to predominant cultural images of women.

The Post–World War II Masculinity Crisis and the Rise of Mass Spectator Sports

Today, according to Naison (1980, 36), "The American male spends a far greater portion of his time with sports than he did 40 years ago, but the greatest proportion of that time is spent in front of a television set observing games that he will hardly ever play." How and why have organized sports increasingly become an object of mass spectatorship? Lasch (1979) has argued that the historical transformation from entrepreneurial capitalism to corporate capitalism has seen a concomitant shift from the Protestant work ethic (and industrial production) to the construction of the "docile consumer." Within this context, sport has degenerated into a spectacle, an object of mass consumption. Similarly, Alt (1983) states that the major function of mass-produced sports is to channel the alienated emotional needs of consumers in instrumental ways. Although Lasch and Alt are partly correct in stating that the sport spectacle is largely a manipulation of alienated emotional needs toward the goal of consumption, this explanation fails to account fully for the emotional resonance of the sports spectacle for a largely male audience. I would argue, along with Sabo and Runfola (1980, xv) that sports in the postwar era have become increasingly important to males precisely because they link men to a more patriarchal past.

The development of capitalism after World War II saw a continued erosion of traditional means of male expression and identity, due to the continued rationalization and bureaucratization of work, the shift from industrial production and physical labor to a more service-oriented economy, and increasing levels of structural unemployment. These changes, along with women's continued movement into public life, undermined and weakened the already shaky breadwinner role as a major basis for male power in the family (Ehrenreich 1983; Tolson 1977). And the declining relevance of physical strength in work and in warfare was not accompanied by a declining psychological need for an ideology of gender difference. Symbolic representations of the male body as a symbol of strength, virility, and power have become increasingly important in popular culture as actual inequalities between the sexes are contested in all arenas of public life (Mishkind et al. 1986). The marriage of television and organized sport—especially the televised spectacle of football—has increasingly played this important ideological role. As Oriard (1981) has stated,

> What football is for the athletes themselves actually has little direct impact on what it means to the rest of America.... Football projects a *myth* that speaks meaningfully to a large number of Americans far beneath the level of conscious perception.... Football does not create a myth for all Americans; it excludes women in many highly significant ways. (33–34)

Football's mythology and symbolism are probably meaningful and salient on a number of ideological levels: patriotism, militarism, violence, and meritocracy are all dominant themes. But I would argue that football's primary ideological salience lies in its ability, in the face of women's challenges to male dominance, to symbolically link men of diverse ages and socioeconomic backgrounds. Consider the words of a thirty-two-year-old white professional male whom I was interviewing: "A woman can do the same job I can do— maybe even be my boss. But I'll be *damned* if she can go out on the field and take a hit from Ronnie Lott."

The fact that this man (and perhaps 99% of all U.S. males) probably could not take a hit from the likes of pro football player Ronnie Lott and live to tell about it is really irrelevant, because football as a televised spectacle is meaningful on a more symbolic level. Here individual males are given the opportunity to identify—generically and abstractly—with all men as a superior and separate caste. Football, based as it is upon the most extreme possibilities of the male body (muscular bulk, explosive power, and aggression) is a world apart from women, who are relegated to the role of cheerleader/sex objects on the sidelines rooting their men on. In contrast to the bare and vulnerable bodies of the cheerleaders, the armored male bodies of football players are elevated to mythical status, and as such give testimony to the

undeniable "fact" that there is at least one place where men are clearly superior to women.

WOMEN'S RECENT MOVEMENT INTO SPORT

By the 1970s, just when symbolic representations of the athletic male body
had taken on increasing ideological importance, a second wave of athletic
feminism had emerged (Twin 1979). With women's rapid postwar movement into the labor force and a revived feminist movement, what had been
an easily ignorable undercurrent of female athleticism from the 1930s
through the 1960s suddenly swelled into a torrent of female sports participation—and demands for equity. In the United States, Title IX became the
legal benchmark for women's push for equity with males. But due to efforts
by the athletic establishment to limit the scope of Title IX, the quest for
equity remained decentralized and continued to take place in the gymnasi-
ums, athletic departments, and school boards of the nation (Beck 1980;
Hogan 1979, 1982).

Brownmiller (1984, 195) has stated that the modern female athlete has
placed herself "on the cutting edge of some of the most perplexing problems
of gender-related biology and the feminine ideal," often resulting in the
female athlete becoming ambivalent about her own image: Can a woman be
strong, aggressive, competitive, and still be considered feminine? Rohrbaugh
(1979) suggests that female athletes often develop an "apologetic" as a strategy for bridging the gap between cultural expectations of femininity and the
very unfeminine requisites for athletic excellence. There has been some disagreement over whether a widespread apologetic actually exists among
female athletes. Hart (1979) argues that there has never been an apologetic
for black women athletes, suggesting that there are cultural differences in the
construction of femininities. And a recent nationwide study indicated that
94% of the 1,682 female athletes surveyed do not regard athletic participation to be threatening to their femininity (Woodward 1985). Yet, 57% of
these same athletes did agree that society still forces a choice between being
an athlete and being feminine, suggesting that there is still a dynamic tension
between traditional prescriptions for femininity and the image presented by
active, strong, even muscular women.

Femininity as Ideologically Contested Terrain

Cultural conceptions of femininity and female beauty have more than aesthetic meanings; these images, and the meanings ascribed to them, inform
and legitimize unequal power relations between the sexes (Banner 1983;

Brownmiller 1984; Lakoff and Scherr 1984). Attempting to be viewed as feminine involves accepting behavioral and physical restrictions that make it difficult to view one's self, much less to be viewed by others, as equal with men. But if traditional images of femininity have solidified male privilege through constructing and then naturalizing the passivity, weakness, helplessness, and dependency of women, what are we to make of the current fit, athletic, even muscular looks that are increasingly in vogue with many women? Is there a new, counterhegemonic image of women afoot that challenges traditional conceptions of femininity? A brief examination of female bodybuilding sheds light on these questions.

Lakoff and Scherr (1984, 110) state that "female bodybuilding has become the first female-identified standard of beauty." Certainly the image of a muscular—even toned—woman runs counter to traditional prescriptions for female passivity and weakness. But it's not that simple. In the film *Pumping Iron II: The Women*, the tension between traditional prescriptions for femininity and the new muscularity of female bodybuilders is the major story line. It is obvious that the new image of women being forged by female bodybuilders is itself fraught with contradiction and ambiguity as women contestants and judges constantly discuss and argue emotionally over the meaning of femininity. Should contestants be judged simply according to how well-muscled they are (as male bodybuilders are judged), or also by a separate and traditionally feminine aesthetic? The consensus among the female bodybuilders, and especially among the predominantly male judges, appears to be the latter. In the words of one judge, "If they go to extremes and start looking like men, that's not what we're looking for in a woman. It's the winner of the contest who will set the standard of femininity." And of course, since this official is judging the contestants according to his own (traditional) standard of femininity, it should come as no surprise that the eventual winners are not the most well-muscled women.

Women's bodybuilding magazines also reflect this ambiguity: "Strong Is Sexy," reads the cover of the August 1986 issue of *Shape* magazine, and this caption accompanies a photo of a slightly muscled young bathing-suited woman wielding a seductive smile and a not-too-heavy dumbell. And the lead editorial in the September 1986 *Muscle and Beauty* magazine reminds readers that "in this post-feminist age of enlightenment . . . each woman must select the degree of muscularity she wants to achieve" (6). The editor skirts the issue of defining femininity by stressing individual choice and self-definition, but she also emphasizes the fact that muscular women can indeed be beautiful and can also "make babies." Clearly, this emergent tendency of women attempting to control and define their own lives and bodies is being shaped within the existing hegemonic definitions of femininity.

And these magazines, full as they are with advertisements for a huge assortment of products for fat reduction, muscle building (e.g., "Anabolic Mega-Paks"), tanning formulas, and so on suggest that even if bodybuilding does represent an attempt by some women to control and define their own bodies, it is also being expressed in a distorted manner that threatens to replicate many of the more commercialized, narcissistic, and physically unhealthy aspects of men's athletics. Hargreaves (1986, 117) explains the contradictory meaning of women's movement into athletic activities such as bodybuilding, boxing, rugby, and soccer:

> This trend represents an active threat to popular assumptions about sport and its unifying principle appears as a shift in male hegemony. However, it also shows up the contradiction that women are being incorporated into models of male sports that are characterized by fierce competition and aggression and should, therefore, be resisted. Instead of a redefinition of masculinity occurring, this trend highlights the complex ways male hegemony works in sport and ways in which women actively collude in its reproduction.

It is crucial to examine the role that the mass sports media play in contributing to this shift in male hegemony, and it is to this topic that I will turn my attention next.

Female Athletes and the Sports Media

A person viewing an athletic event on television has the illusory impression of immediacy—of being there as it is happening. But as Clarke and Clarke (1982, 73) point out,

> The immediacy is, in fact, *mediated*—between us and the event stand the cameras, camera angles, producers' choice of shots, and commentators' interpretations—the whole invisible apparatus of media presentation. We can never see the whole event, we see those parts which are filtered through this process to us....Rather than immediacy, our real relation to sports on television is one of distance—we are observers, recipients of a media event.

The choices, the filtering, the entire mediation of the sporting event, is based on invisible, taken-for-granted assumptions and values of dominant social groups, and as such the presentation of the event tends to support corporate, white, and male-dominant ideologies. But as Gitlin (1980) has demonstrated, the media is more than a simple conduit for the transmission of dominant ideologies. If it were simply that, then the propaganda function of television would be transparent for all to see, stripping the medium of its veneer of objectivity and thus reducing its legitimacy. Rather, television provides frameworks of meaning that, in effect, selectively interpret not only

the athletic events themselves but also the controversies and problems surrounding the events. Since sport has been a primary arena of ideological
legitimation for male superiority, it is crucial to examine the frameworks of
meaning that the sports media have employed to portray the emergence of
the female athlete.

A potentially counterhegemonic image can be dealt with in a number of
ways by the media. An initial strategy is to marginalize something that is too
big to simply ignore. The 1986 Gay Games in the San Francisco Bay Area are
a good example of this. The games explicitly advocate a value system (equality between women and men, for instance) that runs counter to that of the
existing sports establishment (Messner 1984). Despite the fact that the games
were arguably the Bay Area's largest athletic event of the summer, and that
several events in the games were internationally sanctioned, the paltry
amount of coverage given to the games did *not*, for the most part, appear on
the sports pages or during the sports segment of the television news. The
event was presented in the media not as a legitimate sports event but as a
cultural or lifestyle event. The media's framing of the games invalidated its
claim as a sporting event, thus marginalizing any ideological threat that the
games might have posed to the dominant value system.

Until fairly recently, marginalization was the predominant media strategy
in portraying female athletes. Graydon (1983) states that 90% of sports
reporting still covers male sports. And when female athletes are covered—by
a predominantly male media—they are described either in terms of their
physical desirability to men ("pert and pretty") or in their domestic roles as
wives and mothers. Patronizing or trivializing female athletes is sometimes
not enough to marginalize them ideologically: Top-notch female athletes
have often been subjected to overt hostility intended to cast doubts upon
their true sex. To say "she plays like a man" is a double-edged sword—it is,
on the surface, a compliment to an individual woman's skills, but it also suggests that since she is so good, she must not be a true woman after all. The
outstanding female athlete is portrayed as an exception that proves the rule,
thus reinforcing traditional stereotypes about femininity. Hormonal and
chromosomal femininity tests for female (but no masculinity tests for male)
athletes are a logical result of these ideological assumptions about
male–female biology (Lenskyj 1986).

I would speculate that we are now moving into an era in which female
athletes have worked hard enough to attain a certain level of legitimacy that
makes simple media marginalization and trivialization of female athletes
appear transparently unfair and prejudicial. The framing of female athletes as
sex objects or as sexual deviants is no longer a tenable strategy if the media
are to maintain their own legitimacy. As Gitlin (1980) pointed out in reference to the media's treatment of the student antiwar movement in the late

1960s, when a movement's values become entrenched in a large enough proportion of the population, the media maintains its veneer of objectivity and fairness by incorporating a watered-down version of the values of the oppositional group. In so doing, the ideological hegemony of the dominant group shifts, but is essentially maintained. I would argue that this is precisely what is happening today with women and sport in the media. Women athletes are increasingly being covered by "objective" reports that do not trivialize their performances, make references to a woman's attractiveness, or posit the superior female athlete as a sex deviant. The attitude now seems to be, "They want to be treated equally with men? Well, let's see what they can do."

What is conveniently ignored by today's sportscasters—and liberal feminists, intent on gaining equal opportunities for female athletes, sometimes collude in this—is that male and female bodies do differ in terms of their potential for physical strength, endurance, agility, and grace. Despite considerable overlap, the average adult male is about five inches taller than the average female. Can women really hope to compete at the highest levels with men in basketball or volleyball? The average male has a larger and more powerful body. Males average 40% muscle and 15% body fat, while females average 23% muscle and 25% body fat. Can women possibly compete at the highest levels with men in football, track and field, hockey, or baseball? Women do have some physical differences from men that could be translated into athletic superiority. Different skeletal structures and greater flexibility make for superior performances on a balance beam, for instance. And women's higher body fat ratio gives them greater buoyancy in water and greater insulation from heat loss, which has translated into women's best time in swimming the English Channel both ways being considerably faster than the best times recorded by men. But the fact is, the major sports (especially the "money" sports) are defined largely according to the most extreme possibilities of the male body. If cross-sex competition is truly on the agenda, women are going to be competing at a decided disadvantage, "fighting biology all the way" (Brownmiller 1984, 32), on male-defined turf.

Given these physiological differences between the sexes and the fact that major sports are organized around the most extreme potentialties of the male body, "equal opportunity" as the sports media's dominant framework of meaning for presenting the athletic performances of women athletes is likely to become a new means of solidifying the ideological hegemony of male superiority. With women competing in male-defined sports, the sports media can employ statistics as objective measures of performance. Equal opportunity within this system provides support for the ideology of meritocracy while at the same time offers incontrovertible evidence of the "natural" differences between males and females. And male reporters can simply smile and shrug: "We just call 'em as we see 'em."

Male Responses to Female Athleticism

How people receive and interpret the complex and sometimes contradictory ideological messages they receive through the media is an important issue that deserves more analytic attention than can be offered here (Dunn 1986). I would like to make a tentative speculation here that the emerging images of femininity being forged by women athletes and framed by the media are grudgingly becoming accepted by the majority of males. Although there is clearly some resistance— even outright hostility—toward female athleticism expressed by a small minority of the men I have interviewed, the following statement by a thirty-three-year-old blue collar man is typical of the majority:

> I really enjoy the progress they [female athletes] are making now, having bobby-sox baseball and flag football for little girls. And in high school they have whole leagues now like for the boys. I think that's great. You used to watch women's games in the 60s and in the 70s even, and you could watch all these mistakes—errors on routine grounders, things like that. But now they're really sharp—I mean, they can play a man's game as far as mental sharpness. But I think physically they're limited to their own sex. There is still the male part of the game. That is, males have better physical equipment for sports, as for what they can do and what they can't do.

This man's statement expresses many of the basic ambiguities of male consciousness under liberal capitalism in the "postfeminist" 1980s: embedded in the liberal ideal of equal opportunity is a strong belief that inequality is part of the natural order. Thus, it's only fair that women get an equal shot to compete, but it's really such a relief to find that, once given the opportunity, they just don't have the "physical equipment" to measure up with men. "They're [still] limited to their own sex."

CONCLUSION

I have discounted the simplistic notion that women's increasing athleticism unambiguously signals increased freedom and equality for women with the argument that "equal opportunity" for female athletes may actually mark a shift in the ideological hegemony of male dominance and superiority. But it would be a mistake to conclude from this that women's movement into sport is simply having a reactionary effect in terms of the politics of gender relations. It should not be lost on us that the statement made by the above-mentioned man, even as it expresses a continued need to stress the ways that women are different and inferior to men, also involves a historically unprecedented acknowledgment of women's physicality and "mental sharpness."

It has been argued here that gender relations, along with their concomitant images of masculinity and femininity, change and develop historically as a result of interactions between men and women within socially structured limits and constraints. We can see how the first wave of athletic feminism in the 1920s signaled an active challenge to Victorian constraints on women, and we can see that the way this challenge was resisted and eventually marginalized reflected the limits imposed upon women's quest for equality by an emerging industrial capitalism and a crumbling, but still resilient, patriarchy. Similarly, the current wave of women's athleticism expresses a genuine quest by women for equality, control of their own bodies, and self-definition, but within historical limits and constraints imposed by a consumption-oriented corporate capitalism and men's continued attempts to retain power and privilege over women. As Connell (1987, 251) has pointed out, "In sexual ideology generally, ascendant definitions of reality must be seen as accomplishments that are always partial and always to some extent contested. Indeed we must see them as partly defined by the alternatives against which they are asserted."

Organized sport, as a cultural sphere defined largely by patriarchal priorities, will continue to be an important arena in which emerging images of active, fit, and muscular women are forged, interpreted, contested, and incorporated. The larger socioeconomic and political context will continue to shape and constrain the extent to which women can wage fundamental challenges to the ways that organized sports continue providing ideological legitimation for male dominance. And the media's framing of male and female athletes will continue to present major obstacles for any fundamental challenge to the present commercialized and male-dominant structure of organized athletics. It remains for a critical feminist theory to recognize the emergent contradictions in this system in order to inform a liberating social practice.

Part II

Masculinities:
Class, Race,
Sexualities

3

Masculinities and Athletic Careers

Author's note: I grew up in the 1950s and 1960s, the son of a basketball coach, and dreaming of athletic stardom. I did play basketball in high school, but then hit the wall as a freshman in college, when I discovered that I was too short to play forward, too slow to play guard, and just right to sit on the bench and watch everyone else play. Years later, in graduate school at U.C. Berkeley, I was drawn to the earliest developments of pro-feminist men's organizations in the United States, and to the new scholarship that applied a feminist analysis to the study of men. My advisor Bob Blauner suggested that I apply this analysis to something that I cared about—my own experience as a "failed athlete" and what this had meant for my developing masculine identity. At this moment in history—the mid-1980s,—scholars like Ann Hall, Nancy Theberge, and Susan Birrell had begun to lay a foundation of a feminist analysis of women and sport. But thus far, Don Sabo was the only sociologist who had begun to ask feminist questions about men's sports. I drew from these scholarly developments for my study—life-history interviews with men who were former athletes. In analyzing my interviews, I grappled with trying to come up with good generalizations about how these men's identities were shaped and changed from boyhood to adulthood, as they traversed athletic careers, and then reconstructed identities after disengagement from these careers. I found that there were interesting differences among these men—especially those shaped by their social class and racial-ethnic backgrounds. So I struggled with a dilemma: how can I apply a critical feminist analysis of men's power and privilege in sport, while at the same time be attentive to the importance of differences and inequalities among men? Late in the 1980s, as I wrote this essay, I found the ideas of R. W. Connell useful in grappling with this dilemma. Connell argued that

there is no singular "male sex role." Rather, there are multiple masculinities that are constructed in relation to the subordination of women,
and through men's class, racial, and sexual relations with other men. In
this essay, I focus primarily on how social class shaped men's experiences and masculine identities in ways that led them to different outcomes during and after their athletic careers.

The growth of women's studies and feminist gender studies has led to the
emergence of a new men's studies (Brod 1987; Kimmel 1987). But just as
feminist perspectives on women have been justifiably criticized for falsely universalizing the lives and issues of white, middle-class, U.S. women (hooks
1984; Zinn, Cannon, Higgenbotham, and Dill 1986), so, too, men's studies
has tended to focus on the lives of relatively privileged men. As Brod
(1983–1984) points out in an insightful critique of the middle-class basis and
bias of the men's movement, if men's studies is to be relevant to minority and
working-class men, less emphasis must be placed on personal lifestyle transformations, and more emphasis must be placed on developing a structural critique of social institutions. Although some institutional analysis has begun in
men's studies, very little critical scrutiny has been focused on that very masculine institution, organized sports (Messner 1985; Sabo 1985; Sabo and
Runfola 1980). Not only is the institution of sports an ideal place to study
men and masculinity, careful analysis would make it impossible to ignore the
realities of race and class differences.

In the early 1970s, Edwards (1971, 1973) debunked the myth that the
predominance of blacks in sports to which they have access signaled an end to
institutionalized racism. It is now widely accepted in sport sociology that social
institutions such as the media, education, the economy, and (a more recent
and controversial addition to the list) the black family itself all serve to systematically channel disproportionately large numbers of young black men into
football, basketball, boxing, and baseball, where they are subsequently
"stacked" into low-prestige and high-risk positions, exploited for their skills,
and, finally, when their bodies are used up, excreted from organized athletics
at a young age with no transferable skills with which to compete in the labor
market (Edwards 1984; Eitzen and Purdy 1986; Eitzen and Yetman 1977).

While there are racial differences in involvement in sports, class, age,
and educational differences seem more significant. Rudman's (1986) initial
analysis revealed profound differences between whites' and blacks' orientations to sports. Blacks were found to be more likely than whites to view sports
favorably, to incorporate sports into their daily lives, and to be affected by the
outcome of sporting events. However, when age, education, and social class
were factored into the analysis, Rudman found that race did not explain
whites' and blacks' different orientations. Blacks' affinity to sports is best

explained by their tendency to be clustered disproportionately in lower-income groups.

The 1980s ushered in what Wellman (1986, 43) called a "new political linguistics of race," which emphasize cultural rather than structural causes (and solutions) to the problems faced by black communities. The advocates of the cultural perspective believe that the high value placed on sports by black communities has led to the development of unrealistic hopes in millions of black youths. They appeal to family and community to bolster other choices based on a more rational assessment of "reality." Visible black role models in many other professions now exist, they say, and there is ample evidence that proves that sports careers are, at best, a bad gamble.

Critics of the cultural perspective have condemned it as conservative and victim blaming. But it can also be seen as a response to the view of black athletes as little more than unreflexive dupes of an all-powerful system, which ignores the importance of agency. Gruneau (1983) has argued that sports must be examined within a theory that views human beings as active subjects who are operating within historically constituted structural constraints. Gruneau's reflexive theory rejects the simplistic views of sports as either a realm of absolute oppression or an arena of absolute freedom and spontaneity. Instead, he argues, it is necessary to construct an understanding of how and why participants themselves actively make choices and construct and define meaning and a sense of identity within the institutions that they find themselves.

None of these perspectives consider the ways that gender shapes men's definitions of meaning and choices. Within the sociology of sport, gender as a process that interacts with race and class is usually ignored or taken for granted—except when it is *women* athletes who are being studied. Sociologists who are attempting to come to grips with the experiences of black men in general, and in organized sports in particular, have almost exclusively focused their analytic attention on the variable "black," while uncritically taking "men" as a given. Hare and Hare (1984), for example, view masculinity as a biologically determined tendency to act as a provider and protector that is thwarted for black men by socioeconomic and racist obstacles. Staples (1982) does view masculinity largely as a socially produced script, but he accepts this script as a given, preferring to focus on black men's blocked access to male role fulfillment. These perspectives on masculinity fail to show how the male role itself, as it interacts with a constricted structure of opportunity, can contribute to locking black men into destructive relationships and lifestyles (Franklin 1984; Majors 1986).

In this essay, I will examine the relationships among male identity, race, and social class by listening to the voices of former athletes. I will first briefly describe my research. Then I will discuss the similarities and differences in the choices and experiences of men from different racial and social class backgrounds. Together, these choices and experiences help to construct what

Connell (1987) calls "the gender order." Organized sports, it will be suggested, is a practice through which men's separation from and power over women is embodied and naturalized at the same time that hegemonic (white, heterosexual, professional-class) masculinity is clearly differentiated from marginalized and subordinated masculinities.

DESCRIPTION OF RESEARCH

Between 1983 and 1985, I conducted thirty open-ended, in-depth interviews with male former athletes. My purpose was to add a critical understanding of male gender identity to Levinson's (1978) conception of the "individual life-course"—specifically, to discover how masculinity develops and changes as a man interacts with the socially constructed world of organized sports. Most of the men I interviewed had played the U.S. "major sports"—football, basketball, baseball, track. At the time of the interview, each had been retired from playing organized sports for at least five years. Their ages ranged from twenty-one to forty-eight, with the median, thirty-three. Fourteen were black, fourteen were white, and two were Hispanic. Fifteen of the sixteen black and Hispanic men had come from poor or working-class families, while the majority (nine of fourteen) of the white men had come from middle-class or professional families. Twelve had played organized sports through high school, eleven through college, and seven had been professional athletes. All had at some time in their lives based their identities largely on their roles as athletes and could therefore be said to have had athletic careers.

Male Identity and Organized Sports

Earlier studies of masculinity and sports argued that sports socializes boys to be men (Lever 1976; Schafer 1975). Here, boys learn cultural values and behaviors, such as competition, toughness, and winning at all costs, that are culturally valued aspects of masculinity. While offering important insights, these early studies of masculinity and sports suffered from the limiting assumptions of a gender-role theory that seems to assume that boys come to their first athletic experience as blank slates onto which the values of masculinity are imprinted. This perspective oversimplifies a complex reality. In fact, young boys bring an already gendered identity to their first sports experiences, an identity that is struggling to work through the developmental task of individuation (Chodorow 1978; Gilligan 1982). Yet, as Benjamin (1988) has argued, individuation is accomplished, paradoxically, only through relationships with other people in the social world. So, although the major task of masculinity is the development of a "positional identity" that clarifies the boundaries between self and other, this separation must be accomplished through some form of connection with others. For the men in my study, the rule-bound structure of organized sports became a context in which they struggled to construct a masculine positional identity. All of the men in this study described the emotional salience of their earliest experiences in sports in terms of relationships with other males. It was not winning and victories that seemed important at first; it was something "fun" to do with fathers, older brothers or uncles, and eventually with same-aged peers. As a man from a white, middle-class family said, "The most important thing was just being out there with the rest of the guys—being friends." A thirty-two-year-old man from a poor chicano family, whose mother had died when he was nine years old, put it more succinctly: "What I think sports did for me is it brought me into kind of an instant family. By being on a Little League team, or even just playing with kids in the neighborhood, it brought what I really wanted, which was some kind of closeness."

Though sports participation may have initially promised "some kind of closeness," by the ages of nine or ten the less skilled boys were already becoming alienated from—or weeded out of—the highly competitive and hierarchical system of organized sports. Those who did experience some early successes received recognition from adult males (especially fathers and older brothers) and held higher status among peers. As a result, they began to pour more and more of their energies into athletic participation. It was only after they learned that they would get recognition from other people for being a good athlete—indeed, that this attention was contingent on *being a winner*—that performance and winning (the dominant values of organized sports) became extremely important. For some, this created pressures that served to lessen or eliminated the fun of athletic participation (Messner 1987a, 1987b).

While feminist psychoanalytic and developmental theories of masculinity are helpful in explaining boys' early attraction and motivations in organized sports, the imperatives of core gender identity do not fully determine the contours and directions of the life course. As Rubin (1985) and Levinson (1978) have pointed out, an understanding of the lives of men must take into account the processual nature of male identity as it unfolds through interaction between the internal (psychological ambivalences) and the external (social, historical, and institutional) contexts.

To examine the impact of the social contexts, I divided my sample into two comparison groups. In the first group were ten men from higher-status backgrounds, primarily white, middle-class, and professional families. In the second group were twenty men from lower-status backgrounds, primarily minority, poor, and working-class families. While my data offered evidence for the similarity of experiences and motivations of men from poor back-grounds, independent of race, I also found anecdotal evidence of a racial dynamic that operates independently of social class. However, my sample was not large enough to separate race and class, and so I have combined them to make two status groups.

In discussing these two groups, I will focus mainly on the high school years. During this crucial period, the athletic role may become a master status for a young man as he is beginning to make assessments and choices about his future. It is here that many young men make a major commitment to—or begin to back away from— athletic careers.

MEN FROM HIGHER-STATUS BACKGROUNDS

The boyhood dream of one day becoming a professional athlete—a dream shared by nearly all the men interviewed in this study—is rarely realized. The sports world is extremely hierarchical. The pyramid of sports careers narrows very rapidly as one climbs from high school, to college, to professional levels of competition (Edwards 1984; Harris and Eitzen 1978; Hill and Lowe 1978). In fact, the chances of attaining professional status in sports are approximately 4/100,000 for a white man, 2/100,000 for a black man, and 3/1,000,000 for a Hispanic man in the United States (Leonard and Reyman 1988). For many young athletes, their dream ends early when coaches inform them that they are not big enough, strong enough, fast enough, or skilled enough to compete at the higher levels. But six of the higher-status men I interviewed did not wait for coaches to weed them out. They made conscious decisions in high school or in college to shift their attentions elsewhere—usually toward educational and career goals. Their decision not to pursue an athletic career appeared to them in retrospect to be a rational decision based on the growing knowledge of how very slim their chances were to be successful in the sports world. For instance, a twenty-eight-year-old white graduate student said:

> By junior high I started to realize that I was a good player—maybe even one of the best in my community—but I realized that there were all these people all over the country and how few will get to play pro sports. By high school, I still dreamed of being a pro—I was a serious athlete, I played hard—but I knew it wasn't heading anywhere. I wasn't going to play pro ball.

A thirty-two-year-old white athletic director at a small private college had been a successful college baseball player. Despite considerable attention from professional scouts, he had decided to forgo a shot at a baseball career and to enter graduate school to pursue a teaching credential. He explained this decision: "At the time I think I saw baseball as pissing in the wind, really.

I was married, I was twenty-two years old with a kid. I didn't want to spend four or five years in the minors with a family. And I could see I wasn't a superstar; so it wasn't really worth it. So I went to grad school. I thought that would be better for me."

Perhaps most striking was the story of a high school student body president and top-notch student who was also "Mr. Everything" in sports. He was named captain of his basketball, baseball, and football teams and achieved All-League honors in each sport. This young white man from a middle-class family received attention from the press and praise from his community and peers for his athletic accomplishments, as well as several offers of athletic scholarships from universities. But by the time he completed high school, he had already decided to quit playing organized sports. As he said, "I think in my own mind I kind of downgraded the stardom thing. I thought that was small potatoes. And sure, that's nice in high school and all that, but on a broad scale, I didn't think it amounted to all that much. So I decided that my goal's to be a dentist, as soon as I can." In his sophomore year of college, the basketball coach nearly persuaded him to go out for the team, but eventually he decided against it: "I thought, so what if I can spend two years playing basketball? I'm not going to be a basketball player forever and I might jeopardize my chances of getting into dental school if I play." He finished college in three years, completed dental school, and now in his mid-thirtys, is again the epitome of the successful American man: professional with a family, a home, and a membership in the local country club.

How and why do so many successful male athletes from high-status backgrounds come to view sports careers as "pissing in wind," or as " small potatoes"? How and why do they make this early assessment and choice to shift from sports and toward educational and professional goals? The white, middle-class institutional context, with its emphasis on education and income, makes it clear to them that choices exist and that the pursuit of an athletic career is not a particularly good choice to make. Where the young male once found sports to be a convenient institution within which to construct masculine status, the post adolescent and young adult man from a higher-status background simply *transfers* these same strivings to other institutional contexts: education and careers.

For the higher-status men who had chosen to shift from athletic careers, sports remained important on two levels. First, having been a successful high school or college athlete enhances one's adult status among other men in the community—but only as a badge of masculinity that is *added* to his professional status. In fact, several men in professions chose to be interviewed in their offices, where they publicly displayed the trophies and plaques that attested to their earlier athletic accomplishments. Their high school and college athletic careers may have appeared to them as "small potatoes," yet many successful men speak of their earlier status as athletes as having "opened doors" for them in their present professions and in community affairs. Similarly, Farr's (1988) research on "Good Old Boys Sociability Groups" shows how sports, as part of the glue of masculine culture, continues to facilitate "dominance bonding" among privileged men long after active sports careers end. The college-educated, career-successful men in Farr's study rarely express overtly sexist, racist, or classist attitudes; in fact, in their relationships with women, they "often engage in expressive intimacies" and "make fun of exaggerated 'machismo'" (276). But though they outwardly conform more to what Pleck (1982) calls "the modern male role," their informal relationships within their sociability groups, in effect, affirm their own gender and class status by constructing and clarifying the boundaries between themselves and women and lower-status men. This dominance bonding is based largely on ritual forms of sociability (camaraderie, competition), "the superiority of which was first affirmed in the exclusionary play activities of young boys in groups" (Farr 1988, 265).

In addition to contributing to dominance bonding among higher-status adult men, sports remains salient in terms of the ideology of gender relations. Most men continued to watch, talk about, and identify with sports long after their own disengagement from athletic careers. Sports as a mediated spectacle provides an important context in which traditional conceptions of masculine superiority—conceptions recently contested by women—are shored up. As a thirty-two-year-old white professional-class man said of one of the most feared professional football players today: "A woman can do the same job as I can do—maybe even be my boss. But I'll be *damned* if she can go out on the football field and take a hit from Ronnie Lott."

Violent sports as spectacle provide linkages among men in the project of the domination of women, while at the same time help to construct and clarify differences among various masculinities. The statement above is a clear identification with Ronnie Lott *as a man,* and the basis of the identification is the violent male body. As Connell (1987, 85) argues, sports is an important organizing institution for the embodiment of masculinity. Here, men's power over women becomes naturalized and linked to the social distribution of violence. Sports, as a practice, suppresses natural (sex) similarities, constructs differences, and then, largely through the media, weaves a structure of symbol and interpretation around these differences that naturalizes them (Hargreaves 1986, 112). It is also significant that the man who made the above statement about Ronnie Lott was quite aware that he (and perhaps 99% of the rest of the U.S. male population) was probably as incapable as most women of taking a "hit" from someone like Lott and living to tell of it. For middle-class men, the "tough guys" of the culture industry—the Rambos, the Ronnie Lotts who are fearsome "hitters," who "play hurt"—are the heroes who "prove" that "we men" are superior to women. At the same time, they play the role of the "primitive other," against whom higher-status men define themselves as "modern" and "civilized."

Sports, then, is important from boyhood through adulthood for men from higher-status backgrounds. But it is significant that by adolescence and early adulthood, most of these young men have concluded that sports *careers* are not for them. Their middle-class cultural environment encourages them to decide to shift their masculine strivings in more "rational" directions: education and nonsports careers. Yet their previous sports participation continues to be very important to them in terms of constructing and validating their status within privileged male peer groups and within their chosen professional careers. And organized sports, as a public spectacle, is a crucial locus around which ideologies of male superiority over women, as well as higher-status men's superiority over lower-status men, are constructed and naturalized.

MEN FROM LOWER-STATUS BACKGROUNDS

For the lower-status young men in this study, success in sports was not an added proof of masculinity; it was often their only hope of achieving public masculine status. A thirty-four-year-old black bus driver who had been a star athlete in three sports in high school had neither the grades nor the money to attend college, so he accepted an offer from the U.S. Marine Corps to play on their baseball team. He ended up in Vietnam, where a grenade blew four fingers off his pitching hand. In retrospect, he believed that his youthful focus on sports stardom and his concomitant lack of effort in academics made sense:

> You can go anywhere with athletics—you don't have to have brains. I mean, I didn't feel like I was gonna go out there and be a computer expert, or something that was gonna make a lot of money. The only thing I could do and live comfortably would be to play sports—just to get a contract— doesn't matter if you play second or third team in the pros, you're gonna make big bucks. That's all I wanted, a confirmed livelihood at the end of my ventures, and the only way I could do it would be through sports. So I tried. It failed, but that's what I tried.

Similar, and even more tragic, is the story of a thirty-four-year-old black man who is now serving a life term in prison. After a career-ending knee injury at the age of twenty abruptly derailed what had appeared to be a certain road to professional football fame and fortune, he decided that he "could still be rich and famous" by robbing a bank. During his high school and college years, he said, he was nearly illiterate: "I'd hardly ever go to classes and they'd give me Cs. My coaches taught some of the classes. And I felt, 'So what? They *owe* me that! I'm an *athlete!*' I thought that was what I was born to do—to play sports—and everybody understood that."

Are lower-status boys and young men simply duped into putting all their eggs into one basket? My research suggested that there was more than "hope for the future" operating here. There were also immediate psychological reasons that they chose to pursue athletic careers. By the high school years, class and ethnic inequalities had become glaringly obvious, especially for those who attended socioeconomically heterogeneous schools. Cars, nice clothes, and others signs of status were often unavailable to these young men, and this contributed to a situation in which sports took on an expanded importance for them in terms of constructing masculine identities and status. A white, thirty-six-year-old man from a poor, single-parent family who later played professional baseball had been acutely aware of his low-class status in his high school:

> I had one pair of jeans, and I wore them every day. I was always afraid of what people thought of me—that this guy doesn't have anything, that he's wearing the same Levi's all the time, he's having to work in the cafeteria for his lunch. What's going on? I think that's what made me so shy.... But boy, when I got into sports, I let it all hang out—[laughs]— and maybe that's why I became so good, because I was frustrated, and when I got into that element, they gave me my uniform in football, basketball, and base-ball, and I didn't have to worry about how I looked, because then it was *me* who was coming out, and not my clothes or whatever. And I think that was the drive.

Similarly, a forty-one-year-old black man who had a ten-year profes-sional football career described his insecurities as one of the few poor blacks in a mostly white, middle-class school and his belief that sports was the one arena in which he could be judged solely on his merit:

> I came from a very poor family, and I was very sensitive about that in those days. When people would say things like "Look at him—he has dirty pants on," I'd think about it for a week. [But] I'd put my pants on and I'd go out on the football field with the intention that I'm gonna do a job. And if that calls on me to hurt you, I'm gonna do it. It's as simple as that. I demand respect just like everybody else.

"Respect" was what I heard over and over when talking with the men from lower-status backgrounds, especially black men. I interpret this type of respect to be a crystallization of the masculine quest for recognition through public achievement, unfolding within a system of structured constraints due to class and race inequities. The institutional context of education (some-times with the collusion of teachers and coaches) and the constricted structure of opportunity in the economy made the pursuit of athletic careers appear to be the most rational choice to these young men.

The same is not true of young lower-status women. Dunkle (1985) points out that from junior high school through adulthood, young black men are far more likely to place high value on sports than are young black women, who are more likely to value academic achievement. There appears to be a gender dynamic operating in adolescent male peer groups that contributes toward their valuing sports more highly than education. Franklin (1986, 161) has argued that many of the normative values of the black male peer group (little respect for nonaggressive solutions to disputes, contempt for nonmaterial culture) contribute to the constriction of black men's views of desirable social positions, especially through education. In my study, a forty-two-year-old black man who did succeed in beating the odds by using his athletic scholarship to get a college degree and eventually becoming a successful professional said: "By junior high, you either got identified as an athlete, a thug, or a bookworm. It's very important to be seen as somebody who's capable in some area. And you *don't* want to be identified as a bookworm. I was very good with books, but I was kind of covert about it. I was a closet bookworm. But with sports, I was *somebody*; so I worked very hard at it."

For most young men from lower-status backgrounds, the poor quality of their schools, the attitudes of teachers and coaches, as well as the antieducation environment within their own male peer groups, made it extremely unlikely that they would be able to succeed as students. Sports, therefore, became *the* arena in which they attempted to "show their stuff." For these lower-status men, as Baca Zinn (1982) and Majors (1986) argued in their respective studies of chicano men and black men, when institutional resources that signify masculine status and control are absent, physical presence, personal style, and expressiveness take on increased importance. What Majors (1986, 6) calls "cool pose" is black men's expressive, often aggressive, assertion of masculinity. This self-assertion often takes place within a social context in which the young man is quite aware of existing social inequities. As the black bus driver, referred to earlier, said of his high school years:

> See, the rich people use their money to do what they want to do. I use my ability. If you wanted to be around me, if you wanted to learn something about sports, I'd teach you. But you're gonna take me to lunch. You're gonna let me use your car. See what I'm saying? In high school I'd go where I wanted to go. I didn't have to be educated. I was well-respected. I'd go somewhere, and they'd say, "Hey, that's Mitch Harris, yeah, that's a bad son of a bitch!"

Majors (1986) argues that although "cool pose" represents a creative survival technique within a hostile environment, the most likely long-term effect of this masculine posturing is educational and occupational dead ends. As a result, we can conclude, lower-status men's personal and peer-group responses to a constricted structure of opportunity—responses that are rooted, in part, in the developmental insecurities and ambivalences of masculinity—serve to lock many of these young men into limiting activities such as sports.

SUMMARY AND CONCLUSIONS

This research has suggested that within a social context that is stratified by social class and by race, the choice to pursue—or not to pursue—an athletic career is explicable as an individual's rational assessment of the available means to achieve a respected masculine identity. For nearly all of the men from lower-status backgrounds, the status and respect that they received through sports were temporary—it did not translate into upward mobility. Nonetheless, a strategy of discouraging young black boys and men from involvement in sports is probably doomed to fail, since it ignores the continued existence of structural constraints. Despite the increased number of black role models in nonsports professions, employment opportunities for young black males actually deteriorated in the 1980s (Wilson and Neckerman 1986), and nonathletic opportunities in higher education also declined. While blacks constitute 14% of the college-aged (eighteen–twenty-four years) U.S. population, as a proportion of students in four-year colleges and universities, they have dropped to 8%. In contrast, by 1985, black men constituted 49% of all college basketball players and 61% of basketball players in institutions that grant athletic scholarships (Berghorn et al., 1988). For young black men, then, organized sports appears to be more likely to get them to college than their own efforts in nonathletic activities.

But it would be a mistake to conclude that we simply need to breed socioeconomic conditions that make it possible for poor and minority men to mimic the "rational choices" of white, middle-class men. If we are to build an appropriate understanding of the lives of all men, we must critically analyze white middle-class masculinity, rather than uncritically taking it as a normative standard. To fail to do this would be to ignore the ways in which organized sports serves to construct and legitimate gender differences and inequalities among men and women.

Feminist scholars have demonstrated that organized sports gives men from all backgrounds a means of status enhancement that is not available to young women. Sports thus serve the interests of all men in helping to construct and legitimize their control of public life and their domination of women (Bryson 1987; Hall 1987; Theberge 1987). Yet concrete studies are suggesting that men's experiences within sports are not all of a piece. Brian Pronger's (1990b) research suggests that gay men approach sports differently than straight men do, with a sense of "irony." And my research suggests that although sports are important for men from both higher- and lower-status backgrounds, there are crucial differences. In fact, it appears that the meaning that most men give to their athletic strivings has more to do with competing for status among men than it has to do with proving superiority over women. How can we explain this seeming contradiction between the feminist claim that sports links all men in the domination of women and the research findings that different groups of men relate to sports in very different ways?

The answer to this question lies in developing a means of conceptualizing the interrelationships between varying forms of domination and subordination. Marxist scholars of sports often falsely collapse everything into a class analysis; radical feminists often see gender domination as universally fundamental. Concrete examinations of sports, however, reveal complex and multilayered systems of inequality: racial, class, gender, sexual preference, and age dynamics are all salient features of the athletic context. In examining this reality, Connell's (1987) concept of the "gender order" is useful. The gender order is a dynamic process that is constantly in a state of play. Moving beyond static gender-role theory and reductionist concepts of patriarchy that view men as an undifferentiated group that oppresses women, Connell argues that at any given historical moment, there are competing masculinities— some hegemonic, some marginalized, some stigmatized. Hegemonic masculinity (that definition of masculinity that is culturally ascendant) is constructed in relation to various subordinated masculinities as well as in relation to femininities. The project of male domination of women may tie all men together, but men share very unequally in the fruits of this domination.

These are key insights in examining the contemporary meaning of sports. Utilizing the concept of the gender order, we can begin to conceptualize how hierarchies of race, class, age, and sexual preference among men help to construct and legitimize men's overall power and privilege over women. And how, for some black, working-class, or gay men, the false promise of sharing in the fruits of hegemonic masculinity often ties them into their marginalized and subordinate statuses within hierarchies of intermale dominance. For instance, black men's development of what Majors (1986) calls "cool pose" within sports can be interpreted as an example of creative resistance to one form of social domination (racism); yet it also demonstrates the limits of an agency that adopts other forms of social domination (masculinity) as its vehicle. As Majors (1990) points out: "Cool Pose demonstrates black males' potential to transcend oppressive conditions in order to express themselves *as men*. [Yet] it ultimately does not put black males in a position to live and work in more egalitarian ways with women, nor does it directly challenge male hierarchies."

Indeed, as Connell's (1990) analysis of an Australian "Iron Man" shows, the commercially successful, publicly acclaimed athlete may embody all that is valued in present cultural conceptions of hegemonic masculinity—physical strength, commercial success, supposed heterosexual virility. Yet higher-status men, while they admire the public image of the successful athlete, may also look down on him as a narrow, even atavistic, example of masculinity. For these higher-status men, their earlier sports successes are often status enhancing and serve to link them with other men in ways that continue to exclude women. Their decisions not to pursue athletic careers are equally important signs of their status vis-à-vis other men. Future examinations of the contemporary meaning and importance of sports to men might take as a fruitful point of departure that athletic participation, and sports as public spectacle, serve to provide linkages among men in the project of the domination of women, while at the same time help to construct and clarify differences and hierarchies among various masculinities.

4

White Men Misbehaving

Feminism, Afrocentrism, and the Promise of a
Critical Standpoint

Author's note: As the 1990s rolled around, it had become clear to scholars that we can never look simply at gender, that we need always simultaneously to take into account other systems of inequality. Theories of race/class/gender/sexuality offered a language of "intersectionality" and "matrixes of domination"—language that only began to hint at how we might grapple empirically with these complexities. This essay is based on a keynote address I delivered in 1992 to the North American Society for the Sociology of Sport (NASSS), in which I discussed the contradictions of my own position as a privileged white male academic, trying be a responsible public intellectual around complex and sticky issues at the intersections of race and gender. The early 1990s were a time of accelerated concern about young black males in the United States, and sport was a highly visible site of debate about problems, dangers, and possibilities for improvements in the lives of black boys and men. In this essay, I reflected on this contemporary debate by drawing from an idea introduced by feminist epistemologists: that one's standpoint (one's understanding of the world) is structured by one's position within intersecting systems of privilege and subordination. These ideas suggested that for a privileged person like myself to begin to understand race and gender, and then to act in progressive ways, involved trying to see the world through multiple standpoints, especially through the experiences of groups of people with less privilege than I have. I explored the ways that the then-newly-emergent "black feminist thought" of Patricia Hill Collins and others

offered scholars critical points of entrée through which to understand
the limits of standpoints of privileged people, as well as the standpoints
of white feminist women and black male Afrocentrists, while building
the foundation of a progressive coalition politics.

When scholars of sports talk about power and social inequality, they
often advocate "resistance." But I often wonder, "resistance against
what?" On a surface level, the answer to this question is simple: I want my
work to contribute to cultural and political resistance against oppression and
exploitation. But when we actually begin to focus on specific issues, it gets a
lot more complicated.

For instance, some time ago I was called on the phone by a representative of the National Organization for Women Legal Defense and Education
Fund, who was searching for a male academic who would publicly take a
stand against the controversial movement in Detroit to establish all-male
public schools in predominantly African American districts. "Well," I waf-
fled, "I'm not for it, but I do understand how the deteriorating conditions in
urban communities and schools, and the especially devastating impact on
young African American males, have led many African Americans to desperately search for solutions." "Yes," the NOW representative replied, "we know
that too, but our position is that there is no evidence that separating boys
from girls is going to solve those problems. In fact, we are worried that this
approach ignores the problems faced by African American girls, and will jus-
tify tipping more educational resources away from them. Would you be willing to testify on behalf of our position?" "Well," I sidestepped and
back-pedalled, "I really think it's more appropriate that you find African
American scholars to talk about this."

In the end, I passed on the opportunity to take a public stand on this
issue. My gut-level reason was that I felt that it was inappropriate for me, a
white male academic, to take a public stand against a grassroots initiative in
an African American community. But I also felt that in taking no public stand
on this issue, I had failed in my commitment to support women's quest for
equality. After having spent much of my time in the past few years researching, writing, and teaching about the ways that race, class, gender, and sexual
systems of oppression often "intersect," my theories, it seemed, were revealed
as useless ivory tower exercises. I felt, in short, like a bit of a chump.

After pondering this incident for some time, I'm a bit less hard on myself.
I am convinced, though, that it raised some fundamental issues that need to
be explored and publicly discussed more fully. The primary issue that I will
focus on here is the ongoing question of how we can conceptualize the relationships between racial and gender oppression. In particular, I will discuss
how African American males stand in very contradictory manner at the

nexus of intersecting systems of racial and gender oppression (Collins 1990). But conceptualizing and theorizing are clearly not enough. Also at issue is how we, as social scientists, connect our theory and research to the real world. How do we, as Russell Jacoby (1987) asked, serve as responsible "public intellectuals"? This question, it seems to me, is at the heart of recent debates within NASSS about "applied sport sociology" (Chalip 1990; Ingham and Donnelly 1990; Yiannakis 1989). I think the key question is not "should our research be engaged with the real world," but rather, "whose interests should our research serve?" It is quite simple to respond to this question by asserting that we aim for our work to serve "the oppressed," against the interests of the oppressors. But it's clearly not that simple. Many of us have acknowledged that it's necessary to move beyond Marxist class reductionist or radical feminist gender reductionist theories that tend to oversimplify the world by falsely collapsing all forms of oppression into one supposedly "primary" cause. Instead, the current movement in progressive sociology is toward theories that conceptualize multiple, semiautonomous, cross-cutting systems of inequality (Baca Zinn et al. 1986; Collins 1990). Thus far, though, most attempts at grand theories of these interrelated systems of power, or even more modest conceptual efforts (e.g., Messner and Sabo 1990), tend to fall short of the task. One reason is that these models tend to assume— altogether too optimistically—that different forms of oppression are part of the same social or cultural dynamic. As a result of this oversimplification, they also tend to assume an underlying congruence of interests, goals and strategies among the various movements that struggle against these forms of oppression. But when progressive movements perceive their interests as conflicting—as happened in the Detroit case, where an African American community attempting to take control of their schools came into conflict with feminists—our theories are revealed to be inadequate.

In this essay, I will explore this intersection of race and gender by examining two ascendant political discourses about African American males: Afrocentrism, and black feminist thought. The current conversations between these two political discourses, I will suggest, offer new standpoints for the study of sport and culture. A potential outcome of this new standpoint is not only a more clear understanding of how race and gender interact in the lives of African American women and men, but also the establishment of a critical perspective that decenters, and thus problematizes, hegemonic masculinity, rather than taking it as a universal normative standard.

YOUNG BLACK MALES AND AFROCENTRISM

I experienced the Los Angeles Rebellions of 1992 like most everybody else: I watched them on television, though the smell of smoke and the constant sound of helicopters overhead added a troubling dimension of realism to the televised spectacle. One moment in the televised coverage stays with me more than any other. As I watched an image of what appeared to be three white male youths jumping up and down on a car and smashing it with crowbars, the news commentator's voice-over said, "Black youth are rampaging in the South-Central area." At that moment, I was reminded of an article I had recently read by Stuart Alan Clarke (1991), in which he asserts that American society is obsessed with images of "black men misbehaving." Indeed, I thought, even when our eyes clearly show us a scene of young white men "misbehaving," the conventional ideological news frame still tends to construct the black male as the villain. And young black males are all too aware of this. For instance, about two years ago at the University of Southern California, where I teach, there were several attempted rapes in a campus parking structure by a man who was described as a "tall, thin, thirtyish, black male." One of my black male students, twentyish, short, and stout told me that he was put up against the wall and frisked by police on campus. He told me that "all of us black guys know to walk around campus with books and briefcases, dressed like students, or we'll be hassled by the police."

Woody Allen—whom I'm not so sure it's politically correct to quote these days—nevertheless once said that "90% of success in life is just showing up." He had a bit of a point there, but I suspect his statement is more accurate in explaining the accomplishments of white males from privileged backgrounds. There are abundant examples of not-so-talented white males who have managed to parlay their cultural capital into positions of power. In fact, the example of Dan Quayle suggests that Woody Allen may have understated his point. But for women, for poor or blue-collar people, for people of color, for gays and lesbians, just showing up is not nearly enough—they often must fight for rights and for respect. Indeed, in my research with male former athletes, the black men often spoke of the importance of respect as a prime motivating force in their athletic strivings (Messner 1992). They knew, and had directly experienced the reality, that black males, especially in public life, are far more likely to be suspected than respected. This shared experience of suspicion and lack of respect among African American males goes a long way toward explaining the organized—and I am sure in some ways highly ambivalent and agonized—support that Mike Tyson and Clarence Thomas received from some sectors of the African American community. The easy framing of Tyson as a sexual predator and an animal, in particular, played off of and into all of the most destructive and racist stereotypes about black males in American society.

Young black males today are living with the legacy of twenty-plus years of deindustrialization, rising joblessness, declining inner-city schools, and twelve years of Republicanism that simply preaches "just say no" to drugs and gangs, while the only things worth saying "yes" to crumble (Wilson 1987). As

Elijah Anderson (1990) observes, the decline of solid blue-collar jobs for black males, along with the suburban flight of much of the black middle class has left young inner-city black males with few "old heads," a term that refers to adult male community leaders who have traditionally taught young males the value of hard work, family support, and community responsibility. Today, Anderson observes, these traditional "old heads" have been replaced by the more respected "new heads"—young street toughs and drug dealers with wads of cash. For a very limited number of black male youth, one kind of "old head" remains: the inner-city coach. A chillingly moving *Sports Illustrated* photo essay recently featured the Dorsey High School football team in Southwest Los Angeles, and their coach, Paul Knox (Miller and Smith 1992). The text accompanying this photo essay described Coach Knox and his assistants as "strong black men who serve not only as coaches, but as role models. They talk to their players like brothers. They listen to them like fathers. They try like hell to keep their players safe" (46). From this piece, one gets the impression of life on the football team at Dorsey as a bit of an oasis within a war zone. As gunshots sound outside the stadium, teammates who belong to different gangs embrace and support each other. Within this context, it should be no surprise that athletic careers still appear to be the way "up and out" for many young black males. Adult leaders might preach to these youth to emphasize "books first," but the realities they experience every day tend to point them in different directions. For the athletically inclined, sports is one of these directions. And no matter how much parents, teachers, or community leaders stress "books first," the college statistics for nonathlete black males are not encouraging. In the 1990–1991 academic year, the proportion of students in Division I schools who were African American was only 6%, while scholarship athletes were 22.3% black, scholarship football players were 42.7% black, and scholarship men's basketball players were 59.9% black. At my university, where only 4.7% of all students are black, 31.8% of those on athletic scholarships are black, while scholarship football players and men's basketball players are 44.7% and 84.6%, respectively (Lederman 1992).

Educators and sport sociologists can debate the question of whether encouraging young black males to pursue athletic careers is helpful or not. But the reality is, when young boys from the neighborhood surrounding USC walk through campus, they see what must appear to be an ocean of mostly white faces and blonde hair. When they look out on the athletic training fields or in the gym, or watch a game on television, they see a very high proportion of blacks. I suspect that this reality, that they see with their own eyes, speaks more loudly than any words.

African American males' shared knowledge of the increasingly limited structure of opportunity that they face and their day-to-day experience of

Americans' obsession with "black men misbehaving" also go a long way toward explaining the forms that progressive movements in African American communities are taking today. The current Afrocentric move-ment is surely not in the tradition of Martin Luther King's calls for racial integration. Instead, it echoes Malcolm X's calls for community autonomy. And just as with the Muslim and Black Power movements of the 1960s, central to Afrocentrism today is a militant assertion of "black manhood." This concern was depicted in the film *Boyz n the Hood*. The film suggests that the young males in the 'hood are faced with two major options: the first is to follow the lead of the young hoodlum "new heads," and likely end up cycling in and out of prison and eventually getting killed at a young age. A second possibility is suggested in the case of the talented young football player who is being recruited by USC. This option, too, is revealed as a dead end, as the youth's talents and dreams cannot safeguard him from the violence in his community. Indeed, recently, one of USC's football players was struck during practice by a stray bullet from local gang violence, demonstrating in a very real way the thin line between the street and the athletic field for many of these young men. But *Boyz n the Hood* offers a ray of hope. Here, for one of the very few times in American cinema, a positive image of an African American father was presented. And the son of this father, we see, eventually makes the right choices that allow him to escape the violent 'hood and attend college. This was undoubtedly a positive mes-sage, but for me, this film raised the same troubling question that the Detroit all-male schools issue raised: what about the women? In order to make its point that a strong father is the answer to the problem of black male youth, the film went about depicting mothers as either irresponsible crack addicts, unfair bitches, or upwardly mobile professionals who neglect their children for their careers.

BLACK FEMINISM AND THE GENDER POLITICS OF AFROCENTRISM

Twenty years ago, the masculinist gender politics of antiracism organizations were rarely questioned. The few black feminists, such as Michelle Wallace (1978), who challenged assumptions of male superiority by leaders such as Eldridge Cleaver or Stokely Carmichael were accused of undermining the cause of black liberation by dividing women from men. Today, with assertions of black manhood again taking center stage in Afrocentric discourse and political practice, there is a broader, more assertive and sophisticated response from black women. For example, two years ago I attended a session on black males at the American Sociological Association meetings, where

Elijah Anderson presented some of the findings of his ethnographic research that later became *Streetwise*. Anderson told the following story, based on the narrative of a black man, of a late-night street interaction between three black males and a white woman:

> A white lady walkin' down the street with a pocketbook. She start walkin' fast. She get so paranoid she break into a little stride. Me and my friends comin' from a party about 12:00. She stops and goes up on the porch of a house, but you could tell she didn't live there. I stop and say, "Miss, you didn't have to do that. I thought you might think we're some wolf pack. I'm twenty-eight, he's twenty-six, he's twenty-nine. You ain't gotta run from us." She said, "Well, I'm sorry." I said, "You can come down. I know you don't live there. We just comin' from a party." We just walked down the street and she came back down, walked across the street where she really wanted to go. So she tried to act as though she lived there. And she didn't. After we said, "You ain't gotta run from us," she said, "No, I was really in a hurry." My boy said, "No you wasn't. You thought we was gon' snatch yo' pocketbook." We pulled money out. "See this, we work." I said, "We grown men, now. You gotta worry about them fifteen-, sixteen-, seventeen-year-old boys. That's what you worry about. But we're grown men." I told her all this. "They the ones ain't got no jobs; they're too young to really work. They're the ones you worry about, not us." She understood that. You could tell she was relieved and she gave a sigh. She came back down the steps, even went across the street. (Anderson 1990, 167–168)

The point of Anderson's story— that in public places, black males are commonly unfairly suspected of being violent rapists—was well taken. But the woman in the story was a somewhat humorous prop for making this point about the indignities that black males face. Anderson did not appear to have much empathy for her. As he finished telling the story, a white woman sitting in front of me whispered to the white woman next to her, "He acts like she had no reason to be frightened of a pack of men. *Of course she* was scared! Women are attacked and raped every day!" It seemed clear to me that this woman identified and empathized with the white woman in the story, but gave no indication that she understood Anderson's point about the impact of this omnipresent suspicion on the vast majority of black males who do not rape. After the talk, during the discussion session, an African American woman stood up and bridged this chasm by eloquently empathizing with the legitimate fears of the woman *and* with the cumulative public humiliation of the black males in the story. The woman *and* the men in this story, she asserted, were differentially victimized in public space. The solution lies in their learning to empathize with each other, and then building from that common empathy a movement that fights against the oppressive system that dehumanizes them both.

This scene, it seemed to me, demonstrated both the limits of masculinist Afrocentrism and of white feminism, while demonstrating the role that black feminism can play in creating a new standpoint that bridges these two movements. As Patricia Hill Collins (1990) has so eloquently put it, black women are often "outsiders within"—as women, they are outsiders within the Afrocentric movement; as blacks, they are outsiders within feminism. This social position "on the margins," to use bell hooks's (1984) terminology, gives black women a unique standpoint through which the complex mechanisms and interweavings of power and oppression can be more clearly deconstructed and, possibly, resisted. From a black feminist standpoint, African American males' unique experiences of oppression are acknowledged and struggled against. But black feminists do not accept the analysis presented by some men of color (e.g., Peña 1991; Staples 1992) that interprets public displays of misogyny, rape, and other forms of violence against women by men of color primarily as distorted or displaced responses to racism and to class constraints. Instead, gender must be viewed *not* as a "superstructural" manifestation of class and/or racial politics, but as a semi-autonomous system of power relations between women and men (Baca Zinn et al, 1986; Collins 1990).

In an essay on black masculinity, bell hooks (1992) charges that what she calls "conservative Afrocentric males" often draw on "phallocentric masculinity" as a resource to fight racial oppression. And, she observes, public figures such as Eddie Murphy and Spike Lee tend to exploit the commodification of phallocentric black masculinity. But, hooks argues, there exist also what she calls "progressive Afrocentric males," including many gay black men, who are, in her words, "not sitting around worried about castration and emasculation," but are instead exploring more egalitarian relationships with women and with other men. In the concluding section of this essay, I will explore how this emergent dialogue between progressive Afrocentric males and black feminists might inform critical studies of sport.

THE PROMISE OF A CRITICAL STANDPOINT IN SPORT STUDIES

Susan Birrell (1989, 1990) has suggested that we should build theory by listening to the "home truths" of the "critical autobiography" of women of color. Building on Birrell's argument, Yvonne Smith (1992, 228) has argued that more studies of women of color in sport would contribute to a more "inclusive womanist/feminist scholarship and race relations theory." I agree with this, and I am also convinced that it would be most fruitful for sport scholars to listen to the public conversations taking place today between Afrocentric males and black feminist women. An example of this conversation can be found in bell hooks's (1990) dialogue with Cornel West. And those of us who attended the "author meets critics" session at the 1992 American Sociological Association Meetings, where Patricia Hill Collins's book, *Black Feminist Thought* was discussed, witnessed some of this ongoing dialogue between African American female and male scholars. Theory construction is under way in these conversations.

One promise that these conversations hold is that even those of us who are not central players can listen in and learn to ask new, critical questions. Decentered theoretically, we can begin to turn commonly asked questions back on themselves: not "why do black men so often misbehave," but rather, why are we so *obsessed* with this question, and what, in fact, about the everyday misbehaviors of *white* men and *middle and upper-class* men? The invisible presence in Elijah Anderson's street scene, discussed above, is the powerful white men, who, through their control of institutions, have removed jobs from the inner cities, cut aid to schools, allowed police protection for citizens to deteriorate while allowing some police to engage in racist terror tactics, and refused to take the measures that might make public life safe for women, thus imposing a de facto curfew on women. But privileged males are invisible in this story because the race, class, and gendered power of these males is attached to their positions in institutions, not to their personal behaviors in the street. In fact, their everyday actions in political, corporate, or educational institutions are commonly defined as "normal" male behavior. Our task as scholars, it seems to me, is to raise critical questions about the "normal" operation of hegemonic masculinity in such a way that these actions are redefined as "misbehaviors."

I am convinced that black feminist thought offers a critical theoretical framework with which we might better understand the crucial issues of our day. For instance, with many colleges and universities today "downsizing," when women file Title IX suits intended to push educational institutions toward gender equity, one response by universities may be to simply cut sports, as appears to have happened recently at Brooklyn College. Potentially, this sort of situation positions males—especially those poor and black males who see athletic scholarships as their main hope for upward mobility— against equality for women's sports.

This tension between defenders of men's sports—especially football— and advocates of women's sports is already evident. For instance, Donna Lopiano (1992), currently the head of the Women's Sports Foundation, has described a cartoon that she would like to see appear in *The Chronicle of Higher Education*. The cartoon consists of a single frame in which a flock of geese, each with a potbelly and wearing a football helmet, is flying in a "V" formation. The lead goose is plummeting to the earth, a plume of smoke in his wake. Below, standing on the ground, are two women, dressed in athletic uniforms, holding shotguns. One of them is saying to the other, "Don't they know we're just shooting blanks?"

I suggest that Lopiano's cartoon represents a much more complex picture if we take into account more than simply the standpoint of the two women athletes. First, I pictured the flock of geese (who represent men's football programs) as being made up of 42.7% black males, flying over a campus community that is only 6% black. The lead goose, plummeting to the earth, is a young black man whose dream of an NFL contract has been dashed by a serious injury. One of the black geese is saying about the women who are shooting at them, "Don't *they* know that we have to dress up like this and learn to fly in formation in order to be allowed on this campus?" I envision yet a third presence in this picture. Standing just at the margin, barely inside the frame, a black feminist speaks to both the "geese" and to the women athletes, "What are all of you fools *doing*? They've got you young men endangering your lives in a brutal game, so that all of these white people can watch you crash and burn and be carried off on stretchers. And they've got you women taking up arms and shooting at people, as though you were trying to mimic the worst things that men do. Isn't there something terribly wrong with this entire *system* that it ends up pitting its victims against each other?"

In this imaginary picture, each of the three standpoints (the women athletes, the men athletes, the black feminist) offers a partial understanding of reality. But the black feminist standpoint, grounded as it is in the experience of double, and often triple, oppression and marginalization, is likely to offer the most radical view, in the sense of identifying the commonalities between various systems of oppression (gender, race, and class). Black feminist thought invites us to shift our attention away from simplistic bickering between oppressed groups, and, instead, to focus our energies on developing a critical understanding of the power structure that frames and shapes this picture. Through this critical standpoint, we may be able to respond to such issues not by taking stands either with men against women, or with women against men, but by building coalitions that confront the institutional conventions that so often pit us against each other.

5

Studying Up on Sex

Author's note: In 1995, as part of my job as president of the North American Society for the Sociology of Sport (NASSS), I had to deliver an hour-long presidential address. Since I desperately wanted to avoid putting over 200 sport studies scholars to sleep, I decided to deliver a talk entitled "Studying Up on Sex." The title was intended as an attention-getter, but also as a double entendre. "Studying up" has one generally recognizable colloquial meaning, but in sociology it has another. Here it refers to studying "up" in the power structure. Sociologists have most often studied "down"—studying the poor or the incarcerated. But some sociologists have "studied up" as well: C. Wright Mills began in the 1950s a tradition of studying up on corporate and governmental elites; feminist scholars began a critical study of men in the 1980s that flourishes today; the 1990s saw the development of a critical study of whiteness that is now an essential part of the larger field of the study of race. With the blossoming of gay/lesbian studies starting in the late 1970s and the later development of queer studies, a critical "studying up" on heterosexuality had begun to develop by the early 1990s. In this essay, I draw from this emergent literature on the social construction of heterosexuality, and assess its utility in examining sexualities, homophobia, and heterosexism in sport. I also draw on a memory from my youth as a high school athlete that helped me to reflect on the way that my sense of myself as "100% heterosexual" was shaped by my social context, especially the sport context. What the scholarly literature and my story suggest is that it's useful to view heterosexuality not as some individual attribute or orientation that one just naturally "has," but rather, as a historical construct built into modern institutions, and as identities that people actively perform and construct within concrete institutional contexts, like organized sports.

> The threat of precipitous expulsion from the class of heterosexuals,
> and from all the material and discursive privileges enjoyed by mem-
> bers of that class, bribes class members into complicity with a per-
> vasive representation of the class as coherent, stable, exclusively
> loyal to heterosexual eroticism, and pure of any sodomitical desires
> or conduct.
>
> —Janet Halley, *Fear of a Queer Planet*

> As soon as we look into this over-worked, heterosexualized norma-
> tivity, we see what it is working so hard to hide. Sexual relations are
> perhaps the most fraught and troubling of all social relations
> precisely because, especially when heterosexual, they so often
> threaten rather than confirm gender polarity.... Through sex, trou-
> ble looms.
>
> —Lynne Segal, *Straight Sex*

My aim in this essay is to reflect critically on recent scholarship on sexuality in order to explore its relevance to sport studies. And I want to take
a particular slant on this topic that's implied in my title, "Studying Up on
Sex." "Studying up" has one, generally recognizable colloquial meaning, but
in sociology, it has another. It refers to studying "up" in the power structure.
Sociologists have perhaps most often studied "down"—studied the poor, the
blue- or pink-collar workers, the "nuts, sluts, and perverts," the incarcerated.
And though this research sometimes has empowering possibilities for socially
marginalized groups, too often it is delivered to empowered agents who hope
to use this information to further institutionalize their control, subordination,
and exploitation of others.

The very idea of studying up rarely occurs to sociologists unless and until
we are living in a time when those who are "down" have made identity
claims, and have organized movements that challenge the institutional privileges of the elite. In such a politicized historical context, studying up has the
goal of revealing and demystifying the mechanisms of power, identifying their
internal contradictions and cleavages so as to inform movements for change.
There is a long history of this sort of studying up on social class in classical
sociology—for instance, Karl Marx's *Capital* and C. Wright Mills' *The Power
Elite*. In sport studies, several scholars (e.g., Gruneau 1983) have revealed
how capitalist relations are played out within corporate sport institutions.
Over the past twenty-five years, the study of gender relations has increasingly
involved the development of a critical studying up on the social construction
of masculinity. In recent years, this concern has been developed in sport
studies by numerous scholars (e.g., Kidd 1987; Messner 1992; Messner and
Sabo 1990; Sabo 1985). In race relations scholarship, there has been a more
recent turn toward studying up on the social construction of whiteness—
most notably Ruth Frankenberg's (1993) *White Women, Race Matters*. In

sport studies, we have a rich literature on race and ethnicity, but there has been very little studying up on whiteness—studying *race* has meant, for the most part, studying the experiences of African Americans.

Studies of sexuality, especially gay and lesbian studies, have blossomed since the mid-1970s, but only very recently have scholars such as Janet Halley (1993), Chrys Ingraham (1994), Lynne Segal (1994), and Jonathan Katz (1995) begun a systematic examination of heterosexuality. In sport studies, we have benefited from the work of Helen Lenskyj (1986), Brian Pronger (1990), and others who have delineated the experiences of lesbians and gay men in sports. But with a few notable exceptions (e.g., Kolnes 1995), there has been very little extension of these scholars' insights into a consideration of the social construction of heterosexuality in sport. Rather than viewing homophobia as part of a heterosexist system of power relations that serves to construct the heterosexual as a privileged historical identity category, discussions in sport studies of the negative implications of homophobia on "straight" athletes have tended to view it as a shared psychological disease that impedes the development of healthy identities and relationships.

My task here, then, is to draw from a discourse that has recently blossomed outside of sport studies in order to raise questions about the social construction of heterosexuality in sport. I hope to demonstrate that it is crucial to study heterosexuality—not to reify it, but, rather, to expose its constructedness, its internal differentiation and contradiction. I will argue that sexuality—the social organization and deployment of desire—and the attendant social construction of modern sexual identities, is a key linking process in what Patricia Hill Collins (1990) calls a "matrix of domination," structured along lines of race, class, and gender. And I will suggest how this insight might inform our understanding of contemporary sport. The first task, though, is to locate the historical emergence of *the heterosexual*.

LOCATING *THE HETEROSEXUAL*

By the late 1970s, in the face of religious right backlash, the gay and lesbian liberation movement had pragmatically adopted the discourse and strategies of the minority group model, previously developed by the civil rights and women's movements. For many gay men and lesbians, this meant affirming, celebrating, and normalizing gay/lesbian identities, "lifestyles," and communities. Differences among and between gay men and lesbians were often submerged in the face of the need to unite against escalating homophobic violence and institutional heterosexist backlash. For a brief historical moment, "We Are Family" appeared to unite a "gay/lesbian community"— and it was largely successful within the liberal, equal rights parameters of the struggle (Weston 1991). However, the movement's leaders and spokespeople were nearly all white, more often than not men, college educated, and of the professional class. Just as important, much of the sexual and gender diversity that had served as a radically subversive impulse within gay liberation was submerged, even crushed, as gay leaders increasingly attempted to project a straight image to the public: "We are just like you." Through this process, homophobia was challenged, but, ironically, heterosexuality remained the unquestioned, unproblematic norm against which homosexuality attempted to normalize itself.

Radical gay and lesbian writers, though, were criticizing and problematizing this. Lesbians of color, such as Cherrie Moraga (Moraga and Anzaldua 1982), challenged the false universalization of "women" and "lesbians." In 1980, Adrienne Rich attempted to turn heterosexism on its head by arguing that lesbianism is a normal outcome of women's development, but that "compulsory heterosexuality" bombards us with rewards, punishments, and incentives (Rich 1980). Also in 1980, Monique Wittig, in a startling essay entitled "The Straight Mind," argued that there is an "economy of heterosexuality" that serves to construct women as a subordinate social category (Wittig 1992). But by far the most systematic examination of the historical construction of heterosexuality is Jonathan Katz's 1995 book entitled *The Invention of Heterosexuality.* Katz draws from Foucault's (1978) observation that the term *homosexual,* first used in 1868, was subsequently created as a modern identity category. In the decades surrounding the turn of the twentieth century, "heterosexual and homosexual appeared in public as Siamese twins, the first good, the second bad, bound together in public for life in unalterable antagonistic symbiosis" (Katz 1995, 65). The term *heterosexual* was not printed in the United States before 1892, but Katz assures us—with tongue firmly in cheek—that "looking back on past eras before the use of the term 'heterosexual,' we can, of course, find well-documented examples of same-sex erotic acts and emotions" (Katz 1995, 32). However, heterosexuality is "not identical to the reproductive intercourse of the sexes." Rather, it "signifies one particular historical arrangement of the sexes and their pleasures" (Katz 1995, 14).

The heterosexual's birth as a "normal" modern identity category was not lacking in complication. The term's first appearance in the 1901 edition *of Borland's Medical Dictionary* defined heterosexuality as "Abnormal or perverted appetite toward the opposite sex" (as cited in Katz 1995, 86). Freud, who rarely used the term, warned in his 1905 *Three Essays on Sexuality* that the "dangers of heterosexual intercourse" may result in a "fixation" on "homosexuality" (as cited in Katz 1995, 65). In 1923, "heterosexuality" appeared for the first time in *Webster's New International Dictionary* and was defined as a "morbid sexual passion for one of the same sex," but, by 1934, heterosexuality was being defined in *Webster's* in its current mode, as "a manifestation of sexual passion for one of the opposite sex; normal sexuality" (as cited in Katz 1995, 92). In effect, the first quarter of the twentieth century constituted the heterosexual's successful coming out, "a public, self affirming debut" (Katz 1995, 83). What had occurred here? What normalized heterosexuality? The term *heterosexual,* Katz argues, has two parts. First, modernization and feminism had challenged and undermined patriarchal power and sexual divisions of labor, thus leading to widespread anxieties among men. In the context of these upheavals in the social organization of gender, "hetero" served to reconstruct and renaturalize the "oppositeness" of the sexes. Second, the "sexual" in *heterosexual* reflected a "revaluing of pleasure and procreation, consumption and work in a commercial, capitalist society" (Katz 1995, 90).

Scholars of sport are familiar with historical analyses that point to the importance of contested and shifting gender relations, class relations, and race relations as major impulses in the rise of modern sport. But with a few partial exceptions (e.g., Cahn 1994; Crosset 1990), these historical analyses have not attempted to come to grips with the emergence of the heterosexual at precisely the time in history when modern sport was being forged as a social institution. In the late nineteenth and early twentieth centuries, modernization, urbanization, the women's movement, and the influx of black and new immigrant men into the labor force all led to a "crisis" of white middle-class masculinity (Kimmel 1995). The creation of modern sport is one of these men's institutional "responses" to this crisis in class, racial, and gender relations (Messner 1992). An important dimension of this reconstitution of hegemonic masculinity through sport involved a clearly asserted linkage between masculinity and heterosexuality. The creation of heterosexual masculinity in sport and elsewhere enforced a much more clear distinction between what we would now call *homosexuality* and *homosociality* than had previously existed in early nineteenth-century elite men's relationships with each other (Hansen 1992).

Following this thought, a fruitful line of theoretical and historical inquiry might involve an interrogation of how sexuality—and in particular, *the heterosexual*—has served over the past century as a key linking process within a shifting matrix of domination, structured along lines of race, class, and gender. In fact, I would hypothesize that sexuality has been an especially *salient* process when it appears at the intersections of other structures of power. For instance, as Angela Davis (1981) has pointed out, the historical construction of "the myth of the black male rapist" served as a key ideological construct in the continued race and class subordination of black males in the post–Civil War years. When men who had been slaves attempted to move into the paid labor force, they were seen as a threat by many white men, who used terror tactics such as lynchings to enforce a color bar in the workforce. Some people responded to this terror with outrage. So instead of simply lynching black men, the white terrorists successfully invoked the image of an aggressively sexualized black male who threatened White Womanhood: now black men were lynched *and* castrated. According to Davis, once the image of the black male threat was sexualized, most of the outrage expressed earlier by white liberals was silenced. We can see in this example how the imposition of an animalistic, sexualized image onto black men served as a means of control within a system of race and class stratification that had been destabilized by the legal emancipation of slaves. Paul Hoch (1979), employing a radical psychoanalytic perspective, suggests that white males have projected the image of the oversexed "black beast" onto black males as a means of sublimating their own repressed sexual desires. Thus, the "myth of the black male rapist" serves both as a means of holding the black man down economically, and also constructs a deep psychological fear of black men in white men's minds.

Later, especially during the 1960s and early 1970s Black Power Movement, some black men actively took on and purposefully displayed an aggressively heterosexual masculine persona as a way of waging psychological warfare against their white male oppressors (Wallace 1979). This brief example suggests how the imposition, manipulation, and contesting of heterosexualized images and identities becomes a key linking process in battles between men in race/class hierarchies. It should be added, of course, that in these sexualized battles within intermale dominance hierarchies, women often play key roles, either as (white) virgins to be "protected" or "threatened," or as sexualized and debased objects through which to stake a claim to "manhood." Women's sexual agency or pleasure is rarely considered in these phallic wars between men.

Drawing from this same insight, we might ask today, how is sexuality perhaps similarly employed in constructions of black males—both inside and outside of sport—as dangerous sexual deviants? In other words, in the case of black men in the United States, how has the suspicion of sexual deviance served to undercut black men's otherwise ethically powerful claims to equal status within racialized, classed, and gendered hierarchies? And in what ways have black males at times uncritically conspired with, manipulated, and/or contested these sexualized images?

Critical examinations of sexual identity categories in sport can also reveal the ways that sexuality and gender have been differently constructed for women and for men. In particular, the dualities of *lesbian versus heterosexual* and *gay versus heterosexual* have been differently constructed for women and for men in sport. As many people have pointed out, sport participation offers a normalizing equation for men:

athleticism = masculinity = heterosexuality

For women athletes, the equation has nearly always been more paradoxical:

athleticism? femininity? heterosexuality?

Susan Cayleff's (1995) biography of Babe Didrikson Zaharias reveals some of these issues. Didrikson's incredibly successful athletic career spanned several decades, during which women's sports surged in popularity and appeal (the 1920s) and then waned in light of a backlash against female athleticism and women's rights in general (the 1930s through the 1950s). In this context, Cayleff shows how Didrikson's conscious reconstruction of herself as heterosexual and feminine— including radically changing her appearance and marrying a man—paid dividends in public acceptance. But Cayleff also argues that Didrikson was, in fact, a lesbian who had a long-term relationship with a woman. In an insightful review of the book, Mariah Burton Nelson (1995) challenges the straight–lesbian binary. Why must we assume, Nelson argues, that Didrikson was either–or? Maybe she had an emotional and/or sexual relationship with both her husband *and* her female partner? Maybe she was bisexual?

DECONSTRUCTING THE BINARIES?

Nelson's question raises an important theoretical issue. In recent years, postmodernists and deconstructionists have challenged the binary, oppositional thinking that underlies modern social thought, including that of liberation movements and their progressive academic counterparts. To the point of this essay, queer theorists (e.g., Warner 1993) have recently argued that the establishment of gay/lesbian identities and communities has served to buttress the unquestioned normality, and thus the political hegemony, of the heterosexual. The acceptance of the "gay–straight binary" by the gay/lesbian liberation movement inadvertently contributed to the institutionalization of sexuality as a discourse of medical and technical surveillance and control. In other words, as some radical Foucauldians (e.g., Butler 1990; Sedgewick 1990) have argued, the collective agency of "sexual liberationists" has operated conservatively, within the framework of dominant discourses of binary oppositions. There is a great deal of debate over the question of just what "queer theory" is (Gamson 1995; Thomas 1995). But Seidman (1993, 118) provides a useful description of queer theory as a

> revolt of the social periphery against the center, only this time the center was not mainstream America, but a dominant gay culture. From minor skirmishes in the mid-to-late 1970's to major wars through the 1980's, the concept of a unitary lesbian or gay male subject was in dispute. Three major sites of struggle against the gay cultural center have been the battle over race, bi-sexuality, and nonconventional sexualities.

This multifaceted "revolt" has led to new strategies: rather than organizing within the binary categories that have been created by agents of institutional control, queer theorists argue in favor of a new discourse and practice that disrupts and fractures gay and lesbian categories—thus the emergence of "post-gay" organizations like Queer Nation, which celebrate sexual diversity, transgender identities, and transgressive politics. Their aim is not to organize a liberation movement, but, rather, to forge a radical break with what they view as the conventional, even conservative politics of a mostly older genera-tion of gay and lesbian leaders. There is no essential homosexual, new queer theorists and activists are saying—and, by extension, they hope to call into question the essential nature of the heterosexual.

Many sociologists—I among them—have reacted with skepticism or even defensiveness to theories of deconstruction that have originated largely in the humanities. One sociologist, Steven Ward (1995), has gone so far as to argue that postmodern deconstructionism constitutes "the revenge of the humanities" against the modern privileging of empiricism and rational scien-tific epistemologies. Deconstructionists' emphasis on discourse as *the* basis of social reality, some sociologists have argued, falls into a dangerous idealism that ignores material, structured relations of power that shape language and ideology. I am sympathetic to these criticisms, but I think a major reason that what I call "the posties" have been so attractive to many social scientists is that our own theories of social inequality and change have been seriously flawed. In particular, poststructuralists have revealed the limits—and the oppressive implications—of falsely universalized categories like *the working class, women, gays and lesbians, and people of color*. However, though queer theory is powerful in its critique of modernist categories, its activist politics may ultimately tend to rely on "exquisite intellectual and political gesturing [that] draws its power more from its critical force than any positive program for change" (Seidman 1990, 111). As Arlene Stein and Ken Plummer (1994, 184) have argued, the incoherence of queer theory's political project is directly linked to its tendency to be preoccupied with literary and mass media texts:

> Queer theorists…appreciate the extent to which the texts of literature and mass culture shape sexuality, but their weakness is that they rarely, if ever, move beyond the text. There is a dangerous tendency for the new queer theorists to ignore 'real' queer life as it is materially experienced across the world, while they play with the free-floating signifiers of texts. What can the rereading of a nineteenth-century novel really tell us about the pains of gay Chicanas or West Indian lesbians now, for example? Indeed, such postmodern readings may well tell us more about the lives of middle-class radical intellectuals than about anything else! Sociology's key

concerns—inequality, modernity, institutional analysis—can bring a clearer focus to queer theory.

Stein and Plummer put their finger directly on one of the major shortcomings and dangers of poststructuralism: an overemphasis on the causal importance of language and a concomitant underemphasis on material social relations. In short, I would argue that although language is extremely important, simply deconstructing our discourse about binary categories does not necessarily challenge the material basis of master categories to which subordinate categories of people stand in binary opposition: the capitalist class, men, heterosexuals, whites. In fact, quite the contrary may be true. As many feminists have pointed out, although it is certainly true that every woman is at least somewhat uniquely situated, a radical deconstruction of the concept *woman* could lead to a radical individualism that denies similarity of experience, thus leading to a depoliticized subject. In fact, it is around the concept of *woman* that feminists have succeeded in organizing valuable institutions like women's shelters and rape crisis centers, and have succeeded in wresting concessions from the state like Title IX, and laws against sexual harassment and employment discrimination. These kinds of changes, despite their limits, have made real differences in peoples' lives.

Similarly, the forging of gay and lesbian identities and communities, despite the way they mask difference, inequalities, and even oppression within these categories, has been successful in overturning some oppressive legal and medical practices. Deconstructing these categories risks dismantling the basis from which some progress has been won—and indeed, the basis from which more progress might be won in the future. Moreover, I suspect that heterosexuality, as an institution, can quite easily reconstruct itself in light of a bevy of queer public transgressions. *The heterosexual,* as a privileged identity category, does not necessarily need *the homosexual,* as its oppositional counterpart. The heterosexual can just as easily reconstruct itself in opposition to a polymorphously "queer nation."

We do need to take into account the insights that deconstructionists offer us—especially the way they call into question the very categories we take for granted—for example, Cole's (1994) radical challenge to our unquestioned use of the concept of *sport*. These kinds of critiques have contributed to a breaking down, or at least a blurring of, disciplinary boundaries. And this is a good thing; for, like geographical boundaries, disciplinary boundaries are often arbitrary constructions that keep new or opposing ideas out, while protecting and reifying narrow orthodoxies within. But though I agree with the necessity of crossing or eliminating disciplinary borders, I think it is important to assert two ways that sociological insights and concepts can contribute to this emergent multidisciplinary landscape.

A MATERIALIST CONCEPTION OF SOCIAL STRUCTURE

First, it is essential to retain and build upon the utility of the concept of social structure, with its attendant emphasis on the importance of peoples' shared positions within structures of power. Such a materialist analysis reveals how differential access to resources, opportunities, and different relationships to structured constraints shape the contexts in which people think, interact, and constrains political practices and discourse. To be sure, we should reject narrowly defined theories such as crude Marxisms or feminisms that insist there is a singular dynamic (i.e., class or gender) shaping history. These reductionist and hierarchical theories have incorrectly named certain groups of people (the working class, or women) as the subjects of history. The new social movements of the past three decades thoroughly exploded these simplistic formulations and claims (Seidman 1993). In place of a transcendent historical subject, we now have the concept of multiplicity and of fragmented and fractured identity categories: there is no working class; instead, there are gay workers, black gay workers, women workers, heterosexual women workers, lesbian Chicana women workers, and so forth. When facing these complex realities, some postmodernists have argued that modernity has collapsed and with it has evaporated the hope for a transcendent historical subject who can attain a conscious grasp of the totality of social life, who can organize and change it. Within this postmodern view (e.g., Lemert 1994), a sociologist who asserts that her or his work is operating from the standpoint of a commitment social justice is scoffed at as hopelessly mired in passé, modernist thought. Instead, postmodernists argue, we face an increasingly unstable and fragmented world in which knowledge can only be, at best, partial, and in which groups can coalesce temporarily around limited and short-term goals.

Clearly, the world is complex. In fact, the idea of a single, transcendent, revolutionary historical subject (such as the working class or women) who can understand and change the totality of social life was probably always an incorrect naive assumption made by revolutionary intellectuals. The "working-class" and "women" have always been internally differentiated and fragmented groups that, respectively, Marxists and some feminists have falsely universalized. However to abandon the project of human liberation now is to engage in an act of historical capitulation to the forces of greed, violence, and oppression right at a time in history when new social movements have achieved partial (sometimes even dramatic) successes in decolonization, women's rights, gay and lesbian liberation, and antiracism. What is needed now are theories that can inform an alliance politics that is grounded simultaneously in a structural analysis of power and a recognition of multiplicity (e.g., Baca Zinn and Dill, 1996).

COUNTERHEGEMONIC RESISTANCE OR PLAYFUL SUBVERSIONS?

Even as we attempt to transcend (or leave behind us) the limits of a narrow empiricism, it is still crucial to create and utilize systematic ways to come up with good generalizations about groups of people's shared experiences and interests within social structures. This is especially important today, I think, in light of some sexual deconstructionists and queer theorists who are arguing for an escape from oppressive social institutions and the creation of "free zones" where individuals, couples, or groups can perform "playful subversions." Seidman (1993, 133) describes this emphasis on escape from institutions as "a celebration of liminality, of the spaces between or outside structure, a kind of anarchistic championing of 'pure' freedom from all constraints and limits." In sport studies, this perspective has been articulated most eloquently by Brian Pronger (1994, 10), who argues that sport is part of an oppressive cultural practice through which "the free flow of energy is stopped. This restriction of desire is a *process* in which organization, in the codifying interests of capital, resists the free flow of energy." Sport—and its disciplinary body practices—are inherently "fascist," according to Pronger, and thus the idea of struggling within sport to make it more democratic or humane is, in effect, conspiring with fascism. "The issue becomes not one, then, of including more people in sport, but of trying to exclude as many as possible from its fascist project" (Pronger 1994, 10). In light of this perspective, Pronger then asks,

> What does resistance look like? What are the possibilities for refiguring the discourse of sport? These are postmodern questions not of overcoming— but of lines of flight. Because, the problem of sport is the problem of modernity, which is the problem of the overarching fascist territorialization of the body, of desire, of the free-flow of energy in the many regions to which modernity has extended its grasp. Overcoming modernity, I think, is beyond our reach. [We should] explore, instead, strategies that are geared to undermining, thwarting, strangling, subverting, momentarily escaping fascist organizations of the body, rather than overthrowing the structural foundations of our era. (Pronger 1994, 21)

No doubt Pronger is correct that sport—especially in its dominant institutional forms—has contributed to an oppressive territorialization of the body. But Pronger seems to ignore the various collective attempts to change

sport that have taken place largely outside the dominant athletic institutions, as well as the incidents of resistance and emancipatory moments that
sometimes take place even within the dominant sport institutions. These
moments should highlight for us the fact that sport, like all institutions, is
not a seamless totalitarian system. Rather, it is a political terrain characterized by internal contradiction and paradox that leave room for the play of
oppositional meanings, and potentially for the organization of collective
resistance and institutional change. I fear that the view of sport as a thoroughly and hopelessly fascist practice from which we should "escape" represents an historic capitulation to the challenge of struggling within
sport—not only to make sport more democratic, equal, peaceful, and
humane, but also to contribute toward the transformation of other non-
sport institutions such as schools, families, and the economy. Despite its
limitations, I believe that the Gramscian concept of hegemony, with its
attendant focus on structural constraint and collective human agency, is
still the most useful macrotheoretical framework for exploring these historical and political questions about the possibilities for human freedom (e.g.,
Gruneau 1983).

Escape from social institutions to a realm of absolute erotic freedom is
really not possible anyway. Yet, some queer theorists appear to be arguing for
a return to a Rousseauian notion of freedom, unfettered and unmediated by
civilization. Instead, I would argue that in the context of social order—*any*
social order—Eros, like all bodily matters, is always socially mediated. To
paraphrase Connell (1995), the social takes up the body and its desire and
transforms it, without changing the fact that it is a biological body. Thus, the
idea of an unmediated "free flow of erotic energy," is not only impossible, it is
an idea that may mask the very relations of power it is embedded within
rather than illuminating and subverting them. Even radical Freudians such as
Wilhelm Reich in the 1930s and 1940s and Herbert Marcuse in the 1940s,
1950s, and 1960s, who aimed to liberate Eros, saw their Utopian projects as
attempts to eliminate surplus repression (the repression required for people to
be willing to do alienated labor, to wage war, to administer death camps,
etc.), while still arguing that any society will require a partial sublimation of
Eros (Marcuse 1955; Reich 1972).

And so, I pose the following questions concerning erotic desire: How do
institutional power relations shape, mediate, repress, sublimate, and desubli-
mate desire? How do individuals and groups respond in ways that reproduce,
subtly change, or overtly challenge oppressive conventions? How do people
(for instance, athletes and spectators) actively take up the construction of
their own sexual identities and communities? And how do these sexual identities, relations, and practices intersect with other kinds of differences and
inequalities within a socially structured matrix of domination?

Clearly, the framework and questions I have outlined lie largely within what many would call a *modernist* worldview, based on the idea that the project of human liberty, democracy, and equality can be furthered by social movements that are informed by a rational analysis of social structures of power. But after asserting the strengths of a sociological perspective and outlining some of the dangers of deconstruction, I want to emphasize that I do not see my project here as a contribution to battening down the disciplinary hatches to hold off the deconstructionist barbarians. I think deconstruction has a contribution to make, and when it is done well it can illuminate oppressive institutional power dynamics in new and important ways (e.g., Cole and Hribar 1995). A fruitful approach might be to engage in a seemingly contradictory enterprise: First, our scholarly work should critically and intelligently support the identity claims of disenfranchised groups. For instance, when we do research that supports Title IX compliance or sex-equal coverage in the sports media, we are relying on—perhaps even reifying— a male-female binary. There are dangers in reifying categorical views of women and men rather than emphasizing the empirical reality, a "continuum of performance" that reveals an enormous amount of overlap between women's and men's athletic abilities (Kane 1995). On the other hand, since the institution of sport is materially structured along the lines of this binary opposition, the successful deployment of the category *women in sport* can have a real outcome in terms of redistribution of resources and opportunities (Carpenter 1993). And though this in itself is not necessarily revolutionary, it does alter the state of play of the gender order in such a way that makes new challenges possible. This does not mean we should endorse the oppressive use of falsely universalized categories in the name of reform. We need to point out when, for instance, the universalizing category *women* marginalizes women of color, lesbians, poor women, older or differently abled women. Some scholars might argue—correctly—that this minimal change still leaves the dominant category, *men,* essentially unchallenged. Thus, I suggest a second prong to our strategy: we should employ a practice of *strategic deconstruction*—not of the identity categories of subordinate groups, but, rather, of the dominant end of binary categories. In short, our aim should be to study up in order to uncover the mechanisms at work in the social construction of whiteness, of hegemonic masculinity, of heterosexuality.

A SEXUAL STORY

What does this mean concretely in terms of sport studies? First and foremost, it means interrogating our own values, biases, and domain assumptions. Are we operating from a deviance model that only makes sexual orientation visible when it is gays and lesbians we are discussing, but that leaves heterosexuality the unexamined, invisible norm? Second, it means we should analyze current sport institutions (including sport media) as material contexts within which heterosexuality is constructed. There are surely many ways to approach this task. One way is through a sociological analysis of what Ken Plummer (1995) calls "sexual stories." Plummer argues that people's sexual stories, their "narratives of the intimate life, focused especially around the erotic, the gendered and the relational," offer a fascinating sociological window into the "late modern world" (Plummer 1995, 6). I will present one such sexual story here as an example. It is a story that nudged itself out of the recesses of my own memory in the context of a group of men I worked with for two years doing a version of the "memory work" research developed by Frigga Haug (1987) for her book *Female Sexualization*. Our group followed Haug's concerns and methods in a very general way. We were concerned with recalling and reconstructing our own experiences of gendered, sexualized, classed, and racialized embodiment, and then collectively analyzing our stories. Through this process we attempted to reveal similarities and differences among us, and to move toward a theorization of embodiments of masculinity within shifting and changing structured contexts. As R. W. Connell explains the underlying aim of such research, "the theorized life history can be a powerful tool for the study of social structures and their dynamics as they impinge upon (and are reconstituted in) personal life" (Connell 1990, 84). As Haug and Plummer both note, stories based on memories of events that took place years ago do not necessarily reveal an objective "truth" of that moment in time. The memories are mediated and often distorted by time. And the meanings we draw from these kinds of stories, ex-post facto, are often quite different than the meanings the events in the story might have had at the time. But the fact that the story is remembered and reconstructed in the process of group memory work, Haug would argue, means that the events in the story represented a particularly salient moment in life—and this moment is useful for theorizing the complex relationship between agency and social structure.

When I was in the ninth grade, I played on a "D" basketball team, set up especially for the smallest of high school boys. Indeed, though I was pudgy with baby fat, I was a short 5'2," still prepubescent with no facial hair and a high voice that I artificially tried to lower. The first day of practice, I was immediately attracted to a boy I'll call Timmy, because he looked like the boy who played in the Lassie TV show. Timmy was short, with a high voice, like me. And like me, he had no facial hair yet. Unlike me, he was very skinny. I liked Timmy right away, and soon we were together a lot. I noticed things about him that I didn't notice about other boys: He

*said some words a certain way, and it gave me pleasure to try to talk like him. I
remember liking the way the light hit his boyish, nearly hairless body. I thought
about him when we weren't together. He was in the school band, and at the football
games, I'd squint to see where he was in the mass of uniforms. In short, though I
wasn't conscious of it at the time, I was infatuated with Timmy—I had a crush on
him. Later that basketball season, I decided—for no reason I could really articulate
then—that I hated Timmy. I aggressively rejected him, began to make fun of him
around other boys. He was, we all agreed, a geek. He was a "faggot."*

*Three years later, Timmy and I were both on the varsity basketball team, but
had hardly spoken a word to each other since we were freshmen. Both of us now
had lower voices, had grown to around 6 feet tall, and we both shaved, at least a
bit. But Timmy was a skinny, somewhat stigmatized reserve on the team, whereas I
was the team captain and starting point guard. But I wasn't so happy or secure
about this. I'd always dreamed of dominating games, of being the hero. Halfway
through my senior season, however, it became clear that I was not a star, and I figured I knew why. I was not aggressive enough.*

*I had always liked the beauty of the fast break, the perfectly executed pick and
roll play between two players, and especially the long twenty-foot shot that touched
nothing but the bottom of the net. But I hated and feared the sometimes brutal contact under the basket. In fact, I stayed away from the rough fights for rebounds and
was mostly a perimeter player, relying on my long shots or my passes to more
aggressive teammates under the basket. But now it became apparent to me that
time was running out in my quest for greatness: I needed to change my game, and
fast. I decided one day before practice that I was going to get aggressive. While
practicing one of our standard plays, I passed the ball to a teammate and then ran
to the spot at which I was to set a pick on a defender. I knew that one could sometimes get away with setting a face-up screen on a player, and then as he makes contact with you, roll your back to him and plant your elbow hard in his stomach. The
beauty of this move is that your own body "roll" makes the elbow look like an accident. So I decided to try this move. I approached the defensive player, Timmy,
rolled, and planted my elbow deeply into his solar plexus. Air exploded audibly from
Timmy's mouth, and he crumbled to the floor momentarily.*

*Play went on as though nothing had happened, but I felt bad about it. Rather
than making me feel better, it made me feel guilty and weak. I had to admit to
myself why I'd chosen Timmy as the target against whom to test out my net aggression. He was the skinniest and weakest player on the team.*

Years later, I can now interrogate this as a *sexual* story, and as a *gender*
story, unfolding within the context of the heterosexualized and masculinized
institution of sport. It certainly doesn't take a Kinsey Scale to recognize the
fluidity and changeability of sexual desire in this story. It doesn't require the

employment of a Freudian theory of bisexuality to recognize homoerotic desire operating in my story. Nor does it take an Adrienne Rich, a Marcuse, or Reich to see how the institution of compulsory heterosexuality led me to deny and repress my homoerotic desire through a direct and overt rejection of the desired object, through homophobic banter with male peers, and through the resultant stigmatization of the feminized Timmy. And, eventually, we might read the sublimation of the original homoerotic desire into an aggressive, violent act as serving to construct a clear line of demarcation between self and other. In short, the rejection of Timmy and the joining with teammates to stigmatize him in ninth grade stands as what Connell (1987) calls "a moment of engagement with hegemonic masculinity," in which I actively took up the collective project of constructing heterosexual/masculine identities in the context of sport. The elbow in the gut three years later can be seen as a punctuation mark that occurred precisely because of my fears that this project might be failing.

It's also interesting to compare my story with "coming out" stories in sport. Though we have a few lesbian and bisexual coming out stories among women athletes, there are very few gay male coming out stories. When I interviewed Tom Waddell over a decade ago about his sexual identity and athletic career, he made it quite clear that for many years sports *was* his closet (see Messner 1994). He was conscious of entering sports and constructing a masculine/heterosexual athletic identity precisely because he feared being revealed as gay. It was clear to him, in the context of the 1950s, that being revealed as gay would undercut his claims to the status of manhood. Thus, though the athletic closet was hot and stifling, he remained in the closet until several years after his athletic retirement. Waddell's coming out story may invoke a dramaturgical analysis: he clearly attempted to control and regulate others' perceptions of him by constructing a public "frontstage" persona that differed radically from what he believed to be his "true" inner self. My story, in contrast, suggests a deeper, less consciously strategic "going in" with my homoerotic desire. Most likely, I was aware on some level of the dangers of such feelings and was escaping the dangers, disgrace, and rejection that would likely result from being different. But, in retrospect, I can see that perhaps it was not a "closet" I was going into—perhaps I was stepping out into an entire world of heterosexual privilege. My story also suggests that a threat to the promised privileges of hegemonic masculinity might trigger a momentary sexual panic that can lay bare the constructedness, indeed, the instability of the heterosexual/masculine identity.

In either case—Waddell's or mine—we can see how as young male athletes, heterosexuality and masculinity were not things we "were," but things we were *doing*. It is very significant, I think, that as each of us was "doing heterosexuality," neither of us was actually "having sex" with women (though one of us desperately wanted to!). This underscores the point made earlier, that heterosexuality is a constructed identity, a performance, and an institution that is not necessarily linked to sexual acts. Though for one of us it was more conscious than for the other, we were both doing heterosexuality as an ongoing practice through which we sought to link ourselves into systems of power, status, and privilege. In other words, each of us actively scripted our own sexual/gender performances, but these scripts were constructed within the constraints of a socially organized (institutionalized) system of power and pleasure.

QUEER QUESTIONS ABOUT HETEROSEXUALITY

What do heterosexuals, as a category of people, actually share with each other? As it turns out, not very much. Heterosexuals certainly don't share a singular economic status, racial or ethnic identification, or religious or political belief system. In fact, they don't even share the same sexual tastes and practices—we've known that at least since Kinsey in the 1940s and 1950s. Peter Nardi, a prominent gay sociologist, visited my sexuality class this past spring and stumped my class with a question: "I have a gay male friend and a lesbian friend, and occasionally they like to have sex with each other. Is that straight sex? It is, after all, a man and a woman. But they *identify* as a gay man and as a lesbian. So is it gay sex?" We could ask similar questions about people who identify as heterosexuals. What are we to make of heterosexual men who like to dress in women's clothes while masturbating? What about the heterosexual man who rapes other men in prison, or the heterosexual men identified by Laud Humphreys in his classic (1971) study, *The Tea Room Trade*, who occasionally have sex with other men in public restrooms? And what of heterosexual groups of young men who, in fraternities or sport teams engage in group rapes of women? Women tell us that from the woman's perspective, rape is not sex, it's a violent and degrading act of abuse. That's certainly true. But research on gang rape, such as that done by Peggy Sanday (1990), suggests that there is a highly erotic charge for the men involved in gang rapes. But it's not "sex with a woman" that's behind this erotic charge. Rather, the woman serves as a debased object through which the men have sex *with each other*. This is an example of how heterosexism and misogyny work to simultaneously affirm and deny the erotic bond in male groups.

So if we can't identify heterosexuals as a category by their shared sexual desires, practices, or even object choices, what *do* they have in common? What heterosexually identified people do share is, perhaps, a belief that they are categorically different from gays, lesbians, bisexuals, and "queers." And they also share a privileged status that serves to link them into other classed, racialized, and gendered systems of domination and subordination. Heterosexuality as a linking process is evident, for instance, in the vehemence with which many racially subordinated men make claims to heterosexual status so as to shore up a masculinity already undercut by racism, or, in the ways that women in the LPGA or in other elite sports collectively take up the project of constructing an image of heterosexual femininity in order to secure privileges for themselves within an increasingly commercialized professional sport context (Crosset 1990; Kolnes 1995). It is the task of a critical sport studies, 1 think, to explore and demystify these kinds of links, to expose the cracks and fissures in them, and to point to creative possibilities for change.

In 1982, Martin Rochlin published the now widely reprinted "Heterosexual Questionnaire," a one-page, tongue-in-cheek list of eighteen questions that people who identify as heterosexuals might ask themselves (Rochlin 1995). For instance, " What do you think caused your heterosexuality?" "If you have never slept with anyone of the same sex, is it possible that all you need is a good gay lover?" "Why do you insist on flaunting your heterosexuality?" There is a queer, destabilizing impulse in this kind of humor that we might creatively employ in our research and our teaching in sport studies. To boxing fans, we might ask, "Is it possible that you need to watch less violent games in order to get in touch with your homoerotic desire?" Or, we might ask male coaches in women's sports, "Can we really trust a heterosexual male coach to understand the needs and desires of lesbian athletes?" And we might interrogate the entire institution of sport by asking, "If heterosexuality is so natural, why do we all have to work so damned hard to recruit new heterosexuals among every generation of youth?"

Part III
Bodies and Violence

6

When Bodies Are Weapons

Masculinity and Violence in Sport

Author's note: When I conducted life-history interviews with former athletes, I was curious about exploring why many athletes put their own bodies at risk by playing while injured, and put other peoples' bodies at risk in the daily, routine on-field activities of sport. The most obvious answer is that boys learn early on in life to ignore the pain of others and, indeed, to ignore their own pain. If they successfully do so, they are often rewarded and treated as heroes. But in my interviews, the picture that emerged was more complicated than that. Some men were clearly aware of having been hurt—physically and emotionally—by a hypermasculine culture of violence in sports—a culture that is shot-through with misogyny and homophobia. But many expressed what can only be described as a love for aggressive bodily contact within the context of sport, and said that despite serious long-term injuries that still plagued them in later years, they would still "do it all over again." In this essay, I examine, through the words of these men, the ways that sport offered a context of connection with other men that validated their sense of self. We cannot understand men's commitment to risk taking (including athletes' contemporary use of steroids), playing with serious injuries, and constructing their bodies as machines or weapons, unless we understand how sport provides a context for men's emotional connection with other men, and how the larger societal context valorizes, romanticizes, and rewards men's successful use of violence. This tendency of men to be rewarded for being alienated from their own bodies, and for treating others as objects to be defeated, is extreme and obvious in the world of sport, but it offers a more general window into understanding the unhealthy "costs of masculinity" paid by "workaholic" men in nonsports professions.

" **V**iolence in sport" is widely viewed as a social problem. Scholars of sport have typically focused on two clusters of questions, the first being the problem of definition: What is violence? How can we differentiate between aggression and violence? Between legitimate and illegitimate violence? (Bredemeier and Shields 1986; Smith 1986). The second common cluster of questions concern cause and effect: do organized sports offer a socially acceptable context in which to express a naturally aggressive human essence—the catharsis thesis of Moore (1966) and Lorenz (1966)—or is sports violence a socially constructed and learned behavior that actually serves to legitimize and foster more aggressive behaviors? On this question, the weight of social-scientific evidence clearly supports the social construc-tionist argument (Coakley 1978; Schneider and Eitzen 1983). As for the issue of defining aggression and violence, there is a clearly no consensus. In fact, though precise definitions of aggression and violence are necessary for labora-tory experiments common among psychologists, those intent on interpreting the broader social meanings of violence in sport may find that "no single def-inition of sports violence is either possible or desirable" (Goldstein 1983). Instead, it seems reasonable to simply begin with the assumption that in many of our most popular sports, the achievement of goals (scoring and win-ning) is predicated on the successful utilization of violence—that is, these are activities in which the human body is routinely turned into a weapon to be used against other bodies, resulting in pain, serious injury, and even death (Atyeo 1979; Sabo 1986; Underwood 1979).

In any analysis of sport it is crucial to recognize the distinction between, on the one hand, its broader social, cultural and ideological meanings as mediated spectacle, and, on the other hand, the meanings that athletes con-struct as participants (Oriard 1981). This essay will focus on these two levels of meaning, linking them through a feminist analysis of violence and mas-culinities. On the social/ideological level, the analysis will draw on an emer-gent critical/feminist literature that theoretically and historically situates violent sports as a practice that helps to construct hegemonic masculinity. And drawing on my own in-depth interviews with former athletes a feminist theory of masculine gender identity will be utilized to examine the meanings that athletes themselves construct around their own participation in the vio-lent, rule-bound world of sport. Finally, the links between these two levels of analysis will be explored: how does the athlete's construction of meaning sur-rounding his participation in violent sports connect with the larger social construction of masculinities?

SPORT, VIOLENCE, AND THE GENDER ORDER

The modern institution of organized sport, as we now know it, emerged as a male response to social changes that undermined many of the bases of men's traditional partriarchal power, authority, and identity. Proletarianization, urbanization, modernization and (in the United States) the closing of the frontier all served to undermine patriarchal forms of masculinity. And, especially by the turn of the century, the conscious agency of women provided a direct threat to the ideology of male superiority. Within the context of this "crisis of masculinity" (Kimmel 1987), organized sports became increasingly important as "a primary masculinity-validating experience" (Dubbert 1979, 164). Sport was a male-created homosocial cultural sphere that provided (white, middle- and upper-class) men with psychological separation from the perceived "feminization" of society, while also providing dramatic symbolic "proof" of the natural superiority of men over women (Messner 1988). But it is not simply the bonding among men and the separation from women, but the *physicality* of the activity, that gives sport its salience in gender relations. Crossett (1990) traces in the rise of nineteenth-century sport in Britain an ideological elevation of male sexual superiority and, by extension, a naturalization of men's power over women. And women's exclusion from most aspects of this physical activity contributed to men's continued control over women's bodies (Lenskyj 1986).

A number of feminist analyses have suggested that one of the key elements in the elevation of the male-body-as-superior is the use (or threat) of violence. Brownmiller (1975), for instance, argues that although various forms of control (psychological, ideological, etc.) are utilized, ultimately men's control of women rests on violence. According to Dunning (1986), historical and cross-cultural evidence shows that the balance of power tips more strongly toward men when violence and fighting are endemic parts of social life. With industrialization and modernization, as social life became more rationalized and "civilized," more controls were instituted on the use of violence, and thus the balance of power tended to shift more toward women. Men responded to this threat to their power by instituting "combat sports" such as boxing and rugby: "such games were justified ideologically, partly as training grounds for war, partly in terms of their use in the education of military and administrative leaders in Britain's expanding empire, and partly as vehicles for the inculcation and expression of 'manliness'" (Dunning 1986, 271). Clearly, it was not simply a "feminization of society" that men feared: that could have been countered simply by creating homosocial clubs for men. It was also the fear of the *loss of male power and privilege*—especially among middle class men—that formed the basis for the popularization of violent sports (Gorn 1986). Sport, in its present (violent) forms, then, tends to support male dominance not simply through the exclusion or marginalization of females, but through the association of "males and maleness with valued skills and the sanctioned use of aggression/force/violence" (Bryson 1987, 349). In promoting dominance and submission (Bennett et al. 1987), in equating force and aggression with physical strength, domination, and power

(Theberge 1987), modern sport naturalized the equation of maleness with violence, thus lending support and legitimation to patriarchy (Bianchi 1980; Hall 1987; Komisar 1980; Sabo and Runfola 1980).

Yet the simple equation of "male violence" with "patriarchy" is analytically problematic. First, the term "male violence" tends to suggest that violence is an essential feature of maleness, rather than a socially learned feature of a certain kind of masculinity. Indeed, concrete social-scientific examinations of violence show that there is no convincing evidence that men are genetically or hormonally predisposed to violent behavior (Fausto-Sterling 1985; Pleck 1982). In fact, the weight of evidence supports the contention that most males are not comfortable committing acts of violence: violent behavior is learned behavior, and some men learn it better than others (Ewing 1983; Pleck 1982; Scher and Stevens 1987). As Connell (1985, 4) has argued,

> A crucial fact about men is that masculinity is not all of a piece. There have always been different kinds, some more closely associated with violence than others. This is why one should not talk of "male violence" or of "males" doing this or that—phrasing which smuggles back in the idea of a biological uniformity in social behaviour.

The recognition that at any given moment there are various masculinities—some hegemonic, some marginalized, some subordinated—suggests that the term "patriarchy," as it is commonly used, is overly simplistic (Carrigan et. al. 1987; Connell 1987). Not only does the concept of patriarchy tend to view "men" as an undifferentiated category, it tends to downplay the fluidity and contradictions that exist within and between gender categories. Connell suggests instead that we utilize the term "gender order," which can be defined as "the current state of play" in the dynamics of the power relations of sex, gender, and sexuality. Men as a group do enjoy power and privilege at the expense of women. Yet this power and privilege is by no means complete, total, or uncontested, nor is shared equally among all men. Hegemonic masculinity—that form of masculinity that is ascendant—is defined in relation to the subordination of women *and* in relation to other (subordinated, marginalized) masculinities.

The utilization of this more fluid concept of the "gender order" allows us to begin to shed light on an otherwise confusing irony: although men are the major perpetrators of violence, and one overall effect of this violence is the continued subordination of women, a large proportion of men's violence is directed at other men (Connell 1987, 13). Within the world of organized sport, men are almost exclusively the perpetrators as well as the victims of violence (Sabo 1986). Conceptualizing the gender order as a system of competing masculinities allows us to begin to ask the question us to how violence among men contributes to the construction of power relations between men and women. In order to begin to shed light on this issue, it is necessary to explore (1) how and why some men become violent: what meanings do men construct around their own violence against other men? And (2) what is the broader cultural meaning of men's violence against other men? What role does some men's violence against other men play in the current state of play of the gender order?

Organized sport is a perfect place to investigate these questions, since it is an arena in which individual males actively construct meaning around their acts of aggression and violence *and*, given the fact that sport is a public spectacle, these acts often take on important and controversial ideological meanings. Next, the meanings that former athletes have constructed around their own participation in violent sports will be examined. After analyzing these meanings within a feminist social-psychological theory, we will then return to an examination of how these men's actions and self-definitions fit into the current state of play of the present gender order.

ATHLETES: THE MEANING OF VIOLENCE

With the possible exception of boxing, perhaps the position in modern sport that requires the most constant levels of physical aggressiveness is that of lineman in U.S. football. Though television cameras focus primarily on those who carry, throw, catch, and kick the ball, the majority of the players on the field are lining up a few inches apart from each other, and, on each play, snarling, grunting, cursing, and slamming their large, powerful, and heavily armored bodies into each other. Blood, bruises, broken bones, and concussions are commonplace here. Marvin Upshaw, now thirty-six years old, was a lineman in professional football for nine years, following successful high school and college careers. Obviously an intelligent and sensitive man, he seemed a bit stung when asked how he could submit himself to such punishment for so many years.

> You know, a lot of people look at a lineman and they say, "oh, man, you gotta be some kinda *animal* to get down there and beat on each other like that." But it's just like a woman giving birth. A woman giving birth. Everybody says, you know, "That's a great accomplishment: she must be really beautiful." And I do too—I think it's something that's an act of God, that's unreal. *But*, she hasn't done nothing that she wasn't *built* for. See what I'm saying? Now here I am, 260, 270 pounds: and *that's my position.* My physical self helped me. I can *do* that. I can *do* that. I couldn't run out for no pass—I'd have looked like a *fool* runnin' out for a pass, see what I mean? But due to my good speed and my strength and my physical

physique, that's what I'm built for. Just like a truck carrying a big caterpil-lar: you see the strain, but that's what it's built for, so as far as that being a real big accomplishment, it is, but it's not. That's all you were built for.

Upshaw's comparisons of the aggressive uses of his body in football with a woman giving birth and with a truck is telling: it suggests one of the major paradoxes of men's construction of meaning surrounding the uses of their bodies as weapons. On the one hand, so many of the men I interviewed felt a strong need to naturalize their capacities for aggression and violence: men wearing helmets and pads repeatedly engaging in bonecrushing collisions with each other is simply "an act of God," "like a woman giving birth." Yet on the other hand, there is the clear knowledge that the bodies of successful linemen are, like trucks, "built" by human beings to do a specific job. Time after time, I heard former athletes, almost in the same breath, talk of their "natural" and "God-given" talent *and* of the long hours, days, and years of training, work and sacrifice that went into the development of their bodies and their skills. "I was a natural," former professional football star Macarthur Lane told me, "Just about every hour of the day when I wasn't sleeping or eating, I'd be on the playground competing."

Similarly, Jack Tatum, who in his years with the Oakland Raiders was known as "The Assassin" for his fierce and violent "hits" on opposing receivers, described himself as a "natural hitter." But his descriptions of his earliest experiences in high school football tell a different story. Though he soon began to develop a reputation as a fierce defensive back, at first, hitting people bothered him:

> When I first started playing, if I would hit a guy hard and he wouldn't get up, it would bother me. [But] when I was a sophomore in high school, first game, I knocked out two quarterbacks, and people loved it. The coach loved it. Everybody loved it.... The more you play, the more you realize that it is just a part of the game—somebody's gonna get hurt. It could be you, it could be him—most of the time it's better if it's him.

This story suggests that the tendency to utilize violence against others to achieve a goal in the sports context is learned behavior. Two excellent stud-ies of young ice hockey players corroborate this: the combination of violent adult athletic role models as well as rewards from coaches, peers, and the community for the willingness to successfully utilize violence create a context in which violence becomes normative behavior (Smith 1974; Vaz 1980). Athletes who earn reputations as aggressive "hitters" can often gain a certain level of status in the community and among peers, thus anchoring (at least temporarily) an otherwise insecure masculine identity. Louie Gelina, for instance developed a reputation as a very successful high school athlete, largely due to his often ruthless aggressiveness. By his own admission, he would often "do mean things, like beat people up. On the football field, I'd be dirty, like I'd kick guys in the groin...or in basketball, I'd undercut people. And I think it was mainly to earn their respect. It was like I *had* to let them know that, hey, I'm superstud and you, you're second class, you're not as good." But Gelina discovered, as have many athletes, that the use of his body as a weapon—and the support of the community—can cut both ways. His athletic career, and his sense of identity that came with it, unraveled quickly when he injured his knee just before the state championship game.

> I was hurt. I couldn't play, and I got a lot of flack from everybody. The coach, you know: "Are you faking it?" And I was in the whirlpool and [teammate] John came in and said "You fucking pussy!" I still remember that to this day. That hurt more than the injury. Later, people told me it was my fault because we lost, and I just couldn't handle that—not just coaches and other players, but people in the whole town...it hurt, it just really hurt.

Gelina's "sin" was to refuse to conform to what Sabo (1986) calls "the pain principle," so important a part of the structure and values of the sports-world. Gelina had previously found himself rewarded for using his own body to punish other men, but that violence against other men ultimately resulted in violence against his own body. Yet what ultimately "hurt more than the injury" was finding himself ostracized, his masculinity called into question, when he refused to further "give up his body for the good of the team." And it is highly significant that this insult, hurled at him by a teammate, is phrased in relation to a violent reference to a female body-part. Here we can see an illustration of what Kaufman (1987, 2) calls "the triad of men's violence," the three corners of which are violence against women, violence against other men, and violence against one's self.

Louie Gelina never played organized sports again. He had not only lost his status in the community; he had also lost that tentative and precarious sense of masculine identity that he had constructed through his sports successes. Given these high stakes, it is not surprising that many athletes do "choose" to be hitters, and to "give their bodies up for the team." But it is not enough to explain away the use of physical violence in sports as simply the result of rewards and punishments handed out by coaches, peers, and the community for compliance or noncompliance with "the pain principle." Despite the intentions of some coaches and sport psychologists, athletes are not simply the result of some Pavlovian system of reward and punishment. They are human beings, capable of reflection and moral deliberation. Their decisions to participate—or not participate—in violent sports take place within a complex social/psychological context.

And, as we shall see, their decisions—and the meanings that they attribute to them—arc deeply gendered.

MASCULINITY, THE RULES, AND VIOLENCE

In order to properly conceptualize the masculinity/sports relationship, it is crucial to recognize that young males do not come to the institution of sport as "blank slates," ready to be "socialized" into the world of masculinity. Rather, young males come to their first experience as athletes with *already-gendering* identities (Messner 1987a, 1987b). As Chodorow (1978) has argued, early developmental experiences, rooted in the fact that it is women who mother, create a very different balance between separation and attachment in males and females, thus setting the stage for different kinds of problems with relationships, identity, and sexuality throughout the life course (Rubin 1982). One of the results of these differences is that young males tend to approach sports—and violence in sports—differently than females do. Despite the fact that few males truly enjoy hitting, and one has to be socialized into participating in much of the violence that is commonplace in sports, males appear to be predisposed to view aggression, within the rule-bound structure of sports, as legitimate, natural, and even "safe" in a psychological sense.

Gender identity is never a completed project, but always a developmental process that unfolds within a social context. Sport is a fascinating context in which to examine the unfolding of masculine gender identity. One of the most important developmental themes for males is their ambivalence toward intimacy: while craved by males, attachment also constitutes a major threat to the firm psychological boundaries around a fragile masculine identity (Chodorow 1978; Rubin 1982). In fact, males tend to perceive vulnerability, danger, and thus the possibility of violence in situations of close affiliation (Gilligan 1982). Young males bring this ambivalence toward intimacy to all their social interactions, including their first sports experiences. In observing differences between how girls and boys play games and sports, Piaget (1965) and Lever (1976) noted that girls tend to have more "pragmatic" and "flexible" orientations to the rules—they are more prone to make exceptions and innovations in the middle of a game in order to make the game more "fair." Boys, on the other hand, tend to have a more firm, even inflexible orientation to the rules of the game—to them, a clear and consistent set of rules are *what protects* "fairness." This masculine reification of the rules, according to Gilligan (1982), creates a "safe" place for the ambivalent and insecure structure of a developing masculine identity not simply because it meshes with their conception of "fairness," but perhaps more important, because it provides clear-cut boundaries around men's affiliations with each other. Here men can develop a certain kind of closeness with each other while not having to deal with the kinds of (intimate) attachments that they are predisposed to feel fearful of.

Within the athletic context, individuals' "roles" and separate positions within hierarchies are determined by competition within a clearly defined system of rules that govern the interactions of participants. Although most athletes will "stretch" the rules as much as they can to gain an advantage over their opponents, most have a respect, even a reverence, for the importance of rules as a code of conduct that places safe boundaries around their aggression and their relationships with others. Without the rules, there would be chaos—both physically and psychologically; there would be an incredibly frightening need to constantly negotiate and renegotiate relationships. And this is what feels truly dangerous to men. So to Marvin Upshaw, the constant physical aggression that is part of being a lineman in football felt more than "natural" to him—it clearly provided a comfortable context within which he developed a certain kind of relationship with other men.

> I had this guy we played against in Denver by the name of Mike Kern. . . . We battled. He enjoyed it, and I enjoyed it. But never was it a cheap shot, never did he have me down and just drive my head into the ground, you know, unnecessary stuff. We played a good, clean game of football, because we respected each other. Now, if he could knock me on my butt, he'd do it. And I'd do it to him and help him up. Talk to him after the game, sit and talk with him like I'm sittin' here talkin' to you. But while we're out there, now, we go at it. And I loved it. Yeah, I loved it.

For most of the men whom I interviewed, successful competition within the rulebound structure of sport was—at least for a time—the major basis of their relationships with the world, and thus their identities. Aggression "within the rules," then, is considered legitimate and safe (Bredemeier 1983). But what happens when legitimate ("legal") aggression results in serious injury, as it so often does in sport? Two of the men whom I interviewed, football player Jack Tatum (discussed earlier), and former professional baseball player Ray Fosse, were involved in frighteningly violent collisions, each of which resulted in serious injury. In each incident, the play was "legal"— there was no penalty issued by officials. And in the aftermath of each case, there was a lively public controversy concerning "violence in sports." A brief examination of these two men's retrospective definitions of these situations is instructive and helpful in beginning to draw a link between, on the one hand, the athlete's experience and construction of meaning surrounding his participation in violence, and on the other hand, the larger social meanings surrounding such public incidents.

As mentioned, by the time Jack Tatum—"the assassin"—got to the pros, he had become the kind of fearsome hitter that coaches dream of. And though he took pride in the fact that he was not a "dirty" player (i.e., his hits were within the rules), his problem was that he was perhaps *too good* at his craft. "Intimidation" was the name of the game, but there was a growing concern within football and in the sports media that Jack Tatum's "knockouts" were too brutal. In 1978, Tatum delivered one of his hits to an opposing wide receiver, Darryl Stingley. Stingley's neck was broken in two places, and he would never walk again. All of a sudden, Tatum was labelled as part of a "criminal element" in the NFL. Tatum was confused, arguing that this had been a "terrible accident," but was nevertheless simply a "routine play" that was "within the rules."

> I guess the thing that mystified me was that I could play for nine years and one guy gets hurt and then everybody comes down on me, you know. It's just like for nine years I've been playing the game the wrong way: but I've made All-Pro, I've been runner-up for Rookie of the Year, I've got all the honors playing exactly the same way. So, you know, it just kind of mystified me as to why there was just all of a sudden this stuff because a guy got hurt. It wasn't the first time a guy got paralyzed in football, so it really wasn't that unusual. The [NFL] Commissioner told me at one point that I should push people out of bounds instead of hitting them. And nowhere in football have they ever taught you that. As long as the guy's on the football field, you're supposed to hit him.

Ray Fosse was the recipient of a violent hit from Pete Rose in the 1970 All Star game, as an estimated sixty million people watched on television. The situation was simple: it was the twelfth inning, and Pete Rose, steaming around third base, needed only to touch home plate in order to score the winning run; Fosse's job as the catcher was to block the plate with his body and hope that the ball arrived in time to catch it and tag Rose out. Rose arrived a split second before the ball did, and, looking a lot like a football player delivering a "hit," drove his body through Fosse, and touched the plate safely. Fosse's shoulder was separated, and, despite his youth, he never fully regained the powerful home run swing that he had demonstrated earlier that summer. Again a serious injury had resulted from a technically "legal" play. Rose was seen by some as a hero, but others criticized him, asking if it was "right" for him to hurt someone else simply to score a run in what was essentially an exhibition game. Rose seemed as mystified by these questions as Jack Tatum had been. Everyone knew that he was known as "Charley Hustle": "I play to win," responded Rose, "I just did what I had to do."

When I interviewed Fosse years later, well into retirement as a player, he lamented the effect of the injury, but saw it not as the result of a decision on the part of Pete Rose, but, rather, as "a part of the game." It was fate, an impersonal force, that had broken his body—not an individual person. In fact, he felt nothing but respect for Rose.

> I've seen that play a million times since, replays they keep showing and showing, but I never once believed that he hit me intentionally. He's just a *competitor*, and I only wish that every other major league ball player played as hard as he did, 'cause then you wouldn't have fans upset because players were making so much money and they're not performing. But he's a competitor. But I would say that that was the beginning of a lot of pain and problems for me.

Clearly, one of the things that is happening in the Tatum and the Fosse cases is what Bredemeier and Shields (1986) call "contextual morality": the reification of the rules of the game provide a context that frees the participants from the responsibility for moral choices. As long as the participants "play by the rules," they not only feel that they should be free from moral criticism, there is a perhaps subconscious understanding that they are entitled to "respect," that form of emotionally distant connection with others that is so important to masculine identity. Flagrant rule-violators, it is believed, are "violent," and deserve to be sanctioned; others like Tatum and Rose are "aggressive competitors," deserving of respect. But this distinction is shaken when serious injury result from "legal" actions and public scrutiny raises questions about the individual morality of the athletes themselves. Both Tatum and Fosse appear "mystified" by the framing of the issue in terms of individual choice or morality: they just play by the rules.

THE COSTS OF VIOLENCE FOR ATHLETES

I interviewed former pro football star Macarthur Lane in the upstairs office of the health spa that he owns and manages. Retired now for several years, he appears to be in excellent physical condition, and he makes his living helping others achieve strong, healthier bodies. He was relaxed, sitting in a chair and resting his feet on a table, talking about basketball. When I asked him how tall he was, I received a startling reply: "Oh, I used to be about 6'2"—I'm about six even right now. All the vertebraes in my neck, probably from all the pounding and stuff, the vertebraes used to be farther apart—just the constant pounding and jarring. It hurts all the time. I hurt all the time. Right now, that's why I put my legs up here on the table, to take the pressure off my lower back."

Here is one of the ultimate praradoxes of organized combat sports: top athletes, who are often portrayed as the epitome of good physical conditioning and health, are likely to suffer from a very high incidence of permanent injuries, disabilities, alcoholism, drug abuse, obesity, and heart problems. The instrumental rationality that teaches athletes to view their own bodies as machines and weapons with which to annihilate an objectified opponent ultimately comes back upon the athlete as an alien force: the body-as-weapon ultimately results in violence against one's own body. In fact, a former professional football player in the United States has an average life-expectancy of about fifty-six years (roughly fifteen years shorter than the overall average life-expectancy of U.S. males). American football, of course, is especially brutal: Delvin Williams told me that in his pro career, "six of eight off-seasons I had surgery, twice a two-for-one—they cut me twice." In a recent survey of retired professional football players, 78% reported that they suffer physical disabilities related directly to football, and 66% believe that having played football will negatively affect their life-spans (Wojciechowski and Dufresne 1988). But this situation is not limited to football. Baseball has had its share of casualties, too. Ray Fosse's interview with me seemed to be an almost endless chronicle of injuries and surgeries. When someone got injured, he explained, "We had a saying: 'Throw dirt on it, spit on it, go play.'" And Fosse did constantly "play hurt," often with "a lot of cortisone and just anything to kill the pain, just to go out and play. I don't know how many shots I had—I know I had a lot, because it was killing me. And now, as I rotate my left arm, I can hear bone to bone, you know [laughs ironically], because it healed back wrong."

And this parade of injuries is not limited to professional athletes. Nearly every former athlete I interviewed had at least one story of an injury that disabled him, at least for a time. Many had incurred serious injuries that had a permanent impact on their health. Despite the fact that most wore these injuries with pride, like badges of masculine status, there is also a grudging acknowledgment that one's healthy body was a heavy price to pay for glory. But to question their decisions to "give up" their bodies would ultimately mean to question the entire institutionalized system of rules through which they had successfully established relationships and a sense of identity. Since this is usually too threatening, former athletes instead are more likely to rationalize their own injuries as "part of the game," and claim that the pain contributed to the development of "character," and ultimately gained them the "respect" of others.

Other costs paid by athletes who play violent sports are not so easy to measure. But there is strong evidence that the extremely instrumental relationship to self and others that athletes must develop in order to be successful in aggressive competitive sports commonly results in personalities that are more quick to anger (Goldstein 1984), in an increased devaluation of women and gay men (Connell 1990; Sabo 1985), and in an amplification of men's already-existing tendency to have problems developing and maintaining intimate relationships with women and with other men (Messner 1987a, 1987b).

In short, heavy personal and interpersonal costs are paid by those who participate in violent organized sports. And it is absolutely crucial to recognize who these men are. As Edwards (1984) points out, poor and ethnic minority males, because of poverty, institutionalized racism, and lack of other career options are "channeled" disproportionately into sports careers—and into the more dangerous positions within the "combat sports." Males from more privileged backgrounds often play sports while in school, and their experience as athletes may be status-enhancing, but because they face a wider range of educational and career choices, they often opt out of sports at a relatively early age, choosing instead to seek status and respect within less (physically) violent competitive rule-bound structures (Messner 1989). Young men from poor and ethnic minority backgrounds face a constricted range of options (Gibbs 1988). Lacking other resources and choices, sports may appear, as they did for Macarthur Lane, to be the one legitimate context in which a youngster from a disadvantaged background may establish a sense of (masculine) identity in the world: "I'd put my pants on and I'd go out on the football field with the intention that I'm gonna do a job. And if that calls on me to hurt you, I'm gonna do it. It's as simple as that. I demand respect just like everybody else."

As the examples of Fosse and Tatum have illustrated, the meanings that athletes construct around their participation in violent sports may come into conflict with larger cultural meanings when these actions are framed as public spectacle. The final section of this essay will draw some tentative conclusions concerning the larger social meanings of sports violence for the construction of the contemporary gender order.

VIOLENCE, SPORT, AND THE CONTEMPORARY GENDER ORDER

The mythology and symbolism of contemporary combat sports such as football are probably meaningful and salient to viewers on a number of levels: patriotism, militarism, and meritocracy are all dominant themes. But it is reasonable to speculate that gender is a salient organizing theme in the construction of meanings around sports violence. Consider the words of a thirty-two-year-old white professional-class male whom I interviewed: "A woman can do the same job as I can do—maybe even be my boss. But I'll be *damned* if she can go out on the field and take a hit from Ronnie Lott." Embedded in this man's statement are what I will argue are the two sides of the male spectators/sports violence relationship for the construction of the contemporary gender order: violent sports as spectacle provide linkages among men in the project of the domination of women, while at the same time help to construct and clarify differences between various masculinities. The statement by the man above is a clear indication that he is identifying with Ronnie Lott *as a man*, and the basis of the identification is the violent male body. Football, based as it is on the most extreme possibilities of the male body (muscular bulk, and explosive power used aggressively) is clearly a world apart from women, who are relegated to the role of cheerleader/sex objects on the sidelines, rooting their men on. In contrast to the bare and vulnerable bodies of the cheerleaders, the armored male bodies of the football players are elevated to mythical status, and, as such, give testimony to the undeniable "fact" that here is at least one place where men are clearly superior to women. Yet it is also significant that this man was quite aware that he (and perhaps 99% of the rest of the U.S. male population) was probably equally incapable of taking a "hit" from the likes of Lott and living to tell of it. These two themes—identification and difference among men—will briefly be discussed next.

With the decline of the practical relevance of physical strength in work and in warfare, representations of the muscular male body as strong, virile, and powerful have taken on increasingly important ideological and symbolic significance in gender relations (Mishkind 1986). Indeed, the body plays such a central role in the construction of the contemporary gender order because it is so closely associated with the "natural." Yet a concrete examination of athletes shows that the development of their bodies for competition takes a tremendous amount of time, exercise, weight-training, and even use of illegal and dangerous drugs such as steroids. Though the body is popularly equated with nature, it is nevertheless an object of social practice (Carrigan et al. 1987; Connell 1987; 1990).

The embodiment of hegemonic masculinity entails the embedding of force and skill in the body. Men's power over women thus becomes "naturalized," and clearly linked to the social distribution of violence (Connell 1987, 85). Sport is an important organizing institution for this embodiment of masculinity. As a practice, sport suppresses natural (sex) similarities, constructs differences, and then, largely through the media, weaves a structure of symbol and interpretation around these differences that naturalizes them (Hargreaves 1986, 112). Several recent theorists have suggested, though, that the major ideological salience of sport as mediated spectacle may lie not so much in violence as it does in male spectators having the opportunity to identify with the muscular male body. McCormack (1984), for instance argues that boxing films so routinize instrumental violence that the psychological impact of the violence is diminished. The films are really more about "jock appeal"—a narcissistic preoccupation with the male body. Morse (1983), in a fascinating analysis of the use of slow-motion instant replays in football, argues that the visual representation of violence is transformed by slow-motion replays into "gracefulness." The salience for gender relations of the image of male power and grace lies not in identification with violence, Morse argues, but, rather, in the opportunity to engage in an identificatory male gaze that is both narcissistic and homoerotic. An additional interpretation is possible here. Rather than concluding that the violence has no meaning, it is reasonable to speculate that if men are using sports spectatorship to narcissistically identify with the male body as a thing of beauty, perhaps the violence is an important aspect of the denial of the homoerotic element of that identification.

It is also possible that the violence plays another important role: the construction of difference among men. As previously stated, it is disproportionately males from lower socioeconomic and ethnic minority backgrounds who pursue athletic careers in violent sports. Privileged men might, as Woody Guthrie once suggested, commit violence against others "with fountain pens," but with the exception of domestic violence against women and children, physical violence is rarely a part of the everyday lives of these men. Yet violence among men may still have important ideological and psychological meaning for men from privileged backgrounds. There is a curious preoccupation among middle-class males with movie characters who are "working class tough guys" (Biskind and Ehrenreich 1980), with athletes who are fearsome "hitters" and who heroically "play hurt." These violent "tough guys" of the culture industry—the Rambos, the Jack Tatums, the Ronnie Lotts—are at once the heroes who "prove" that "we men" are superior to women *and* they play the role of "other," against whom privileged men define themselves as "modern." They are, in a very real sense, contemporary gladiators who are sacrificed in order that the elite may have a clear sense of where they stand in the pecking order of intermale dominance. Their marginalization as men—signified by their engaging in the very violence that makes them such attractive spectacles—contributes to the construction of hegemonic masculinity. In the United States, a particularly salient feature of this contemporary construction of masculinities in sport is racism: it is indeed ironic that so many young black males are attracted to sports as an arena in which to become "respected," yet once there, to be successful, they must become intimidating, aggressive, and violent in order to survive. And then, the media images of, for instance, Jack Tatum "exploding" Darryl Stingley, become symbolic "proof" of the racist stereotype that black males are indeed "naturally more violent and aggressive."

This research has demonstrated that contemporary "combat sports" provide a context in which a certain type of (violent) masculinity is embodied. The athletes themselves often pay a heavy price in terms of health and relationships for their participation in violent sports. Yet it has been suggested here that, as cultural symbols, these men serve to stabilize a structure of domination and oppression in the gender order. The media's framing of violent sports as public spectacle serves both to unite men in the domination of women and to support the ascendence of hegemonic masculinity and the continued marginalization of other masculinities. Future research should focus on sports violence as an important axis through which class, race, sexual preference, and gender difference and inequalities are constructed and naturalized.

7

Scoring without Consent

Confronting Male Athletes' Sexual
Violence against Women

(with Mark Stevens)

Author's note: Incidents of male athletes' sexual violence against women seem continually to be in the news. Why does this problem continue to recur, and what can we do about it? In this essay, I joined with my colleague Mark Stevens, one of the leading clinical psychologists in the United States working in the field of men's violence prevention, to sketch out an answer to these two questions. In the 1970s, the women's movement began to put men's violence against women on the map as a social problem and as a political issue. This naming of a problem had important reverberations in terms of public policies, laws, and popular culture, and less formal institutional developments like women's shelters in the 1970s and 1980s. These important changes, however, were limited in their effectiveness because they dealt essentially with the outcomes of men's violence against women, not the causes. Thus, in the 1980s and 1990s, scholars began to try to understand how gender relations shape men's tendencies to commit acts of violence against women. In this 2002 essay, we examine four common aspects of the culture of boys' and men's sports—homophobic and misogynistic "dominance bonding" in the male peer group; heterosexual "voyeuring" that erotically bonds members of the male group; a suppression of empathy toward self and others; and a "culture of silence" in the peer group—which together tend to enable some men's sexual violence against women. We then turn to a discussion of clinical violence prevention interventions with men's athletic teams. Drawing from our own experiences, and from the work of various campus-based antiviolence programs that emerged from 1990s to the present, we discuss concrete strategies that we have used in workshops with athletes. We end by asking to what extent such strategies can be successful in the absence of more radical restructuring of the ways that sport shapes boys' and men's identities, relationships, attitudes and orientations toward women.

In recent years, increased public attention has focused on incidents of violence against women perpetrated by high-profile college and professional male athletes. Although not long ago, accusations of sexual assault, sexual harassment, or wife abuse by a high-profile athlete may have been ignored, downplayed, or considered to be outside the frame of legitimate media coverage (Messner and Solomon 1993), increasingly in recent years, the issue of athletes' violence against women has moved squarely into the realm of public and media discourse (McDonald 1999). As reporters are increasingly moved to cover accusations (and sometimes convictions) of male athletes assaulting women, they have understandably turned to scholars of sport with a key question: are male athletes more likely than nonathletes to engage in acts of sexual violence or battery against women, or do we just notice it more when some athletes do assault women, because of their high-profile public status?

The question of male athletes' relationship to violence against women is a difficult but very important one to answer. Some activists (e.g., McPherson 2002) argue that men's violence against women is a broad social problem that is proportionately reflected, like all other social problems, in sport. Perhaps fearing that pointing the finger at high-profile athletes will reinforce destructive and oppressive stereotypes of African American males (who make up about 80% of the NBA, for instance) as sexual predators, these activists prefer instead to pull male athletes into positions of responsibility to educate peers to prevent violence against women.

Although programs based on these assumptions, like the Mentors in Violence Prevention (MVP) program at Northeastern University, are laudable, it is important to examine whether they are based on sound assumptions, since faulty assumptions could ultimately serve to limit or undercut their effectiveness. An examination of recent research on the relationship between athletic participation and violence against women is illustrative. A number of studies of college athletes in recent years have pointed to statistically significant relationships between athletic participation and sexual aggression (Boeringer 1996; Fritner and Rubinson 1993; Koss and Gaines 1993). In what is widely considered the most reliable study to date, Crosset, Benedict, and McDonald (1995) surveyed twenty

universities with Division 1 athletic programs, and found that male athletes, who constituted 3.7% of the student population, were 19% of those
reported to campus Judicial Affairs Offices for sexual assault. Crosset
(2000) argues that researchers have more than likely been using far to
broad a brush in examining "men's sports" and violence against women.
Studies that have compared across sports have found vast differences. Koss
and Gaines (1993) found a much stronge relationship in men's "revenue-
producing sports," and Crosset et al. (1996) found that the majority of
reported assaults concerned athletes in "contact sports" like basketball,
football, and hockey. These data suggest the dangers of "clumping all sport
environments together under the rubric of athletic affiliation" (Crosset
2000). When the focus is on specific kinds of athletic contexts, we may be
able to better understand the causes of some athletes' violence against
women, and thus intervene more effectively.

Crosset (2000) argues that although the empirical research does show
some correlations between participation in certain kind of sports with violent
and misogynous attitudes and behaviors, more research is needed to establish
clear causal connections. He concludes that the current debate over whether
athletes commit more violence than nonathletes do against women is
"unproductive." It "detracts from the fact that some athletes are violent
against women," a fact that calls for active preventative efforts. Crosset's
pragmatic point is well taken, and we take it a step further. It is important to
confront male athletes' violence against women not simply because "some
athletes are violent against women," but also because the world of sports is a
key institutional site for the construction of hegemonic masculinity, and thus
a key potential site for its contestation (Bryson 1987; Kidd 1990; Messner
1988). The institution of sport tends not only to "reflect," but also to *amplify*
everything about masculinity that is generally true in the larger gender order.
Values of male heroism based on competition and winning, playing hurt,
handing out pain to opponents, group-based bonding through homophobia
and misogyny, and the legitimation of interpersonal violence as a means
toward success are all values undergirding hegemonic masculinity in the
larger gender order that are amplified in men's sport. Thus, confronting these
issues within sport not only might help make the world safer for some
women, as Crosset suggests; a fundamental confrontation with the root
causes of athletic men's violence against women is likely to have a positive
ripple effect throughout the larger gender order.

It is necessary to distinguish beween direct and complicit involvement
in violence. The vast majority of male athletes *do not engage* in violence
against women, but an unknown, and certainly larger percentage are complicit by their silence. We will argue that intervention strategies must confront the root causes of men's violence against women, and a key way to
accomplish this is to provide a context in which the "silent majority" of men

move affirmatively away from being quietly complicit in a culture of misogyny, homophobia, and violence.

The question of what enables, encourages, or even rewards certain
men's violence against women is a complex one. Certainly, there are multiple factors at work. Broad, contextual factors such as the degree to which
boys experience life as a pedagogy of legitimate violence (Canada 1995),
combined with the degree of gender inequality in the culture or community
(Sanday 1981) can enable or constrain men's violence against women.
Researchers have only begun to explore the possible links between men's
violence against women with the experience of some men—especially in
homosocial institutions like sports, the military, or fraternities—of being
routinely rewarded for successfully using their bodies as weapons against
other men (Messner 1992, Nixon 1997). Furthermore, researchers have
begun to explore links between male athletes' violence against women with
their experience of being rewarded for ignoring their own pain and injuries,
and "giving one's body up for the team" (Messner 1992; Sabo 1994; Young
and White 2000). With these issues in mind, we will focus this essay on one
key element underlying male athletes' violence against women: the peer
group dynamics of the team. Following our analytic discussion of these
dynamics, we will raise some critical questions about educational intervention strategies with male athletes.

LOCKER ROOM TALK AND ACTIONS

In a riveting and insightful account of the infamous 1989 Glen Ridge gang
rape case, journalist Bernard Lefkowitz (1997) describes how twelve popular
white high school athletes lured a seventeen-year-old "slightly retarded" girl
into a basement. The dynamics of the sexual assault that ensued are instructive for our purposes here: first, the boys set up chairs—theatre style—in
front of a couch. As some boys sit in the chairs to watch, others lead the girl
to the couch and induce her to begin to give oral sex to one of the most popular and respected boys. As this happens, one sophomore boy notices "puzzle-
ment and confusion" in the girl's eyes, turns to his friend and says, "Let's get
out of here" (Lefkowitz 1997, 23). Another senior baseball player "feels
queezy" and thinks "I don't belong here," and climbs the stairs to leave with
another baseball player. On the way out, he tells another guy, "It's wrong.
C'mon with me," but the other guy stays (24). In all, six of the young men
leave, while six—five seniors and one junior—remain in the basement. As
the girl is forced to continue giving oral sex to the boy, other boys laugh,
shout encouragement to their friends, and derisively shout "You whore!" at
the girl (24). One boy decides it would be amusing to sexually abuse her with

a baseball bat. As he does this (and follows it with a broomstick), the girl hears one boy's voice say "Stop. You're hurting her," but another voice says, "Do it more" (25). Later, the girl remembers that the boys were all laughing, while she was crying. When they were done, they warned her not to tell anyone, and concluded with an athletic ritual of togetherness by standing in a circle and clasping "One hand on top of the other, all their hands together, like a basketball team on the sidelines at the end of a timeout" (25).

In his description and analysis of the Glen Ridge community in which the boys and their victim grew up, Lefkowitz points to a number of factors that enabled the gang rape to happen, and these are the very same factors that the recent social scientific literature on men, sexual violence, and sport has pointed to:

- The role of competitive, homophobic, and misogynistic talk and joking as a form of "dominance bonding" in the athletic male peer group.
- "Voyeuring" whereby boys would set up situations where they seduce girls in places and situations in which their friends watch the sex act, and sometimes take an active part in it.
- The suppression of empathy—especially toward girls who are the objects of the competitive dominance bonding that the boys learned from each other.
- The "culture of silence" among peers, in families, and in the community that enables some men's sexual violence against women.

In examining these four enabling factors, we will keep in the forefront Lefkowitz's observation that the actual physical assault in this case was conducted by four football players and wrestlers. Two others, apparently, sat and watched—perhaps laughed and cheered—but did not actually physically join in the assault. The other six boys who left the scene as the assault was beginning felt uncomfortable enough to leave, but they did not do anything significant at the time to stop their friends. They did not leave the basement and report the assault to parents, teachers, or the police, and they all refused throughout the subsequent long and painful years of litigation to "turn on" their male friends and provide incriminating evidence. It is the *complicity* of these boys that we take as the centerpiece of our analysis here. As R.W. Connell (1995) has argued, the dominant, or "hegemonic" form of masculinity is usually expressed and embodied by a relatively small majority of men; what helps hegemonic masculinity sustain itself in a system of power relations is the consent of many women, but especially the complicity of other men— some (or many) of whom may be uncomfortable with some or all of the beliefs and practices that sustain hegemonic masculinity. Although legal interventions in sexual assaults obviously need to target the behaviors of boys and men who are the perpetrators, intervention strategies that aim to prevent future sexual assaults should also target those boys and men who may be marginal to the group, but whose complicit silence enables their teammates' assaultive behaviors.

SEXUAL TALK AND DOMINANCE BONDING

Gary Alan Fine (1987) found that one of key ways that eleven- and twelve-year-old boys in Little League Baseball learn to bond with each other is with sexually aggressive banter. Wood (1984) argues that this sort of competitive sexual talk among boys is a sort of group pedagogy through which boys are "groping toward sexism" in their attitudes and practices toward girls and women. These same tendencies are evident among postadolescent and young adult men. In a study of talk in a college men's athletic locker room, Curry (1991) observed that a dominant mode of conversation inclined toward the dual themes of competition and boasting of sexual conquests of women. Such conversation is characterized by high volume—it is clearly intended as a performance for the group—and by its centrality in the geography of the locker room. This kind of talk has consequences. First, as Curry's (2000) subsequent research of college athletes' violence in a sports bar shows, aggressive talk can often be connected to violent off-the-field actions. And, according to Farr (1988), sexually aggressive talk provides a means of "dominance bonding" for young males. Internal hierarchies are constructed and contested as the boys and young men simultaneously mark the boundaries of the "insider" and the "outsider" (e.g., women, gay men, nonathletic men). And dominance bonding—based as it is on humorous, aggressive, sometimes violent talk about sex—has an erotic base to it, as Lyman's (1987) research on joking among fraternity members indicates.

Curry's (1991) locker room study indicated another important discourse dynamic. On the margins of the locker room, other men were engaged in other kinds of conversations. They spoke in hushed tones about personal issues, problems, even insecurities about dating or relationships with girlfriends. These quiet and private conversations stand in contrast to the loud and public conversation that dominates the locker room. We speculate that these more personal conversations remain private partly because boys and young men have had the experience of being (or seeing other boys) humiliated in male groups for expressing vulnerability, or for expressing care for a particular girl (Sabo 1994).

The main policing mechanisms used to enforce consent are misogyny and homophobia: boys and men who make themselves vulnerable by revealing personal information are targeted as the symbolic "women," "pussies," and "faggots" on athletic teams (and, indeed, in many other male groups). In fact, it is a key part of the group process of dominance bonding that one or more members of the male group are made into the symbolic debased and degraded feminized "other" through which the others can bond and feel that their status as "men" is safely ensured. Early on, most boys learn to avoid at all costs offering one's self up as a target for this kind of abuse. The power of this group dynamic was illustrated in Messner's (1992) interview with a former athlete who, during his successful athletic career, had been a closeted gay man. One of the best ways that this man found to keep his secret within this aggressively homophobic world was to participate in what he called "locker room garbage" talk about sexual conquests of women.

"VOYEURING": WOMEN AS OBJECTS OF CONQUEST

Lefkowitz (1997, 183–184) shows that by the time they were teens, the "jocks" of Glen Ridge used more than talk for their erotic dominance bonding. They would sometimes gather together in a home when parents were away to watch pornographic films and masturbate together. The next step was the development of a group form of entertainment that they called "voyeuring" whereby a plan would be made for one guy at a party to "convince a girl to go upstairs to a bedroom for a sexual encounter." But first, "his buddies would go up and hide in a closet, under the bed, or behind a door" where they could watch. Sex with a girl, for these guys, was less an intimate encounter with a valued human being than it was the use of a woman's body as a platform for sexual performance for one's male buddies. It was, in Lefkowitz's words, "a way for these guys to create their own porn movie" (184). Though it is difficult to say how widespread similar group practices of voyeuring among male athletes might be, this erotic bonding dynamic is found elsewhere. For instance, the California white high school football players known as the "Spur Posse" had multiple sexual encounters with girls and young women as a competition among the boys to see who could "score" the most times (Messner 1994). Similarly, Sanday's (1990) research suggests that misogynistic denigration of women and erotic male bonding underlies fraternity gang rapes.

A key to the understanding of the group process by which males use women's bodies to erotically bond with each other is that most heterosexual boys and young men go through a period of intense insecurity and intense discomfort when learning to establish heterosexual relations with girls and women. Former male athletes reported that when they were in high school, or even in college, talking with girls and women raised intense anxieties and feelings of inadequacy (Messner 1992). As these young men immersed themselves in the peer pedagogy of heterosexual relations, they learned to put on a performance for girls that, surprisingly for some of them, seemed to "work." Their successful utilization of this learned dramaturgy of the hetero-sexual come-on allowed them to mask or overcome a sense of insecurity and "lameness." It also intensified—at a deep psychological level—adherence to the group process of erotic dominance bonding with other members of the male peer group by collectively constructing women as objects of conquest.

SUPPRESSION OF EMPATHY

An important lessons that an athlete—especially one in the more aggressive "combat sports"—must learn in order to survive and thrive is to suppress one's empathy for one's opponent (Messner 1992). Nixon's (1997) research suggests that male athletes who learn to accept that their participation in sports will routinely result in injuries to others are more likely to engage in physical aggression outside of the sport context. Cross-cultural research on rape has pointed to the importance *of the degree and type of contact that boys and men have with girls and women* as a variables that correlate with rates of rape. Rape rates tend to be higher in societies with rigid divisions of labor between the sexes, especially where these divisions are marked by male dom-inance and female subordination (Sanday 1981). Homosocial bonding among men, especially when the bond is the sort of sexualized dominance bonding just discussed, is a very poor environment for the development of empathy for women. Lefkowitz (1997) observes that the boys most central to the Glen Ridge rape grew up without sisters in families dominated by strong male fig-ures. Their peer group, family, and community experiences taught them that boys' and men's activities were more highly prized than those of girls and women. "The immediate environment," Lefkowitz (280) argues, "did not cul-tivate great empathy for women." In contrast, some of the boys who left the scene due theior discomfort with the gang rape were unable to suppress their empathy for the victim. Most of these boys grew up in homes with sisters.

THE CULTURE OF SILENCE

A question that plagued Lefkowitz in his examination of the Glen Ridge rape was why the six boys who left the scene remained complicit in their silence, both the day of the rape, and during the subsequent years of litigation. At least some of these young men were very uncomfortable with what hap-pened—even thought it was "wrong"—but nobody in the group raised a hand or voice to stop it. Significantly, two other young men did. The case "broke" when another male athlete who had not been at the scene of the assault reported to teachers that he had overheard other guys laughing and bragging about the rape. This African American whistle-blower felt excluded from the tightly knit, high-status clique of white athletes. A second nonparticipant young man became an activist in a quest to see that the jocks did not get away with their crime. He was a long-haired *Gigger*, a term used to identify the small minority of radical, artsy, antijock crowd at the school. Both of these boys—one an athlete, one not—were *outsiders* to the dominant athletic male peer group. Those inside—even those who were marginal within the group—maintained a complicit silence that enabled the assault to occur.

This culture of silence is built in to the dynamics of the group's spoken and unspoken codes and rituals. Boys have years of experience within the group that has taught them that there are rewards for remaining complicit with the code of silence, and, indeed, there are punishments for betraying the group. A whistle-blower might be banished from the group, be beaten up, or he might remain in the group, but now with the status of the degraded, feminized "faggot" who betrayed the "men" in the group.

EMPOWERING MARGINAL DISCOURSES

How might coaches, teachers, counselors, and parents intervene with young male athletes to encourage changes in the attitudes and relations that lead to assaults on girls and women? Confronting a male athletic team—especially as an adult "outsider"—is a daunting task. The difficulty of this task is compounded by the fact that all too often, professionals are brought in to consult with athletic departments and to run workshops with athletes because assaultive behaviors have already occurred. There is often in these situations an atmosphere of resentment and defensive silence among the athletes. The intervention strategies discussed in the next section aim to use what little time there is to provide a safe place for talk, but also an enabling place for the emergence of new forms of talk. We explicitly try to "decenter" the dominant misogynistic conversations, while empowering the nonsexist conversations that otherwise might remain marginal.

Contextual and Facilitation Issues

Male student athletes approach our workshops in much the same way that most people anticipate spending an evening at traffic school. They resent having to attend, anticipate a critical finger being pointed in their direction, and often enter the room with an air of unfriendliness and bravado. On the other hand, we have found a detectable amount of curiosity is usually hidden beneath this veneer of aloofness. Understanding male student athletes' resistance while expanding their curiosity helps the engagement process. The facilitator needs to be prepared for a unique type of intimidation that may take the form of loud side conversations, off-the-wall questions, insider jokes, and loud silences accompanied by non-expressive staring. We have attempted to meet these challenges by using a variety of facilitation tools designed to create a safe learning environment, which reduces resistance and increases positive engagement.

- *Get their attention:* We provide statistics, show some video clips, and ask rhetorical questions, such as "How many of you would like to know with 99% certainty that you will never be accused or convicted of being a date or acquaintance rapist?" Almost all participants raise their hands in response to this question. With most eyes on the facilitators, we then tell them that there are some simple principles and practices to use in order to know when one has full consent, which we will be discussing later on in the workshop.
- *Self-disclosure:* We strategically and selectively share our own personal sexual and athletic experiences to create a safe context for risk taking, and to lessen the us-versus-them mentality.
- *Reward honesty:* Participants are more verbal when they feel that they are respected and will be heard. When they are rewarded for taking the risk of sharing their thoughts and feelings, even if they happen to be "politically incorrect," they engage the workshop instead of shutting down.
- *Be firm, but flexible:* Groups of male student athletes can be quite loud, and this group dynamic can create a chaotic learning environment. We try to demonstrate that we expect them to treat us with the same respect that they treat their coaches. On the other hand, we find that it is important to allow room for laughter and some level of chaos, and even to join in at appropriate times.
- *Respectfully challenge:* Participants often present opinions that need to be challenged. It is an essential part of the educational process to find ways to challenge the participants in a manner that will lead to continued dialogue. One way to accomplish this is to become curious, rather than critical, concerning how a participant developed a certain opinion or belief.

The Workshop Agenda

Increasing Empathy. Empathy is the ability to take into consideration and respond accordingly to the feelings of another person. Empathy allows one to measure the impact and consequences that a certain behavior will have on another human being. Men who sexually violate others have been shown to have limited empathy skills (Stevens 1993). As we have argued, athletes are often immersed in peer contexts in which they are rewarded for suppressing their empathy toward others. Increasing empathy skills is thus key to the success of any rape prevention program, but especially important when dealing with male student athletes. Most men give little thought to how the fear of rape can be so incredibly consuming for women. Additionally, most men are unaware that most women feel neither flattered nor safe when whistled at, or made the target of lewd propositions and ogling. In fact, many men have been socialized to view these behaviors both as essential to the mating ritual and as an important component of the bonding process in the male group. Furthermore, men have been systematically taught—partly, but not exclusively within athletics—to hide, avoid, or deny their own feelings of pain, embarrassment, or hurt. When boys are told not to cry, they are also being denied the opportunity to learn how to empathize and feel for the other. We employ a variety of tools and exercises to help motivate men to improve their empathy skills:

1. *Twenty-four hours without rape:* We ask the group to imagine what their life would be like if they knew there was no such thing as rape. We then ask them to imagine how women would feel and act if they knew there was no such thing as rape.
2. *Being bullied:* We ask the participants to recall an experience when they were threatened or picked on by someone who was bigger or more powerful. We ask them to describe how they felt after the attack.
3. *What if this happened to your sister or girlfriend?* After we ask the participants to discuss the variety of ways that they try to "hit on" or "pick up" women, we ask them to imagine other guys using the same behaviors toward their sisters or girlfriends. In response to their discussion of their feelings and reactions, we attempt to pierce the implicit madonna–whore view of women that often pervades male peer groups. We challenge them to be aware of the fact that every woman has a brother, a boyfriend, and/or other family who cares about her.
4. *Gaining full consent.* Sexual assault cannot occur if there is full and mutual consent. How to know that full consent exists appears to be a complicated process. We approach this topic by suggesting the concept of a "consent table" upon which certain variables need to be clearly placed before one can be certain that consent exists. These variables include: permission, sobriety, a truthful statement of one's intentions, and any other pieces of information that would influence one's decision to become sexually involved.

The idea of making these variables explicit *before* becoming fully sexually involved tends to run against the grain of men's taken-for-granted notions of a "proper sexual script," and often brings up strong fears of rejection and embarrassment. Most men have been taught to believe that they just automatically "know" when a woman is aroused and willing to become sexually involved. The idea of asking for permission or clarification of some ambiguity seems unromantic, and seems to raise the risk of rejection. Several exercises are designed to clarify the importance of having unambiguous consent. For instance, we relate various scenarios, and ask them to discuss whether consent was clear or not in the scenarios. Two of our most successful are as follows.

The Traffic Light Metaphor. We begin by asking the men how they respond as drivers to a red, yellow, or green light. They usually say that they know what to do with a red or green light, but when approaching a yellow light, there is often a moment of confusion, usually followed by their speeding up rather than slowing down. Sexual encounters, the men tell us, are far too often experienced as a yellow light. We extend the metaphor by noting that a yellow light is supposed to signal to a driver to slow down and show caution; speeding up is a major cause of crashes in intersections. We explain that a sexual encounter is very much like an intersection—ripe with both excitement and danger—a "yellow light" should be a sign that danger looms, and that one should slow down; show caution. We ask participants to brainstorm ways they can respond to yellow light situations in ways that are respectful and that assure consensual sex.

Speaking Out. We have found that many men are disgusted when they see other men verbally and/or physically degrade women. Yet when confronted with this reality, they often say nothing or signal their approval. One root of this complicit silence is that men are afraid of other men. As with most all-male groups, male student athletes are reluctant to break the silence in fear of being humiliated, ostracized, or beaten up. One way that we confront this issue in workshops is to utilize the concept of team loyalty. For instance, we ask them what is likely to happen *to the team* if, at a party, two or three of their teammates take a very drunk woman into a room and have sex with her when she is clearly not in a condition to give her full consent? Isn't it part of the loyalty to the team, to each other, and to themselves to bravely step in and stop something like this from happening before it happens? Responses to these sorts of questions suggested that some of the previously more marginal men on the teams are empowered to speak out. And, interestingly, when one teammate does speak out—at least in the context of the workshop—others on the team seem to listen, and other marginal teammates then feel empowered to add their voices to the mix.

CONCLUSIONS

Current intervention programs with male athletes (e.g., the Mentors in Violence Program, Athletes for Sexual Responsibility at the University of Maine, as well as our work in various colleges) need to be empirically evaluated to assess their effect, if any, on sexist attitudes and dynamics of male athletic peer groups that enable the assaultive behaviors of some male athletes. We suspect that interventions that are not organically linked to longer-term institutional attempts to address men's violence at its psychological, peer group, and organizational roots will have little if any effect. At their best, such programs may provide a context in which some individual boys and men will be empowered to remove themselves from the role of passively complicit (but not fully comfortable) participants in the daily practices that feed an athletic rape culture. Boys and young men who have suppressed empathy for girls and women might be reawakened and validated, especially if they come to understand the links between their own marginalization within the male peer group and that group's denigration and victimization of women. These young men might be moved to risk "breaking the silence" to speak out against the dominant discourse and practices of the group. The result of this might be that a few girls and women—and, indeed, some boys and men—will be safer than they might otherwise have been.

But intervention programs that do not directly confront these contextual factors are unlikely to radically alter the annual reproduction of sport as a pedagogical site for boys' and men's learning of violence against women. In fact, "rape awareness sessions" for athletes may serve as a school or university's public relations window dressing, while allowing the athletic department and its teams to continue with business as usual. A commitment to address the root causes of men's violence against women will ultimately run up against the need to fundamentally rethink both the dominant conceptions of gender in the society, as well as the specific ways that gender difference and hierarchy continue to be constructed in sport.

Part IV
Gendered Imagery

8

Outside the Frame

Newspaper Coverage of the Sugar Ray Leonard
Wife Abuse Story

(*with William S. Solomon*)

Author's note: Before the rise of the modern women's movement, stories of wife abuse were treated more as jokes than as serious issues, much less as crimes. But feminism put this issue on the public agenda as a social problem. As incidents of famous male athletes' violence against girlfriends and spouses began to receive attention in the 1980s and 1990s, scholars began carefully to scrutinize the ways that the mass media covered these stories. In 1991, when the *Los Angeles Times* broke the story that the famous and popular boxing champion Sugar Ray Leonard had admitted not only to having taken drugs, but to having beaten up his wife, and threatened her life, media studies scholar Bill Solomon and I decided this would be an interesting case study of how the print media covers this story, from start to finish. In examining the coverage of the story in three major newspapers, we deployed the common method of looking at the ways that reporters and editors "framed" the story. In short, we found that the papers quickly dismissed the "wife abuse" part of the story, and shifted the story to a "drug abuse" frame. From there, the news stories within a few days were able to move through a very familiar sequence of sin-apology-and-redemption for Leonard. Almost entirely lost in the story was the potential for exploring how participation in a violent sport might have been linked to "intimate violence" against a woman. We wonder now, a decade and a half later, if writers and editors in the mass media—especially sports-

writers—have developed more critical and sophisticated ways of dealing with stories of athletes' violence against women. We suspect that
this kind of story is now so common that is not so much ignored, but,
rather, delivered with a ho-hum sigh, before moving quickly back to the
daily headlines of wins, losses, and championships.

On March 30, 1991, the *Los Angeles Times* broke a story, based on divorce
court documents, that Sugar Ray Leonard had admitted to physically
abusing his wife, including hitting her with his fists, and to using cocaine and
alcohol over a three-year period while temporarily retired from boxing.
Despite the fact that stories of sexual violence, drug abuse, and other criminal
activities by famous athletes have become common items in the sports pages,
these particular revelations were shocking to many people because Leonard
had been an outspoken public advocate for "just say no to drugs" campaigns,
and he publicly had traded on his image *of* a good family man. Thus, revelations of his family violence and drug abuse left him open to charges of
hypocrisy, to public humiliation, and to permanent loss of his hero status.

This essay explores how this story was framed by three major newspapers. We will argue that despite the fact that the "wife abuse" part of the
story was potentially every bit as important as the "drug abuse" part, all
three newspapers rapidly framed the Sugar Ray Leonard story as a drug story
and ignored or marginalized the wife abuse part of the story. This, we will
suggest, is a result of two factors. First, by the late 1980s, sports media had
developed a prepackaged news frame that presented "jocks-on-drugs" stories
as scripted moral dramas of sin and redemption. This news frame offered
reporters and commentators a ready-made formula for packaging, presenting, and analyzing the social and moral meanings of the Sugar Ray Leonard
story. Second, there is no such familiar formula for reporting and analyzing
wife abuse by a famous athlete. In fact, despite the fact that domestic violence has been redefined by the women's movement as a public issue, it is
still a stubbornly persistent aspect of patriarchal ideology to view wife abuse
as a private matter (Kurz 1989).

NEWS FRAMES AND PATRIARCHAL IDEOLOGY

For public issues, the social construction of a problem occurs in good part
through the mass news media. In reporting an occurrence, the media define it
and explain how it is to be understood through the use of a "frame," a context for viewing the story (Gitlin 1979; Goffman 1974). A news frame is how
the media assign meaning to an event or occurrence; the news frame deter-
mines what is highlighted, emphasized, ignored, or marginalized. A news

frame is therefore an inherently ideological construct, but it rarely appears so. This is because although news frames ultimately impose preferred meanings on a public story, these meanings are commonly drawn from socially shared (hegemonic) understandings of the world (Gitlin 1979).

The news framing process itself is often a contested process, wherein different groups may have "differing and sometimes competing uses for the same occurrence" (Molotch and Lester 1974, 103). News coverage of an occurrence, then, reflects in part the ability of various social or political interests to influence the news framing process so that it is compatible with their beliefs and values. For instance, because the U.S. corporate sector and the federal government are closely linked, economically and ideologically, to the mainstream U.S. media (Bagdikian 1990; Dreier 1982), they are at a powerful advantage, relative to other collectivities or individuals, in influencing this process. This corporate/governmental advantage in shaping news frames is illustrated in analyses of news coverage of "accidents" at nuclear power plants (Mazur 1984) and the U.S.-sponsored war in El Salvador (Solomon 1992). Rather than a mirror of reality, the national news agenda may be seen as a construct of a highly centralized apparatus embedded in the political and economic structure.

The framing of sports stories is less likely to be directly linked to the daily concerns of political and economic elites. But this is not to say that sports reporting is not steeped in dominant values and ideologies (John Hargreaves 1986). In fact, a number of scholars have argued that sports media tend to reflect—and help to reconstruct—patriarchal ideologies (Bryson 1987; Clarke and Clarke 1982; Jennifer Hargreaves 1986; Messner 1988; Willis 1982). Feminist scholars have illuminated the asymmetrical and masculine-biased ways that electronic and print media cover women's and men's sports and female and male athletes (Boutilier and San Giovanni 1983; Duncan 1990; Duncan and Hasbrook 1988; Duncan and Sayaovong 1990; Messner Duncan, and Jensen 1993; Rintala and Birrell 1984; Sabo and Jansen 1992; Trujillo 1991).

Although studies of newspaper coverage of sports have consistently demonstrated the paucity of coverage of women's sports (Bryant 1980; Duncan, Messner, and Williams 1991), there has been very little analysis of the ways that patriarchal ideologies inform the framing of particular stories on the sports pages. One notable exception is Theberge's (1989) analysis of media coverage of a violent brawl in the 1987 World Junior Hockey Championships. Theberge observes that in the immediate aftermath of the incident, there were "competing interpretations" of the causes and meanings of the brawl. In the public debates that followed, feminists argued that the incident was "an instance of a systemic malaise in the sport" that illustrated, in part, "the centrality of violence to the construction of masculine hegemony" (Theberge 1989, 253–254). But, ultimately, this feminist interpretation of the violent event was marginalized in the popular press, and the media's "primary interpretation" (or frame) for the event, drawn mostly from statements by leaders and experts within the sport of hockey, was that the fight was the unfortunate result of a "technical and individual failing" (Theberge 1989, 253). The sport itself, the hegemonic masculine (and corporate) values underlying it, and the "natural" equation of masculinity with violence, thus remained unchallenged.

Theberge demonstrates how an analysis of media coverage of a "deviant event" (an event that demands that sportswriters step outside the conventions of everyday reporting and engage themselves in discussion and debate about the social meanings of events) can lay bare the ideological mechanisms that underlie everyday reporting. Theberge makes two important claims that form the theoretical basis of our examination of the Sugar Ray Leonard story. First, patriarchal ideology appears to be a key mechanism in the process of framing sports news. Second, feminism has created a context through which alternative interpretations of news stories have begun to contend with taken-for-granted patriarchal frames. What is the state of play of these two contending ideologies for framing the meaning of contemporary U.S. sports stories? An analysis of the coverage of a story of wife abuse by a popular athlete, we reasoned, might shed light on this question.

DESCRIPTION OF RESEARCH

We chose to analyze coverage of the Sugar Ray Leonard story in two national dailies, the *Los Angeles Times* (*LAT*), and the *New York Times* (*NYT*), as well as in the now-defunct *National Sports Daily* (*NSD*). We chose the *LAT* because it is the major West Coast daily and because it is the paper that broke the story, the *NYT* because it is the major East Coast daily, and the *NSD* because we thought it might be informative to compare a national paper that specialized in sports coverage. We collected all news stories and editorial columns in the three papers until the story died out as a major news item (see the appendix for a complete list of news stories and editorial columns). This took nine days, from March 30, 1991, until April 7, 1991. Next, we analyzed the content of the stories.

Our overriding concern was to examine how the story was framed, as a drug story, as a domestic violence story, or as both. Was there a coherent, shared frame in all three papers? What kinds of headlines and subheads were used to introduce the story? What was the content of the photos and their captions? How much space in each story was devoted to discussion of drugs, and how much to discussion of domestic violence? To what extent were experts drawn upon by reporters and commentators in analyzing the drug or domestic violence issues as social problems? How was the dominant news frame developed, interpreted, solidified, or contested by sports columnists in the days following the breaking of the story?

Framing the Story

Our analysis of the three newspapers revealed three stages in the development of the news frame. Stage 1 was Day 1, when *LAT* broke the story. Stage 2 was Days 2 and 3, when all three papers covered Sugar Ray Leonard's press conference and reactions inside and outside of the boxing world. Stage 3 was Days 3 through 9, when follow-up stories and editorial commentary discussed the meanings of the story.

Stage 1: The Breaking Story. The *LAT* broke the story and featured it as the top sports story of the day. The headline read, "Leonard Used Cocaine, His Former Wife Testifies," while the subhead stated, "Sugar Ray confirms he abused her physically, acknowledges drug and alcohol abuse." The accompanying photo, of the couple smiling and about to kiss each other, was captioned, "Juanita and Sugar Ray Leonard, pictured before their divorce, testified about marital violence and substance abuse." Although the wife abuse issue clearly was a central part of the story, the headlines and the paragraphs that followed revealed a subtle asymmetry in the coverage of the drug angle and the violence angle. The opening paragraph stated that although Leonard "appeared in nationally televised anti-drugs public service announcements in 1989 [he] has used cocaine himself." When Leonard's violence toward his wife was introduced in the third paragraph of the story, we read that Leonard confirmed that "he abused her physically *because of* alcohol and drug abuse" (our emphasis). This was a key moment in the initial framing of the story: Leonard admits to abusing drugs and alcohol, which in turn caused him to abuse his wife.

Now tentatively framed as a drug abuse story, the article cut to several paragraphs of sometimes graphic testimony from Maryland divorce court records. In these statements, Juanita Leonard said that over a two-year period, Sugar Ray Leonard often struck her with his fists, would "throw me around" and "harass me physically and mentally in front of the children." He had a gun and threatened to kill himself; he threw lamps and broke mirrors. He once scared her so much that she attempted to leave the house with the children: "I was holding my six-month-old child and [Leonard] spit in my face. He pushed me. He shoved me....I was on my way out the door. He wouldn't let me out. He took a can of kerosene and poured it on the front foyer floor in our house. He told me he was going to burn the house down...that he wasn't going to let me leave the house or anything." Sugar

Ray Leonard, in his testimony, did not deny any of this. He agreed that he sometimes struck her with his fists, threatened, and abused her.

Basic to the initial framing of this breaking story is the way in which the question of why Leonard abused his wife is answered. Juanita Leonard stated that she believed that Leonard's physical abuse of her was caused by his use of alcohol and cocaine. Sugar Ray Leonard also stated that the only times he hit her were when he had been drinking. But when he was asked directly if the "problems between you and your wife" were caused by "the fact that you drank or used drugs," he flatly stated, "No. There was a period in my life when my career had ended temporarily and I was going through a state of limbo, and I wasn't particularly happy with my marital situation." This is a strand of the testimony that apparently was ignored by the reporter who wrote the breaking story. Wife abuse was presented as a secondary issue, caused by the drug and alcohol abuse. Despite this initial drug story frame, the graphic, emotionally gripping testimony about domestic violence left open the possibility that this could have developed into a story about wife abuse. As the story broke, then, the drug story frame was still very fluid, still very much in the making, and potentially open to contest.

Stage 2: Public Issues and Private Matters. On Days 2 and 3, the drug story news frame was solidified, and the wife abuse story was rapidly marginalized. On Day 2, the *LAT* and *NYT* ran major articles covering the press conference that Sugar Ray Leonard held to discuss the revelations about his drug abuse and family violence. On Day 3, the *NSD* ran a story covering the news conference. The headlines of these stories stated, "Leonard Says He Used Cocaine After Injury" (*LAT*), "Leonard Tells of Drug Use" (*NYT*), and "Sugar Ray Tells Bitter Tale of Cocaine Abuse" (*NSD*). None of the headlines, subheads, or lead paragraphs mentioned wife abuse. The photos that ran with the articles showed a somber Leonard apparently wiping a tear from his cheek as he spoke at the press conference. None of the photo captions mentioned wife abuse.

The first seven paragraphs of the *LAT* story detailed Leonard's explanations for how and why he began to abuse drugs and alcohol after his eye injury and retirement, and chronicled his statements that his drug use was "wrong...childish...[and] stupid." The story also highlighted the fact that "as a role model, he advised that cocaine use is 'not the right road to take,' adding, 'it doesn't work. I'll be the first to admit it. I hope they look at my mistake—and don't use it.'" Finally, in the eighth paragraph, the writer noted that Leonard "declined [to discuss] the physical abuse or suicide threats alleged by his former wife, Juanita, last summer during questioning under oath before the couple reached a multimillion-dollar divorce settlement." The story did not mention Leonard's corroboration, under oath, of his wife's allegations of abuse. Instead, it quoted Leonard's statement at the press conference that he would "be lying" if he were to say that he and his wife never "fought, argued, or grabbed each other," but that "that was in our house, between us. Unfortunately, during the proceedings, which are very emotional and very painful, certain things are taken out of context or exaggerated." At that point, the violence issue was dropped from the story for good. For the next eight paragraphs, the story returned to explanations of Leonard's drug abuse. The final six paragraphs chronicled his statements of remorse for his drug abuse ("I stand here ashamed, hurt") and his statements that his drug abuse is now a thing of the past ("I grew up").

The NYT essentially followed suit in framing this as a drug story and almost entirely ignored the wife abuse angle. In the fourth paragraph, the story asserted that "his former wife, Juanita, [said that] Leonard used cocaine on occasion and physically abused her while under the influence of alcohol." The story noted that' 'Leonard admitted to substance abuse," but it did not mention his admission of wife abuse. After nine more paragraphs that discussed the possible reasons for Leonard's drug abuse, the wife abuse issue was briefly touched upon again, and the "I'd be lying...taken out of context or exaggerated" quote closed the issue. Significantly, the NYT did not mention (as did the LAT) Leonard's refusal at the press conference to answer questions about the violence issue and his assertion that his physical abuse of his wife is a private matter, "that was in our house, between us." The story closed just as the LAT story did, with Leonard's message to fans and youths not to take drugs and his assurances that "thank God I'm matured and became productive again and I'm happy again."

The NSD story on the press conference went even further than the LAT and NYT in framing the story almost exclusively as a drug story. The first eight paragraphs discussed his admission of drug and alcohol abuse, and noted that once he came out of his retirement and boxed again, his drug abuse ended. "I was again doing what I loved best—fighting," Leonard stated in the story, "I became a better father and person without the use of a substitute." The only mention of wife abuse was in the ninth paragraph: "He also physically abused his wife, Juanita, according to sealed divorce documents." Immediately following this sentence, the story cut to "Leonard said he did not go to a treatment center to stop." This is a jarring transition. But it is a testament to the extent to which this story had become almost entirely a drug story that the writer did not see a need to explain, after mentioning wife abuse, that he was not referring to a treatment center for stopping wife abuse but, rather, for stopping drug use. Wife abuse was outside the frame.

Stage 3: Redemption. For the next week, all three papers ran follow-ups and editorial commentaries on the Sugar Ray Leonard story. The dominant

theme of nearly all of these stories was that Leonard's redemption from his
drug abuse could now be viewed as simply another stage in a heroic career.
On April 1, the *NSD* ran a column headline, "This Is the Truth About Sugar
Ray: He's Not Perfect, But, Then, Who Is?" The column celebrated the "love
affair" that the people of the United States had had with Leonard: "In
Montreal, he fought for us.... We applauded [his] courage and we were
intoxicated with inspiration.... We loved Leonard. We truly did." The
column went on to describe the "shock" we all felt at the revelations of
Leonard's cocaine use. But the entire tone of the column was of Leonard's
redemption and our compassion for him. When we make heroes of athletes,
the writer argued, we set them up to fall down. Nowhere in the column was
there mention of wife abuse.

The next day, the *LAT* ran a column by the reporter who originally
broke the story, headlined "Act of Courage Didn't Involve a Single Punch."
In the column, the writer admiringly recalled Leonard's many "acts of
courage" in the ring, and argued that Leonard showed this courage again at
his press conference, "under the most difficult of circumstances, when he
admitted he had used cocaine." In an almost breathless tone, the writer
continually evoked images of Leonard's courage (nine times), his bravery
(three times), and his intelligence. Wife abuse was never mentioned in the
column. Leonard was more than redeemed in the eyes of this writer. In fact,
this "difficult" incident appears to have further elevated Leonard's status:
"The man and his courage. It was a class act." The same day, the *NYT* a
similar story, "Leonard Hears Words of Support," in which wife abuse was
mentioned only in passing. The first paragraph expressed the focus of the
article: "The reaction of the boxing world to Sugar Ray Leonard's acknowl-
edgement that he used cocaine and drank heavily in the early 1980's has
been mostly sympathetic."

The dominant news frame clearly had solidified: wife abuse was either
completely ignored or marginalized as outside the drug story frame, in all
three newspapers. But the dominant drug story frame did not go entirely
unchallenged. Three editorial sportswriters gave potentially (and partially)
oppositional readings to the Sugar Ray Leonard story. An April 4 *NYT* article, headlined "The Danger of 'Arena' Addiction," did not mention wife
abuse, but it did draw a connection between the trauma of retirement from
sport and the abuse of alcohol and cocaine by athletes. And in an April 3
NSD column headlined "Sugar's Confession Can't Blot Bitter Taste,"
Leonard's press conference was portrayed as a cynical attempt to manipulate
public opinion. The writer noted that Leonard "shoved his wife around," but
the major thrust of the column was to criticize the ways that the media and
the public so easily "forgive our fallen heroes." Leonard's press conference,
and its aftermath, the writer argued, can be viewed as a sort of "20th century

confessional, the sinner spilling the beans into live microphones. He practices damage control and hopes we see it as contrition. He speaks in a halting voice and weeps on camera. The public relations consultants get big bucks for this advice. Tell all. Throw yourself at the public's feet. People are kind. They'll forgive."

By far the most critical editorial column in our sample appeared on April 7 in the *LAT* (reprinted from the *Washington Post*), headlined "Leonard Roped In: It's All in the Game." Like the April 3 *NYT* article, this editorial was critical of the staging of Leonard's press conference. But this was the only article or editorial in our sample that even began to draw connections (albeit, even in this case, carefully tentative connections) between Leonard's participation in the sport of boxing and his acts of wife abuse: "A common experience among boxing champions has been, like Leonard's, wife trouble. Their history is full of it. It grabbed Sugar Ray Robinson, Jack Dempsey, Joe Louis, Sonny Listen, and even the family man, Rocky Marciano. The multi-wived Muhammed Ali begged the courts that the alimony payments were too great. And Mike Tyson is of course famous for slugging his wife and others, for his vulgar talk." But, the writer concluded, the boxing world and the sports media have failed to view Leonard's case as another in a pattern of similar occurrences. As a result, the overall impact of Leonard's "fall from grace" amounts to "nothing whatsoever, not even a ripple."

WITHIN THE FRAME: SIN AND REDEMPTION

Stuck (1988) notes that in recent years, public interest in drugs-in-sports stories "seems to rise when yet another 'big name' athlete, collegiate or professional, had died of an overdose of some illicit drug or has been sent to a rehabilitation facility, then seems to subside after the media has had its fill of the story" (i). On the other hand, Donohew, Helm, and Haas (1989) observed that following the drug deaths of celebrated athletes Len Bias and Don Rogers, attention to drugs-in-sports stories actually *declined* in newspapers. The authors speculated that the reason for this decline is that by the end of the 1980s, "the newsworthiness of drug use . . . had run its course. ... It was no longer news because drug use in the athletic community had come to be viewed as more commonplace." By then, for instance, "revelations that the New York Giants' Lawrence Taylor had undergone treatment at a drug rehabilitation center perhaps no longer seemed as important" (Donohew, Helm, and Haas 1989, 236).

We would add that by the end of the 1980s, not only was the drugs-in-sports story no longer big news, but in addition, the sports media had constructed a common news frame for jocks-on-drugs stories that presented "the facts" as well as "the meanings" of these stories as moral dramas of individual sin and redemption. The jock-on-drugs drama became a familiar set of scripted stages: revelations of sin and subsequent public humiliation, shameful confession and promises to never take drugs again, public evangelism to children to say no to drugs, and public redemption.

This script resonates with the ideology underlying the Reagan administration's "just say no to drugs" campaigns of the 1980s. These campaigns were largely successful in ideologically framing drug problems (and their solutions) as issues of individual moral choice, not as social problems resulting from growing poverty, deterioration of cities and schools, or general alienation and malaise. Sports reporters appear to have accepted uncritically this individual framework of meaning and adapted it to frame the otherwise thorny social issue of jocks on drugs. Moreover, athletes quickly learned to act out their own parts in this scripted morality play, as Sugar Ray Leonard's tearful press conference aptly demonstrated. When the script is properly played out, within a year or so following the initial public revelation of drug use, public redemption often is accompanied by reinstatement in sport participation. And, as demonstrated by baseball player Steve Howe and others, some athletes have managed to cycle through this script several times. A bonus to Leonard in the media's largely uncritical reliance on this scripted framework of meaning was the fact that (unlike most jock-on-drugs cases) the public revelation of Leonard's drug and alcohol abuse occurred several years after his "sins" took place. That he could tearfully (and, we are left to assume, honestly) claim that these were indeed sins that he committed *in the past* meant that there could be a blurring simultaneity to the movement through the drama's stages: the day after the public revelations, Leonard himself shamefully confessed, apologized, promised that he had not taken drugs for a long time, and evangelized to youths to say no to drugs. Within a few days, playing out their own part in the scripted drama, the sports media granted Leonard full redemption from his sins.

It is important to note, though, that the April 3 *NSD* and April 4 *NYT* editorials offered partially oppositional readings of the Sugar Ray Leonard story. Although they did not challenge the drug frame (one didn't even mention wife abuse; the other mentioned it in passing), they did challenge the sports media's complicity in what we are calling the moral drama of individual sin and redemption. In viewing Leonard's press conference as a cynical manipulation aimed at public redemption, and in discussing athletes' drug and alcohol problems in terms of the *social* pressures and strains of athletic careers and retirement trauma, these readings at least challenged the narrow individualism of the dominant drug story frame. These readings hold the potential for broadening the drug story frame to include critiques of commercialized athletic hero worship, including the stress and strain this puts on the heroes themselves. On the other hand, these oppositional readings do not challenge the unspoken patriarchal ideology that led to the ignoring or marginalization of the wife abuse story.

OUTSIDE THE FRAME

By the third day of the Sugar Ray Leonard story, wife abuse was so entirely outside the dominant drug story frame that several follow-up stories and editorials did not mention it at all. But the wife abuse story did not go away entirely. It continued to appear, albeit always very briefly, in some follow-up stories and commentary. When wife abuse was mentioned, it usually was framed in language similar to the following sentence from a follow-up *NYT* story: "his former wife, Juanita, [said] that Leonard used cocaine on occasion and physically mistreated her while under the influence of alcohol." This sentence demonstrates the three ways that the wife abuse story was ideologically managed when it did appear within the drug story news frame:

1. Violence was presented in neutralizing language. The graphic descriptions of Sugar Ray Leonard's violence, threats with guns and kerosene, his spitting in his wife's face, and hitting her with his fists that appeared in the original divorce testimony were replaced with more vague and neutral language: Leonard "physically mistreated" his wife.
2. Sugar Ray Leonard's admitted acts of violence were presented simply as Juanita Leonard's "claims." Although Leonard clearly had acknowledged in the divorce testimony that he had committed the acts of violence that his wife accused him of, in nearly all of the follow-up stories, these facts were presented as something that Juanita Leonard said, claimed, or alleged had occurred. The writers did not add that Sugar Ray Leonard himself had acknowledged having committed these acts, thus leaving the impression, perhaps, that these were merely Juanita Leonard's claims, or allegations, not facts.
3. A causal relationship between drug and alcohol abuse and wife abuse was incorrectly implied. Nearly every mention of the wife abuse incidents in the follow-up commentaries implied that drug and alcohol abuse caused Leonard to be violent to his wife. Most often, these articles did not make a direct causal argument ("drugs made him hit her") but, rather, implied the causal relationship by always directly linking any mention of his acts of violent "mistreatment" of his wife with the observation that Leonard had been abus-

ing drugs. Astonishingly, reporters appear to have relied entirely on the self-reporting of Sugar Ray and Juanita Leonard to conclude, all too easily and quickly, that the drug and alcohol abuse caused the wife abuse to happen. The writers apparently never consulted experts on domestic violence, who undoubtedly would have made two important points.

First, self-reports of perpetrators of wife abuse or of their victims as to why wife abuse occurs are suspect (Dobash, Dobash, Wilson, and Daly 1992). Wayne Ewing, who works with and studies men who batter, argues that in relationships where husbands batter wives, there is a common "cycle of violence" that includes "the building of tension and conflict; the episode of battering; the time of remorse; the idyllic time of reconciliation" (Ewing 1982, 5–6). For the male batterer, a key aspect of the stage of remorse is denial of responsibility for the act of battery. As Ewing puts it, "There is no shock of recognition in the cycle of violence. It is not a matter of 'Oh my god, did I do that?' It is a matter of *stating*, 'Oh my god, I couldn't have done that,' implying that '*in fact did not do it*'.... Remorse, in this model of 'making things right' again literally wipes the slate clean" (Ewing 1982, 6). For the victim who decides (for whatever reason) to remain in a relationship with her batterer, the stage of reconciliation in the cycle of violence often involves at least a partial acceptance of this denial of responsibility: "The man that hit me is not the *real* man that I love, and who loves me." Within this context of denial, alcohol or other drugs can become convenient scapegoats: "It was the booze talking" (and hitting), not the man.

Second, research on domestic violence indicates that while alcohol abuse and wife abuse are statistically correlated, there is no evidence that alcohol abuse causes wife abuse. Numerous studies have shown a statistical correlation between (especially binge-type) alcohol abuse and wife abuse (Coleman and Straus 1983; Hotaling and Sugarman 1986; Kantor and Straus 1987). But the drunken bum theory of wife abuse is largely a myth, as only about one out of four instances of wife abuse involve alcohol (Kantor and Straus 1987). In fact, in cases when binge drinking and wife abuse occur together, there is considerable evidence that both binge drinking and wife abuse might be a result of what researchers have called a frustrated "power motivation" in husbands (Brown, Goldman, Inn, and Anderson 1980; Cahalan 1970; McClelland, Davis, Kalin, and Wanner 1972). Indeed, Kantor and Straus's research suggests that men who are most likely to commit acts of wife abuse are those men who are most firmly enmeshed in "the cultural tradition which glorifies violence, assumes male dominance, and tolerate violence by men against women" (Kantor and Straus 1987, 225). This sounds remarkably like a description of the world of men's sports, in general, and of boxing in particular (Foley 1990; Corn 1986; Kidd 1987; Messner 1992; Sabo 1985; Whitson 1990).

Similarly, Ewing points to a general culture of male dominance and "civic advocacy of violence" as the main antecedents of men's violence against women. He argues, "With respect to the psychological makeup of the abusive male, there is considerable consensus that these men evidence low self-esteem dependency needs, unfamiliarity with their emotions, fear of intimacy, poor communication skills and performance orientation" (Ewing 1982, 5). This description of the male batterer sounds quite similar to the psychological profile of male career athletes (Messner 1992). As Horsefall (1991) puts it,

> Both wife battering and alcohol use/abuse may be attempts by men with low self-esteem and gender insecurity to decrease both of these deficits by indulging in "appropriate" activities available to them.... If their gender identification is positional, their self-esteem shaky, work or sport are closed to them or work is a frustration in itself, then drinking with the boys may make them feel like "men." Behaving in an authoritarian way at home may also provide a similar opportunity. Thus alcohol use/abuse and violence towards wives may have similar roots and therefore present as correlation in some studies. (85–86)

The idea that masculine emotional socialization, toleration of violence, along with plummeting self-esteem brought on by an insecure public status might be at the root of both Leonard's drug and alcohol abuse *and* his abuse of his wife was apparently never entertained by the sports media. To take this approach, of course, would have entailed questioning the patriarchal values system that underlies the institution of sport. Moreover, this line of analysis inevitably would invite serious questioning of the role of violence in sports and the possible links between sports violence with violence in personal life. Young U.S. males do grow up in a society that accepts, even valorizes, violence as a legitimate means of last resort. Sports such as boxing, football, and hockey are surely conveying this pro-violence message to young males (Messner 1990; Sabo 1985; Sabo and Panepinto 1990; Vaz 1980). And given the misogyny that is built into the dominant culture of men's sports (Curry 1991; Foley 1990), the advocacy and celebration of men's athletic violence against each other too often become directly translated into (often sexualized) violence against women (Kaufman 1987; Koss and Dinero 1988; Melnick 1992; Messner 1992; Sabo 1986; Warshaw 1988).

Differential Salience of the Two Frames

In the case of Sugar Ray Leonard, we argue that it would have been analytically fruitful to examine the possible links between two facts: first, here is a man who won fame and fortune by successfully battering other men with his fists; second, once out of the sports limelight, because of what then appeared to be a career-ending injury, he turned to battering his own body with drugs and alcohol, and the body of his wife with his fists. This line of reasoning would draw together what Michael Kaufman (1987) has called "the triad of men's violence": violence against other men, violence against oneself, and violence against women.

That these questions were never acknowledged, much less seriously addressed, is a testament to the extent to which newspapers still form a symbiotic economic alliance with organized sports (Koppett 1981). But it is probably wrong to suspect a conscious conspiracy to cover up the wife abuse issue. The adoption of the drug story frame and the marginalization of the wife abuse frame are probably largely a function of the saliency of the drug frame as well as the lack of saliency of the wife abuse frame in the public domain. As Gamson and Modigliani (1989) argue, the news media construct, and then draw upon, "media packages" that provide ready-made frameworks of meaning for stories. We have suggested that by the time the Sugar Ray Leonard story broke, a jocks-on-drugs media package was already in place and available for use by reporters. Indeed, there was no apparent difference in the extent to which the writers in all three newspapers that we examined in this study relied on this jocks-on-drugs media package. This package, a moral drama of individual sin and public redemption, framed individual cases of jocks on drugs in such a way that the structure and values of the institution of sport—and boxing in particular—were never called into question. But the narrow parameters of the jocks-on-drugs media package did not go entirely uncontested. We have noted that two follow-up editorials insisted on viewing Leonard's case—at least with respect to drug abuse—within its social context, thus challenging the narrow individualism of the hegemonic jocks-on-drugs package.

In addition to the convenience and ideological saliency of the jocks-on-drugs media package, the wife abuse story was probably ignored or marginalized because no such ready-made media package exists for wife abuse stories. That no such package exists is probably a result of the fact that both inside and outside the world of sport, there is still a widespread social denial of men's violence against women, especially that which occurs in families (Kurz 1989). In the Leonard case, the marginalization of the wife abuse story may also be a reflection of the extent to which newspaper sports departments still are relatively unaffected by feminism. Newspaper sports departments, still overwhelmingly male in their gender composition, have been much slower to admit women than other news departments (Mills 1988). The Association for Women in Sports Media estimates that approximately 9,650 of the 10,000 U.S. print and broadcast journalists are men (Nelson 1991). And it is likely that a disproportionate number of the approximately 350 women in sports media are in televised sports, not in newspaper sports departments.

Would adding more women reporters change the way that sports news is reported and analyzed? There is some evidence that female sports reporters approach their stories from a more human, less technical point of view than male sports reporters (Mills 1988). But we tend to concur with Theberge and Cronk (1986) that simply changing the sex composition of the sports newsroom would not drastically change the higher value that reporters tend to place on covering men's sports over women's sports, nor would it drastically change the underlying values and content of the media packages commonly utilized by sports reporters, unless women's sports simultaneously become more highly valued and rewarded than they now are. Indeed, it is difficult to imagine a more gender-equal sports newsroom in the absence of a more general feminist revolution in the sports world.

Appendix: Newspaper Stories and Editorials

E. Gustkey, "Leonard Used Cocaine, His Former Wife Testifies," *Los Angeles Times*, March 30, 1991, p. C-1. (news story)

R. J. Ostrow, "Leonard Says He Used Cocaine After Injury," *Los Angeles Times*, March 31, 1991, p. C-1. (news story)

"Leonard Tells of Drug Use," *New York Times*, March 31, 1991, Section 8, p. 3. (news story)

D. Steele, "Sugar Ray Tells Bitter Tale of Cocaine Use," *The National Sports Daily*, April 1, 1991, p. 33. (news story)

T. Egan, "This Is the Truth About Sugar Ray: He's Not Perfect But, Then, Who Is?" *The National Sports Daily*, April 1, 1991, p. 47. (editorial)

E. Gustkey, "Act of Courage Didn't Involve a Single Punch," *Los Angeles Times*, April 2, 1991, p. C-2. (editorial)

P. Berger, "Leonard Hears Words of Support," *New York Times*, April 2, 1991, Section B, p. 11. (news story)

D. Anderson, "The Danger of 'Arena' Addiction," *New York Times*, April 4, 1991, Section D, p. 21. (editorial)

D. Kindred, "Sugar's Confession Can't Blot Bitter Taste," *The National Sports Daily*, April 3, 1991, p. 7. (editorial)

S. Povich, "Leonard Roped In: It's All in the Game," *Los Angeles Times*, April 7, 1991, p. C-3. (editorial reprinted from the *Washington Post*)

9

The Televised Sports Manhood Formula

(with Michele Dunbar and Darnell Hunt)

Author's note: In 1999, my USC colleagues Darnell Hunt and Michele Dunbar and I were contracted by Children Now, a national organization concerned with children and mass media, to do a content analysis of the televised sports programs that boys watch. We analyzed key telecasts of NFL, NBA, and Major League baseball games, Extreme Sports, ESPN's popular highlights show *SportsCenter*, the pseudosport of professional wrestling, and the commercials that accompanied these broadcasts. We were concerned with asking: In what ways does sports programming provide a pedagogy for boys about manhood, about women, about sex, and about being a consumer? Though we found some real differences across various sports, we identified common themes that cut across different sports and their commercials, together forming a consistent pattern of gender messages about violence, bodies, success, women, and consumption that we called the "Televised Sports Manhood Formula." We know that media research suggests that audiences who are differently situated by factors like age, social class, education, race/ethnicity, sexual orientation, and religion often interpret and make meanings with the same media text in different ways. So we do not conclude simplistically in this essay that sports media "cause" all boys to be violent beer-guzzling misogynists. However, we do think that the "televised sports manhood formula"—especially through its links to commercial marketing strategies that purposely tweak common insecurities among boys and young men—is a potentially powerful pedagogy that serves to stabilize a dominant cultural conception of masculinity—a masculinity that works against the interests of women for respect and equality, and that ultimately does not serve the interests of boys and men to live happy, healthy and safe lives.

A recent national survey found eight- to seventeen-year-old children to be avid consumers of sports media, with television most often named as the preferred medium (Amateur Athletic Foundation of Los Angeles 1999). Although girls watch sports in great numbers, boys are markedly more likely to report that they are regular consumers of televised sports. The most popular televised sports with boys, in order, are pro football, men's pro basketball, pro baseball, pro wrestling, men's college basketball, college football, and Extreme sports. Although counted separately in the Amateur Athletic Foundation (AAF) study, televised sports highlights shows also were revealed to be tremendously popular with boys.

What are boys seeing and hearing when they watch these programs? What kinds of values concerning gender, race, aggression, violence, and consumerism are boys exposed to when they watch their favorite televised sports programs, with their accompanying commercials? This essay, based on a textual analysis, presents the argument that televised sports, and their accompanying commercials, consistently present boys with a narrow portrait of masculinity, which we call the Televised Sports Manhood Formula.

SAMPLE AND METHOD

We analyzed a range of televised sports that were identified by the AAF study as those programs most often watched by boys. Most of the programs in our sample aired during a single week, May 23–29, 1999, with one exception. Because pro football is not in season in May, we acquired tapes of two randomly chosen National Football League (NFL) *Monday Night Football* games from the previous season to include in our sample. We analyzed televised coverage, including commercials and pregame, halftime, and postgame shows (when appropriate), for the following programs:

1. Two broadcasts of *SportsCenter* on ESPN (2 hours of programming).
2. Two broadcasts of Extreme sports, one on ESPN and one on Fox Sports West (approximately ninety minutes of programming).
3. Two broadcasts of professional wrestling, including *Monday Night Nitro* onTNT and *WWF Superstars* on USA (approximately two hours of programming).

4. Two broadcasts of National Basketball Association (NBA) playoff games, one on TNT and the other on NBC (approximately seven hours of programming).

5. Two broadcasts of NFL *Monday Night Football* on ABC (approximately seven hours of programming).

6. One broadcast of Major League Baseball (MLB) on TBS (approximately three hours of programming).

We conducted a textual analysis of the sports programming and the commercials. In all, we examined about twenty-three hours of sports programming, nearly one-quarter of which was time taken up by commercials. We examined a total of 722 commercials, which spanned a large range of products and services. We collected both quantitative and qualitative data. Although we began with some sensitizing concepts that we knew we wanted to explore (e.g., themes of violence, images of gender and race, etc.), rather than starting with preset categories we used an inductive method that allowed the dominant themes to emerge from our reading of the tapes.

Each taped show was given a first reading by one of the investigators, who then constructed a preliminary analysis of the data. The tape was then given a second reading by another investigator. This second independent reading was then used to modify and sharpen the first reading. Data analysis proceeded along the lines of the categories that emerged in the data collection. The analyses of each separate sport were then put into play with each other and common themes and patterns were identified. In one case, the dramatic pseudosport of professional wrestling, we determined that much of the programming was different enough that it made little sense to directly compare it with the other sports shows; therefore, we only included data on wrestling in our comparisons when it seemed to make sense to do so.

DOMINANT THEMES IN TELEVISED SPORTS

Our analysis revealed that sports programming presents boys with narrow and stereotypical messages about race, gender, and violence. We identified ten distinct themes that, together, make up the Televised Sports Manhood Formula.

Table 9.1

Race and Sex of Announcers

White Men	White Women	Black Men	Black Women
24	3	3	1

White Males Are the Voices of Authority

Although one of the two *SportsCenter* segments in the sample did feature a white woman co-anchor, the play-by-play and ongoing color commentary in NFL, wrestling, NBA, Extreme sports, and MLB broadcasts were conducted exclusively by white, male play-by play commentators.

With the exception of *SportsCenter*, women and blacks never appeared as the main voices of authority in the booth conducting play-by-play or ongoing color commentary. The NFL broadcasts occasionally cut to field-level color commentary by a white woman but her commentary was very brief (about three and one-half minutes of the nearly three hours of actual game and pregame commentary). Similarly, one of the NBA broadcasts used a black man for occasional on-court analysis and a black man for pregame and half time analysis, whereas the other NBA game used a white woman as host in the pregame show and a black woman for occasional on-court analysis. Although viewers commonly see black male athletes—especially on televised NBA games—they rarely hear or see black men or women as voices of authority in the broadcast booth (Sabo and Jansen 1994). In fact, the only black commentators that appeared on the NBA shows that we examined were former star basketball players (Cheryl Miller, Doc Rivers, and Isaiah Thomas). A black male briefly appeared to welcome the audience to open one of the Extreme sports shows but he did not do any play-by-play; in fact, he was used only to open the show with a stylish, street, hip-hop style for what turned out to be an almost totally white show.

Sports Is a Man's World

Images or discussion of women athletes is almost entirely absent in the sports programs that boys watch most. *SportsCenter*'s mere 2.9% of news time devoted to women's sports is slightly lower than the 5% to 6% of women's sports coverage commonly found in other sports news studies (Duncan and Messner 1998). In addition, *SportsCenter*'s rare discussion of a women's sport seemed to follow men's in newsworthiness (e.g., a report on a Professional Golfers' Association [PGA] tournament was followed by a more brief report on a Ladies Professional Golf Association [LPGA] tournament). The baseball, basketball, wrestling, and football programs we watched were men's contests so could not perhaps have been expected to cover or mention women athletes. However, Extreme sports are commonly viewed as "alternative" or "emerging" sports in which women are challenging masculine hegemony (Wheaton and Tomlinson 1998). Despite this, the Extreme sports shows we watched devoted only a single fifty-second interview segment to a woman athlete. This segment constituted about 1% of the total Extreme sports programming and, significantly, did not show this woman athlete in action. Perhaps this limited coverage of women athletes on the Extreme sports shows we examined is evidence of what Rinehart (1998) calls a "pecking order" in alternative sports, which develops when new sports are appropriated and commodified by the media.

Men Are Foregrounded in Commercials

The idea that sports is a man's world is reinforced by the gender composition and imagery in commercials. Women almost never appear in commercials unless they are in the company of men, as Table 9.2 shows.

Men Only	Women Only	Women and Men	No People
Table 9.2			
Sex Composition of 722 Commercials			
279 (38.6%)	28 (3.9%)	324 (44.9%)	91 (12.6%)

That 38.6% of all commercials portray only men actually understates the extent to which men dominate these commercials for two reasons. First, nearly every one of the ninety-one commercials that portrayed no visual portrayals of people included a male voice-over. When we include this number, we see that more than 50% of commercials provide men-only images and/or voice-overs, whereas only 3.9% portray only women. Moreover, when we combine men-only and women and men categories, we see that men are visible in 83.5% of all commercials and men are present (when we add in the commercials with male voice-overs) in 96.1% of all commercials. Second, in the commercials that portray both women and men, women are often (although not exclusively) portrayed in stereotypical, and often very minor, background roles.

Women Are Sexy Props or Prizes for Men's Successful Sport Performances or Consumption Choices

Although women were mostly absent from sports commentary, when they did appear it was most often in stereotypical roles as sexy, masculinity-validating props, often cheering the men on. For instance, "X-sports" on Fox Sports West used a bikini-clad blonde woman as a hostess to welcome viewers back after each commercial break as the camera moved provocatively over her body. Although she mentioned the show's sponsors, she did not narrate the actual sporting event. The wrestling shows generously used scantily clad women (e.g., in pink miniskirts or tight Spandex and high heels) who overtly displayed the dominant cultural signs of heterosexy attractiveness to escort the male wrestlers to the ring, often with announcers discussing the women's provocative physical appearances. Women also appeared in the wrestling shows as sexually provocative dancers (e.g., the "Gorgeous Nitro Girls" on TNT).

Table 9.3

Incidences of Women Being Depicted as Sexy Props or Prizes for men

	Sports Center	Extreme	Wrestling	NBA	MLB	NFL
Commercials	5	5	3	10	4	6
Sports programs	0	5	13	3	0	4
Total	5	10	16	13	4	10

Note: NBA = National Basketball Association, MLB = Major League Baseball, and NFL = National Football League.

In commercials, women are numerically more evident, and generally depicted in more varied roles, than in the sports programming. Still, women are underrepresented and rarely appear in commercials unless they are in the company of men. Moreover, as Table 9.3 illustrates, the commercials' common depiction of women as sexual objects and as "prizes" for men's successful consumption choices articulates with the sports programs' presentation of women primarily as sexualized, supportive props for men's athletic performances. For instance, a commercial for Keystone Light Beer that ran on *SportsCenter* depicted two white men at a baseball game. When one of the men appeared on the stadium big screen and made an ugly face after drinking an apparently bitter beer, women appeared to be grossed out by him. But then he drank a Keystone Light and reappeared on the big screen looking good with two young, conventionally beautiful (fashion-model-like) women adoring him. He says, "I hope my wife's not watching!" as the two women flirt with the camera.

As Table 9.3 shows, in twenty-three hours of sports programming, viewers were exposed to fifty-eight incidents of women being portrayed as sexy props and/or sexual prizes for men's successful athletic performances or correct consumption choices. Put another way, a televised sports viewer is exposed to this message, either in commercials or in the sports program itself, on an average of twice an hour. The significance of this narrow image of women as heterosexualized commodities should be considered especially in light of the overall absence of a wider range of images of women, especially as athletes (Duncan and Messner 1998; Kane and Lenskyj 1998).

Whites Are Foregrounded in Commercials

The racial composition of the commercials is, if anything, more narrow and limited than the gender composition. As Table 9.4 shows, black, Latino, or Asian American people almost never appear in commercials unless the commercial also has white people in it (the "multiracial" category).

Table 9.4
Racial Composition of 722 Commercials

White Only	Black Only	Latino/a Only	Asian Only	Multiracial	Undeter-mined	No People
377 (52.2%)	28 (3.9%)	3 (0.4%)	2 (0.3%)	203 (28.1%)	18 (2.5%)	91 (12.6%)

To say that 52.2% of the commercials portrayed only whites actually understates the extent to which images of white people dominated the commercials for two reasons. First, if we subtract the ninety-one commercials that showed no actual people, then we see that the proportion of commercials that actually showed people was 59.7% white only. Second, when we examine the quality of the portrayals of blacks, Latinos, and Asian Americans in the multiracial commercials, we see that people of color are far more often than not relegated to minor roles, literally in the background of scenes that feature whites, and/or they are relegated to stereotypical or negative roles. For instance, a Wendy's commercial that appeared on several of the sports programs in our sample showed white customers enjoying a sandwich with the white owner while a barely perceptible black male walked by in the background.

Aggressive Players Get the Prize; Nice Guys Finish Last

As Table 9.5 illustrates, viewers are continually immersed in images and commentary about the positive rewards that come to the most aggressive competitors and of the negative consequences of playing "soft" and lacking aggression.

Table 9.5
Statements Lauding Aggression or Criticizing Lack of Aggression

Sports Center	Extreme	NBA	MLB	NFL
3	4	40	4	15

Note: NBA=National Basketball Association, MLB=Major League Baseball, and NFL=National Football League.

Commentators consistently lauded athletes who most successfully employed physical and aggressive play and toughness. For instance, after having his toughness called into question, NBA player Brian Grant was awarded redemption by *SportsCenter* because he showed that he is "not afraid to take it to Karl Malone." *SportsCenter* also informed viewers that "the aggressor usually gets the calls [from the officials] and the Spurs were the ones getting them." In pro wrestling commentary, this is a constant theme (and was therefore not included in our tallies for Table 9.5 because the theme permeated the commentary, overtly and covertly). The World Wrestling Federation (WWF) announcers praised the "raw power" of wrestler "Shamrock" and approvingly dubbed "Hardcore Holly" as "the world's most dangerous man." NBA commentators suggested that it is okay to be a good guy off the court but one must be tough and aggressive on the court: Brian Grant and Jeff Hornacek are "true gentlemen of the NBA...as long as you don't have to play against them. You know they're great off the court; on the court, every single guy out there *should* be a killer."

When players were not doing well, they were often described as "hesitant" and lacking aggression, emotion, and desire (e.g., for a loose ball or rebound). For instance, commentators lamented that "the Jazz aren't going to the hoop, they're being pushed and shoved around," that Utah was responding to the Blazers' aggression "passively, in a reactive mode," and that "Utah's got to get Karl Malone toughened up." *SportsCenter* echoed this theme, opening one show with a depiction of Horace Grant elbowing Karl Malone and asking of Malone, "Is he feeble?" Similarly, NFL broadcasters waxed on about the virtues of aggression and domination. Big "hits"; ball carriers who got "buried," "stuffed," or "walloped" by the defense; and players who get "cleaned out" or "wiped out" by a blocker were often shown on replays, with announcers enthusiastically describing the plays. By contrast, they clearly declared that it is a very bad thing to be passive and to let yourself get pushed around and dominated at the line of scrimmage. Announcers also approvingly noted that going after an opposing player's injured body part is just smart strategy: In one NFL game, the Miami strategy to blitz the opposing quarterback was lauded as "brilliant"—"When you know your opposing quarterback is a bit nicked and something is wrong, Boomer, you got to come after him."

Previous research has pointed to this heroic framing of the male body-as-weapon as a key element in sports' role in the social construction of narrow conceptions of masculinity (Messner 1992; Trujillo 1995). This injunction for boys and men to be aggressive, not passive, is reinforced in commercials, where a common formula is to play on the insecurities of young males (e.g., that they are not strong enough, tough enough, smart enough, rich enough, attractive enough, decisive enough, etc.) and then attempt to convince them to avoid, overcome, or mask their fears, embarrassments, and apparent shortcomings by buying a particular product. These commercials often portray men as potential or actual geeks, nerds, or passive schmucks who can overcome their geekiness (or avoid being a geek like the guy in the commercial) by becoming decisive and purchasing a particular product.

Boys Will Be (Violent) Boys

As we show in Table 9.6, announcers often took a humorous "boys will be boys" attitude in discussing fights or near-fights during contests, and they also commonly used a recent fight, altercation, or disagreement between two players as a "teaser" to build audience excitement. Fights, near-fights, threats of fights, or other violent actions were overemphasized in sports coverage and often verbally framed in sarcastic language that suggested that this kind of action, although reprehensible, is to be expected. For instance, as *SportsCenter* showed NBA centers Robinson and O'Neill exchanging forearm shoves, the commentators said, simply, "much love." Similarly, in an NFL game, a brief scuffle between players is met with a sarcastic comment by the broadcaster that the players are simply "making their acquaintance." This is, of course, a constant theme in pro wrestling (which, again, we found impossible and less than meaningful to count because this theme permeates the show). We found it noteworthy that the supposedly spontaneous fights outside the wrestling ring (what we call unofficial fights) were given more coverage time and focus than the supposedly official fights inside the ring. We speculate that wrestling producers know that viewers already watch fights inside the ring with some skepticism as to their authenticity so they stage the unofficial fights outside the ring to bring a feeling of spontaneity and authenticity to the show and to build excitement and a sense of anticipation for the fight that will later occur inside the ring.

Table 9.6

Humorous or Sarcastic Discussion of Fights or Near-Fights

Sports Center	Extreme	NBA	MLB	NFL
10	1	2	2	7

Note: NBA=National Basketball Association, MLB=Major League Baseball, and NFL=National Football League.

Give Up Your Body for the Team

Athletes who are "playing with pain," "giving up their body for the team," or engaging in obviously highly dangerous plays or maneuvers were consistently framed as heroes; conversely, those who removed themselves from games due to injuries had questions raised about their character, their manhood.

Table 9.7

Comments on the Heroic Nature of Playing Hurt

Sports Center	Extreme	NBA	MLB	NFL
9	12	6	4	15

Note: NBA=National Basketball Association, MLB=Major League Baseball, and NFL=National Football League.

This theme cut across all sports programming (see Table 9.7). For instance, *SportsCenter* asked, "Could the dominator be soft?" when a National Hockey League (NHL) star goalie decided to sit out a game due to a groin injury. Heroically taking risks while already hurt was a constant theme in Extreme sports commentary. For instance, one bike competitor was lauded for "overcoming his fear" and competing "with a busted up ankle" and another was applauded when he "popped his collarbone out in the street finals in Louisville but he's back on his bike here in Richmond, just two weeks later!" Athletes appear especially heroic when they go against doctors' wishes not to compete. For instance, an X Games interviewer adoringly told a competitor, "Doctors said don't ride but you went ahead and did it anyway and escaped serious injury." Similarly, NBA player Isaiah Rider was lauded for having "heart" for "playing with that knee injury." Injury discussions in NFL games often include speculation about whether the player will be able to return to this or future games. A focus on a star player in a pregame or halftime show, such as the feature on 49ers' Garrison Hearst, often contain commentary about heroic overcoming of serious injuries (in this case, a knee blowout, reconstructive surgery, and rehabilitation). As one game began, commentators noted that thirty-seven-year-old "Steve Young has remained a rock... not bad for a guy who a lotta people figured was, what, one big hit from ending his career." It's especially impressive when an injured player is able and willing to continue to play with aggressiveness and reckless abandon: "Kurt Scrafford at right guard—bad neck and all—is just out there wiping out guys." And announcers love the team leader who plays hurt:

> Drew Bledso gamely tried to play in loss to Rams yesterday; really admirable to try to play with that pin that was surgically implanted in his finger during the week; I don't know how a QB could do that. You know, he broke his finger the time we had him on Monday night and he led his

team to two come-from-behind victories, really gutted it out and I think he took that team on his shoulders and showed he could play and really elevated himself in my eyes, he really did.

Sports Is War

Commentators consistently (an average of nearly five times during each hour of sports commentary) used martial metaphors and language of war and weaponry to describe sports action (e.g., battle, kill, ammunition, weapons, professional sniper, depth charges, taking aim, fighting, shot in his arsenal, reloading, detonate, squeezes the trigger, attack mode, firing blanks, blast, explosion, blitz, point of attack, a lance through the heart, etc.); see Table 9.8.

Table 9.8

Martial Metaphors and Language of War and Weaponry

Sports Center	Extreme	Wrestling	NBA	MLB	NFL
9	3	15	27	6	23

Note: NBA=National Basketball Association, MLB=Major League Baseball, and NFL=National Football League.

Some shows went beyond commentators' use of war terminology and actually framed the contests *as* wars. For instance, one of the wrestling shows offered a continual flow of images and commentary that reminded the viewers that "RAW is WAR!" Similarly, both NFL *Monday Night Football* broadcasts were introduced with explosive graphics and an opening song that included lyrics "Like a rocket burning through time and space, the NFL's best will rock this place . . . the battle lines are drawn." This sort of use of sport/war metaphors has been a common practice in televised sports commentary for many years, serving to fuse (and confuse) the distinctions between values of nationalism with team identity and athletic aggression with military destruction (Jansen and Sabo 1994). In the shows examined for this study, war themes also were reinforced in many commercials, including commercials for movies, other sports programs, and in the occasional commercial for the U.S. military.

Show Some Guts!

Commentators continually depicted and replayed exciting incidents of athletes engaging in reckless acts of speed, showing guts in the face of danger, big hits, and violent crashes. This theme was evident across all of the sports programs but was especially predominant in Extreme sports that continually depicted crashing vehicles or bikers in an exciting manner (see Table 9.9).

For instance, when one race ended with a crash, it was showed again in slow-motion replay, with commentators approvingly dubbing it "unbelievable" and "original." Extreme sports commentators commonly raised excitement levels by saying "he's on fire" or "he's going huge!" when a competitor was obviously taking greater risks. An athlete's ability to deal with the fear of a possible crash, in fact, is the mark of an "outstanding run": "Watch out, Richmond," an X-games announcer shouted to the crowd, "He's gonna wreck this place!" A winning competitor laughingly said, "I do what I can to smash into [my opponents] as much as I can." Another competitor said, "If I crash, no big deal; I'm just gonna go for it." NFL commentators introduced the games with images of reckless collisions and during the game a "fearless" player was likely to be applauded: "There's no chance that Barry Sanders won't take when he's running the football." In another game, the announcer noted that receiver "Tony Simmons plays big. And for those of you not in the NFL, playing big means you're not afraid to go across the middle and catch the ball and make a play out of it after you catch the ball." Men showing guts in the face of speed and danger was also a major theme in forty of the commercials that we analyzed.

Table 9.9				
Depictions of Guts in Face of Danger, Speed, Hits, Crashes				
Sports Center	*Extreme*	*NBA*	*MLB*	*NFL*
4	21	5	2	8

Note: NBA=National Basketball Association, MLB=Major League Baseball, and NFL=National Football League.

THE TELEVISED SPORTS MANHOOD FORMULA

Tens of millions of U.S. boys watch televised sports programs, with their accompanying commercial advertisements. This study sheds light on what these boys are seeing when they watch their favorite sports programs. What values and ideas about gender, race, aggression, and violence are being promoted? Although there are certainly differences across different kinds of sports, as well as across different commercials, when we looked at all of the programming together, we identified ten recurrent themes, which we have outlined above. Taken together, these themes codify a consistent and (mostly) coherent message about what it means to be a man. We call this message the Televised Sports Manhood Formula:

What is a Real Man? A Real Man is strong, tough, aggressive, and above all, a winner in what is still a Man's World. To be a winner he has to do what needs to be done. He must be willing to compromise his own long-term health by showing guts in the face of danger, by fighting other men when necessary, and by "playing hurt" when he's injured. He must avoid being soft; he must be the aggressor, both on the "battle fields" of sports and in his consumption choices. Whether he is playing sports or making choices about which snack food or auto products to purchase, his aggressiveness will net him the ultimate prize: the adoring attention of conventionally beautiful women. He will know if and when he has arrived as a Real Man when the Voices of Authority—white males—say he is a Real Man. But even when he has finally managed to win the big one, has the good car, the right beer, and is surrounded by beautiful women, he will be reminded by these very same Voices of Authority just how fragile this Real Manhood really is: After all, he has to come out and prove himself all over again tomorrow. You're only as good as your last game (or your last purchase).

The major elements of the Televised Sports Manhood Formula are evident, in varying degrees, in the football, basketball, baseball, Extreme sports, and *SportsCenter* programs and in their accompanying commercials. But it is in the dramatic spectacle of professional wrestling that the Televised Sports Manhood Formula is most clearly codified and presented to audiences as an almost seamless package. Boys and young men are drawn to televised professional wrestling in great numbers. Consistently each week, from four to six pro wrestling shows rank among the top ten rated shows on cable television. Professional wrestling is not a real sport in the way that baseball, basketball, football, or even Extreme sports are. In fact, it is a highly stylized and choreographed "sport as theatre" form of entertainment. Its producers have condensed—and then amplified—all of the themes that make up the Televised Sports Manhood Formula. For instance, where violence represents a thread in the football or basketball commentary, violence makes up the entire fabric of the theatrical narrative of televised pro wrestling. In short, professional wrestling presents viewers with a steady stream of images and commentary that represents a constant fusion of all of the themes that make up the Televised Sports Manhood Formula: this is a choreographed sport where all men (except losers) are Real Men, where women are present as sexy support objects for the men's violent, monumental "wars" against each other. Winners bravely display muscular strength, speed, power, and guts. Bodily harm is (supposedly) intentionally inflicted on opponents. The most ruthlessly aggressive men win, whereas the passive or weaker men lose, often shamefully. Heroically wrestling while injured, rehabilitating oneself from former injuries, and inflicting pain and injury on one's opponent are constant and central themes in the narrative.

GENDER AND THE SPORTS/MEDIA/COMMERCIAL COMPLEX

In 1984, media scholar Sut Jhally pointed to the commercial and ideological symbiosis between the institutions of sport and the mass media and called it the sports/media complex. Our examination of the ways that the Televised Sports Manhood Formula reflects and promotes hegemonic ideologies concerning race, gender, sexuality, aggression, violence, and consumerism suggests adding a third dimension to Jhally's analysis: the huge network of multibillion-dollar automobile, snack food, alcohol, entertainment, and other corporate entities that sponsor sports events and broadcasts. In fact, examining the ways that the Televised Sports Manhood Formula cuts across sports programming and its accompanying commercials may provide important clues as to the ways that ideologies of hegemonic masculinity are both promoted by—and in turn serve to support and stabilize—this collection of interrelated institutions that make up the sports/media/commercial complex. The Televised Sports Manhood Formula is a master discourse that is produced at the nexus of the institutions of sport, mass media, and corporations who produce and hope to sell products and services to boys and men. As such, the Televised Sports Manhood Formula appears well suited to discipline boys' bodies, minds, and consumption choices within an ideological field that is conducive to the reproduction of the entrenched interests that profit from the sports/media/commercial complex. The perpetuation of the entrenched commercial interests of the sports/media/commercial complex appears to be predicated on boys accepting—indeed glorifying and celebrating—a set of bodily and relational practices that resist and oppose a view of women as fully human and place boys' and men's long-term health prospects in jeopardy.

At a historical moment when hegemonic masculinity has been destabilized by socioeconomic change, and by women's and gay liberation movements, the Televised Sports Manhood Formula provides a remarkably stable and concrete view of masculinity as grounded in bravery, risk taking, violence, bodily strength, and heterosexuality. And this view of masculinity is given coherence against views of women as sexual support objects or as invisible and thus irrelevant to men's public struggles for glory. Yet, perhaps to be successful in selling products, the commercials sometimes provide a less than seamless view of masculinity. The insecurities of masculinity in crisis are often tweaked in the commercials, as we see weak men, dumb men, and indecisive men being eclipsed by strong, smart, and decisive men and sometimes being humiliated by smarter and more decisive women. In short, this commercialized version of hegemonic masculinity is constructed partly in relation to images of men who don't measure up.

This analysis gives us hints at an answer to the commonly asked question of why so many boys and men continue to take seemingly irrational risks, submit to pain and injury, and risk long-term debility or even death by playing hurt. A critical examination of the Televised Sports Manhood Formula tells us why: the costs of masculinity (especially pain and injury), according to this formula, appear to be well worth the price; the boys and men who are willing to pay the price always seem to get the glory, the championships, the best consumer products, and the beautiful women. Those who don't—or can't—pay the price are humiliated or ignored by women and left in the dust by other men. In short, the Televised Sports Manhood Formula is a pedagogy through which boys are taught that paying the price, be it one's bodily health or one's money, gives one access to the privileges that have been historically linked to hegemonic masculinity—money, power, glory, and women. And the barrage of images of femininity as model-like beauty displayed for and in the service of successful men suggest that heterosexuality is a major lynchpin of the Televised Sports Manhood Formula, and on a larger scale serves as one of the major linking factors in the conservative gender regime of the sports/media/commercial complex.

On the other hand, we must be cautious in coming to definitive conclusions as to how the promotion of the values embedded in the Televised Sports Manhood Formula might fit into the worlds of young men. It is not possible, based merely on our textual analysis of sports programs, to explicate precisely what kind of impact these shows, and the Televised Sports Manhood Formula, have on their young male audiences. That sort of question is best approached through direct research with audiences. Most such research finds that audiences interpret, use, and draw meanings from media variously, based on factors such as social class, race/ethnicity, and gender (Hunt 1999; Whannel 1998). Research with various subgroups of boys that explores their interpretations of the sports programs that they watch would enhance and broaden this study.

Moreover, it is important to go beyond the preferred reading presented here that emphasizes the persistent themes in televised sports that appear to reinforce the hegemony of current race, gender, and commercial relations (Sabo and Jansen 1992). In addition to these continuities, there are some identifiable discontinuities within and between the various sports programs and within and among the accompanying commercials. For instance, commercials are far more varied in the ways they present gender imagery than are sports programs themselves. Although the dominant tendency in commercials is either to erase women or to present them as stereotypical support or sex objects, a significant minority of commercials present themes that set up boys and men as insecure and/or obnoxious schmucks and women as secure, knowledgeable, and authoritative. Audience research with boys who watch sports would shed fascinating light on how they decode and interpret these more complex, mixed, and paradoxical gender images against the dominant, hegemonic image of the Televised Sports Manhood Formula.

10

This Revolution Is Not
Being Televised

(with Margaret Carlisle Duncan and Nicole Willms)

Author's note: This chapter written with sports media scholar Margaret Carlisle Duncan and USC graduate student Nicole Willms, is the latest installment in a longitudinal study of gender in televised sports. In the late 1980s, Margaret and I went to a conference put on by the Amateur Athletic Foundation of Los Angeles (AAF), attended mostly by representatives of the sports media. The AAF showed the audience clips from recent televised sports coverage that illustrated some extremely racist and sexist language and values projected by reporters and commentators. When the media people at the conference responded defensively, and dismissed the clips they were shown as "anecdotal," Margaret and I volunteered to conduct a systematic social scientific study of gender in televised sports. Our first study was released in 1989. We have since done follow-up studies in 1993, 1999, and again in 2004. Our findings have mostly documented a lack of change between 1989 and 2004 in the quantity and quality of coverage of women's sports in network news shows and (in the past two iterations of the study) sports highlights shows. Due to the strong connections that the AAF has with the sports world, and with the sports media, this study has reverberated outside of academia much more widely than has much of our other scholarly work. The Women's Sports Foundation and other advocacy groups have made use of these media studies. In short, the AAF studies have provided a good entreé for us to become "public sociologists," who use research to advocate for greater equity and fairness in media coverage of women's sports.

"Well, if you're like me, these are going to be three great days," gushed the news anchor on Los Angeles KCBS evening news, as he introduced the sports report and passed the anchor to Jim Hill (who was reporting live, courtside from Staples Center before a Lakers game). "We got the Lakers tonight, we've got March Madness on Thursday and Friday. Jim, it doesn't get any better than this!" As predicted, that evening's sports news focused entirely on men's college and pro basketball, with a short interlude for men's ice hockey. The sports news reports over the next few evenings offered a steady stream of men's NBA and men's NCAA basketball stories, each with a single token men's ice hockey story. Women's sports were ignored in all of these reports. Apparently, neither the women's professional golf (LPGA) tournament, women's NCAA basketball, nor any other women's sports that were taking place on those days were deemed important enough to interrupt the excitement of "three great days" of men's basketball and ice hockey.

This example is indicative of the larger patterns of noncoverage of women's sports that we have found consistently in our research on sports news and highlights shows. The news anchor's apparent throwaway opening comment, "If you're like me..." is especially telling. Nearly all of the sports anchors and ancillary reporters, in the weeks of sports news and highlights shows that we studied, are *just like him*, in that they are men. And these men continue to offer up a steady stream of verbal reports and visual images that focus on men's sports, while largely ignoring women's sports.

BOOMING PARTICIPATION, A TRICKLE OF NEWS COVERAGE

During the 2004 year, the latest in our longitudinal study of sports media that stretches back to 1989, we analyzed how televised sports news and highlights shows cover women's and men's sports. In 1989, 1993, 1999, and now again in 2004, we sampled two weeks in March, two weeks in July, and two weeks in November to study both the quantity and quality of coverage of women's and men's sports news by the three local L.A. network affiliates. In 1999, we added ESPN's popular highlights show, *SportsCenter* to our study. And in 2004, we added for the first time a regional highlights show, Fox's *Southern California Sports Report*.

The dominant finding in our 2004 study is the lack of change over the past fifteen years. In our 1989 study, the three network affiliates devoted only 5% of their air time to coverage of women's sports. Ten years later, in 1999, there was a grudging increase to 8.7%. In 2004, the proportion of news coverage devoted to women's sports had dropped back to 6.3%. In short, there has been virtually no change in the proportion of network affiliate sports news shows' reporting on women's sports since we began collecting data in 1989 (see Figure 10.1). The two sports highlights shows are even worse, with ESPN's *SportsCenter* devoting only 2.1% of its air time to women's sports, and Fox's *Southern California Sports Report* only 3%.

Figure 10.1
Network sports news 1989–2004, by sex

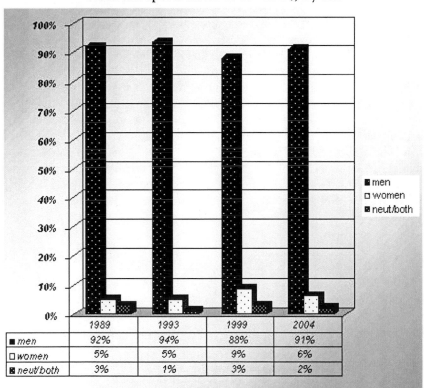

	1989	1993	1999	2004
■ *men*	92%	94%	88%	91%
□ *women*	5%	5%	9%	6%
▣ *neut/both*	3%	1%	3%	2%

The mainstream electronic media's continued silence surrounding women's sports is stunning. Since our 1989 study, girls' and women's sports participation has continued its dramatic growth that began in the 1970s. Each year, millions of girls enthusiastically participate in youth soccer, softball, and other community sports. High school sports are no longer totally dominated by boys. In 1971, only 294,000 U.S. high school girls played interscholastic sports, compared with 3.7 million boys. In 1989, the first year of our sports media study, high school boy athletes still outnumbered girls, 3.4 million to 1.8 million. By 2004, the high school sports participation gap had closed further, 4.0 million boys to 2.9 million girls. This trend is echoed in college sports participation rates. In 1972, the year Title IX was enacted, there were only a little over two women's athletics teams per school at the college level. By 2004, the number had risen to 8.32 teams per NCAA school. From 2000 to 2004, 631 new women's teams were added in U.S. universities, and in the last six years, a total of 1,155 new women's teams have been added. Women's participation rates in the Olympic Games have risen dramatically over the past three decades, and women's professional sports have also grown.

Clearly, the world of sports is no longer a "male preserve," in which boys and men enjoy privileged and exclusive access to participation opportunities and to community and school resources. Though girls' and women's sports are still generally underfunded, and girls and women still too often have to fight for full and equal access, it is also true that in the past three decades we have witnessed an historic sea change in sport's gender dynamics. But one would never know this, if one simply got one's sports information from the network affiliates' evening and late-night news shows, or from the sports highlights shows on ESPN and Fox. The mass media's continued marginalization of women's sports serves to maintain the myth that sports are exclusively by, about, and for men. Women's athletics is booming as never before. However, if it is not covered in the mass media, we can conclude that in a very real way, it simply did not "happen."

GAG FEATURES, SEX APPEAL, AND TENNIS

Against this backdrop of near-silence concerning women's sports, it is especially important to examine how women are shown and talked about, on the rare occasion that they do come into focus on sports news and highlights shows. In our previous studies, we observed that when sports news or highlights shows did place women in the picture, there were certain patterned ways that women appeared. First, we noted that news and highlights shows tended to focus periodically on a nonserious gag feature, or a story on a marginal, but entertaining pseudosport (e.g., a long feature on a woman's nude bungee jump in 1999). We also noted in past studies that women appeared in the sports shows when they were seen as opportunities for commentators (and presumably viewers) to engage in sexualized humor and voyeurism. For instance, in 1999, news and highlights shows frequently focused stories on tennis player Anna Kournikova, usually accompanied by visual footage and some sexually suggestive joking by the commentators. A third pattern that we saw in past studies was a tendency during July men's baseball stories for commentators to make sexually humorous comments as cameras presented close-ups of women spectators in skimpy bathing suits.

In 2004, we saw less of this kind of trivialization of women athletes, and generally less sexualization of women than in past studies. Most of the (still very sparing) stories on women's sports in 2004 were straightforward, respectful stories, rather than gag features, stories on marginal sports, or opportunities for sexual voyeurism and humor. However, there were notable instances of this kind of reporting.

Gag Features. Sports news and highlights shows are often peppered with humor, which tends to make the reports more entertaining for viewers. Gag features—often on marginal sports or pseudosports—are one form that this humor tends to take. For instance, on a March 24 report that included no coverage of women's sports, during a report on Dodgers' spring training camp, KABC showed video for a few seconds on middle-aged women who had been invited to take batting practice at the camp. Ron Fukuzaki jokingly said to the news anchors, "Now we know the Dodgers are looking for a high-priced hitter, the way these ladies are hittin' the ball, hey, who knows, Marc and Michelle?" A second example is *SportsCenter's* thirteen-second long March 18 story on a "weight-lifting granny." Accompanying visuals of a woman lifting weights, Steve Berthiaume quipped, "We've been waiting forever for a sequel to the governor of California's hit, *Pumping Iron.* We have it: here she is, the star of the show, the weight-lifting grandmamma. Granny, you made us proud." No information was offered on the woman's name, or where the weight-lifting event occurred. This was the only coverage of a "women's sport" during this broadcast of *SportsCenter.*

Sexualization Themes. Commentators seem to find appeal in stories that are both humorous gag features and opportunities for sexual titillation. For instance, on November 15, during a sports report that ran no coverage of conventional women's sports, KABC ran a story on a promotional "football game" in which the women players would compete while wearing lingerie. And a common practice is for sports shows to focus a large proportion of their small coverage of women's sports on an individual athlete who is positioned as an icon of white, heterosexual feminine attractiveness. In 2004, sports news and highlights shows had largely replaced Anna Kournikova with Maria Sharapova as their featured young sex symbol. Several times, WTA stories focused on Sharapova (only Serena Williams approached the amount of coverage devoted to Sharapova). This focus on Sharpaova was legitimate: she had recently won Wimbledon, and had become a highly ranked player. But the fact that commentators rarely seemed to report on Sharapova without also commenting (often jokingly) on her appearance indicated a continuation of the sexualization themes from past studies. For instance, on November 11, KABC's Rob Fukuzaki introduced the day's only women's sports story—a fifty-six second feature on the WTA—with this teaser: "They slapped her on a billboard that read 'the closer you get the *hotter* it gets.' Seventeen-year-old Maria Sharapova may have the same appeal as Anna Kournikova but the young Russian can actually play tennis. . . . Sharapova is a poster girl for the event." On one occasion, the Fox commentators went beyond mere reference to Sharapova's sex appeal. On their July 12 broadcast, a thirty-three-second long story on Sharapova accompanied by footage of her win at Wimbleton, Barry LeBrock paused during his commentary on Sharapova as Van Earl Wright peppered the report with lusty howls: "In tennis news tonight . . . seventeen-year-old Wimbledon champ Maria Sharapova—[*howl*]—who has withdrawn from the tournament citing need for rest and recuperation—[*howl*]—now you know why—the Chase Open was to have been Sharapova's first tournament since beating Serena Williams in the Wimbledon final. Sharapova did add though that she plans to rejoin the tour on July 26—[both commentators together *howl*]."

Scantily clad women sometimes provide a visual backdrop for the reporting of men's sports. We saw fewer instances than in past studies of commentators joking about bikini-clad women at baseball games during the July segment of our sample. But we did note a pattern of the use of visual shots of women cheerleaders during reports on various men's sports. For instance, on March 20, KNBC's report on NCAA men's basketball included a two to three second shot of Alabama's female cheerleaders shaking their pom-poms. This was a common part of the package of visual imagery during March reports on men's college basketball, on the three network affiliates, ESPN, and Fox. In fact, Fox promoted their own programs using various shots of college cheerleaders (often wearing local USC and UCLA outfits) doing bump-and-grind dances, wearing short skirts, with exposed midriffs in tight-fitting cropped tops, accompanied by a voice-over saying, "The only sports network where Southern California fans come first. You're watching Fox Sports Network." Images of sexy female cheerleaders represent Fox as a network, while images of women athletes are largely absent in its coverage.

If it's women's sports, it must be tennis

Television news and highlights shows delivered to viewers a steady staple of men's college basketball and football, professional basketball and football, and professional baseball, peppered with generous doses of men's ice hockey, auto racing, golf, tennis, boxing, and occasional reports on other sports. Together, these reports made up an almost continuous stream of information, images, and commentary on men athletes and men's sports. Women's sports reports, by contrast, were occasional, and seemed to interrupt the steady flow of reporting on men's sports. Not only were reports on women's sports far less frequent, they were less varied. When women's sports stories did appear in our sample, 42.4% of them were tennis (WTA) stories. Track and field stories were a distant second, accounting for 16% of all women's sports stories.

Those who make decisions about what to cover on sports news and highlights shows are apparently most comfortable covering men's sports. And when they do cover women's sports, they prefer to cover women in ways that pigeonhole women into conventional roles that are not threatening to a patriarchal gaze: as trivialized jokes and/or as sexualized objects of consumption. But there is a tension here. Women's sports are so clearly here to stay. A whole generation of women—and, indeed, of men—have now come of age since Title IX. Young adults and children now know (and usually support the idea) that sports participation is good for girls and women. Moreover, due to increased opportunities, skilled, competitive, strong, and powerfully athletic girls and women are a growing reality in our daily lives. But much of the mass media lags behind in reflecting this broad social change. And some parts of the mass media can be seen as presenting a backlash against the women's athletic revolution.

WELCOME TO THE MEN'S CLUB

If sport, as an institution, is no longer an exclusive preserve for men, the particular realm of televised sports highlights shows still appears to be. ESPN's *SportsCenter* and Fox's *Southern California Sports* Report consistently offer up a standard staple of men's baseball, men's basketball, men's football, with occasional smidgens of men's hockey, auto racing, and some golf and tennis. Women's sports are rarely included, and if they are, they usually appear as an afterthought. These sports highlights shows offer viewers the most consistent, almost seamless vision of sport as an exclusive territory set up by and for men.

SportsCenter's ironic, often snide humorous style has successfully set the tone for the growth of other sports highlights shows like Fox's *Southern California Sports Report*. This relatively new genre of televised sports entertainment meshes neatly with broader trends in contemporary popular culture that aim to entertain (and sell products to) young-to-middle-aged men. Men's traditional privileges, and the cultural meanings of masculinity, have been destabilized in recent decades, resulting in new insecurities, especially among younger men. Television shows like *The Man Show*, new soft-core porn magazines like *Maxim* and *FHM*, radio talk shows like the nationally syndicated "Tom Leykus Show," and many sports radio and television sports talk shows share similar themes and are targeted to similar audiences of young men. These media typically present sports as a realm apart from women, where men can connect with each other, "as men." This media genre depicts and encourages a young male lifestyle that is saturated with images of, and explicit talk about, sexy women as objects of consumption. A range of consumer products that includes—often centrally, as in *The Man Show*—consumption of beer as part of the young male lifestyle stitches together the bonds among men.

Strong, competent, decisive women (like most women athletes) have no legitimate space in this cultural field. Those kinds of women are either ignored or disparaged. The treatment of women on *SportsCenter* and on Fox's *Southern California Report* meshes neatly with this broader cultural trend. These programs are a "male space" (despite the occasional appearance of a woman announcer). For the most part, they refrain from talking about or depicting the athletic accomplishments of real sportswomen. Women appear on these shows primarily as jokes, as sexual objects that prop up the men (e.g., Fox's use of dancing cheerleaders in its ads), or as athletes who fit conventional stereotypes of heterosexual femininity, like tennis player Maria Sharapova.

AUDIENCE-BUILDING AND MINI-SPIKES

Sociologists often tell students in introductory classes to walk into an elevator, and face the other people, rather than the doorway. The resulting feeling of awkwardness is a clear indicator that a social rule has been breached. Institutional patterns like facing the door in the elevator are often so well-engrained that they are invisible to all of the actors, until someone doesn't conform. The irregularity, the moment of resistance, or the deviant act tend to illustrate the rule. So, too, with moments in the mass media that contradict the dominant patterns.

Well over half (58%) of the combined three network affiliates news shows in our 2004 study had no coverage of women's sports. There were zero sports news or highlights shows in our sample that had no coverage of men's sports. The coverage of women's sports on the news and highlights shows that we sampled was almost uniformly low, but we did note two mini-spikes, or small surges in the coverage of women's sports. The first mini-spike was by KNBC during March, and the second (less dramatic) mini-spike was during the November sample of the Fox *Southern California Sports Report*.

In July, KNBC devoted 15.4% of its sports news time to the coverage of women's sports. This was far more time than KNBC devoted to women's sports in the March sample (5.7%) or in the November sample (5.1%). In July, KNBC also devoted 20.8% of its ticker time (the scrolling text at the bottom of the television screen) to women's sports. This was far more than the 4.6% and 1.6% of ticker time that they devoted to women's sports in

March and November, respectively. Three times in July, KNBC led off a broadcast with a women's sports story. KNBC did not have a lead women's sports story in any of the other two time periods sampled in the study. Twenty of KNBC's thirty-six women's sports stories in July focused on U.S. women's sports in the Olympics, and all three of the lead women's sports stories were Olympics stories. By comparison, neither of the other two network affiliate news shows, nor the sports highlights shows in our sample evidenced such a dramatic expanded focus on women's sports during the Olympic Games (KCBS had two women's Olympics stories during the March sample, KABC had six, ESPN three, and Fox three). KNBC's expanded coverage of the Olympics on its news reports corresponded with the parent network NBC's live and taped coverage of the Olympics.

In the November segment of our sample, Fox devoted 6.8% of its *Southern California Sports Report* coverage to women's sports (compared with Fox's 1.3% combined women's coverage in March and July). This mini-spike in women's sports coverage was largely due to a surge in coverage of women's tennis. Five of Fox's six women's sports stories during the November sample were women's tennis stories. This expanded coverage of women's tennis corresponded with a series of ads that Fox ran during the program, promoting a local WTA tournament, played at LA's Staples Center.

When asked why they don't cover more women's sports, producers, editors and sports reporters will often say that they would really like to do so, but that they are just "giving the audience what they want." Our observation of the two mini-spikes in the coverage of women's sports suggests that something more complicated is going on. Though our content analysis cannot show how producers decide what to show or what not show, we suspect that it is not coincidental that KNBC's March surge in the coverage of women's Olympics sports coincided with the parent NBC network's live and taped coverage of the Olympics. Similarly, Fox's small burst of coverage of women's tennis in November corresponded with the network's running of advertisements for a local WTA event.

KNBC's July surge in coverage of women's Olympics sports is especially noteworthy. When compared with the low levels of coverage on KABC, KCBS, ESPN and Fox, KNBC's surge in Olympics news stories puts into relief the more general claim by producers of sports news and highlights shows that their usual programming choices are based simply on responding to audience demand for men's sports. Sometimes, it seems, when they perceive it to be in their interests, producers of television sports news and highlights shows give us not what they think *we* want, but what *they want us to want*. The producers' party line asserts that the daily stream of stories and images of men's sports is simply the programmers' rational response to audience demand for men's sports. This supply-and-demand line obscures a more complicated reality: producers of sports news and highlights shows actively and consciously attempt to *build audience demand* for events in which they have a vested interest.

Audience-building, grounded in interlocking interests between television networks, news and highlights shows, commercial sponsors, and athletic organizations is routinely built in to men's sports. Audience-building appears to happen for women's sports, though, only when the producers of a show see a direct link between their interests and the promotion of a particular women's sporting event. The interlocking interests in women's sports appear to be simple and linear: when there is a *direct* interest in promoting a *particular* women's sports event (as KNBC did with the Olympics, and Fox did with WTA), then we see a surge in news or highlights coverage of this particular women's sports event. But this kind of surge is both temporary and local (confined to the particular network with the direct interest in promoting the women's sports event). By contrast, the interlocking interests in the men's sports/media/commercial complex permeate the mass media in a seemingly organic, multinodal, manner. As such, these promotional efforts are more easily taken for granted and, ironically, may be less visible *as* promotion. News and highlights shows are two important links in an overall apparatus of audience-building for men's sports. But they rarely operate this way for women's sports. Similar to the person who faces the wrong direction in the elevator, the "mini-spikes" in televised coverage of women's sports that we observed are unique exceptional moments of local and temporary promotion of women's sports events that serve to illustrate the rule.

How can this "rule" be broken or changed? Clearly, the longitudinal data from our studies shows that there is no "evolutionary" growth in media coverage of women's sports that just automatically happens. The proportion of coverage of women's sports on televised news over the past fifteen years is absolutely flat, and there is no reason to believe that this will change in the next fifteen years, unless producers decide that it is in their interests to do so. Of course, producers would have us believe that they are simply responding to audience demand, and that they will give us more women's sports when we ask for it. For instance, on November 19, 2004, KNBC's Fred Roggin ended a broadcast that had otherwise included only stories on men with an eighteen second report on women's golf that included game footage, with this commentary: "And finally: got a call from a viewer last hour, [asking] why don't we show women's golf very often? Well, your wish is our command. Anneke Sorenstam, the leader after two rounds of the ABT Championships. The Swedish superstar who was seeking her eighth win of the year fired a 4-under 68 to grab a three-shot lead heading into the weekend. You call, we listen: there you go!"

Though viewers should phone television stations to protest sexism and to ask for more equitable coverage of women's sports, it would be a mistake to assume that the lack of coverage of women's sports can be explained so simply. A shift toward fair and equitable coverage of women's sports will not result from a few phone calls by viewers, but will involve changes and pressures from a number of directions. One important source of such change within the mass media would involve an affirmative move toward developing and supporting more women sports reporters and commentators. Sports organizations, too, can contribute to change by providing the sports media with more and better information about women athletes. Indeed, a 2005 longitudinal study by Mary Jo Kane and Jo Ann Buysse shows that in recent years, university sports information departments have vastly improved their presentation of women's sports in their annual media guides. But a dramatic change will have to be premised on a critical examination of the ways that sports organizations and media are grounded in masculinist traditions and assumptions. Sport has tended to be one of the last institutional bastions of men's traditional power and privilege. As women have stormed the playing fields by the millions, they have contested this patriarchal institution. But televised sports has continued to juxtapose images of powerful male bodies against sexualized images of women's bodies in ways that affirm conventional notions of male superiority and female frailty. Sport is not a separate "world." It is intertwined with other aspects of social life in important ways. Thus, for the gender imagery of sports media to change in ways that reflect and support this revolution of female athleticism, power relations and perceptions of gender will have to continue to change within sport organizations, within commercial sponsors who promote and advertise sports, within schools and universities, and within the mass media. For this kind of social change to occur will take a renewed feminist movement, both inside and outside sport.

11

The Male Consumer as Loser

Beer and Liquor Ads in Mega Sports Media Events

(with Jeffrey Montez de Oca)

Author's note: My 1999 sports media study for Children Now had sparked my interest in advertising images, and I further developed this interest in my 2002 book *Taking the Field*. I joined with then-USC graduate student Jeffrey Montez de Oca to conduct a study of beer and liquor advertising in major sports media events. We chose beer and liquor ads because they have for many years been central sponsors of sporting events and broadcasts, and also because liquor consumption is so centrally implicated in many of the problems associated with boys and men (within and outside of sports). And we chose to focus on two annual "mega sports media events"—the televised Super Bowl, and the print *Sports Illustrated* swimsuit issue—because these events draw huge audiences, and in some ways set the tone for sports advertising aimed at boys and men. Jeff and I examined Super Bowls and *SI* swimsuit issues from years past, but focused our analysis on the beer and liquor ads that appeared in two years of these events, 2002 and 2003. The patterned themes and stories about men, women, and sex that we found were similar in some ways to the "Televised Sports Manhood Formula." But here we found more consistently a pattern of men being depicted as "losers," as chumps, whose shortcomings and insecurities could be best overcome, the ads suggested, through non-emotional bonding with other guys, preferably over a few beers. Women are absent from many of these ads. But when they do appear, they are depicted either as wives or girlfriends who threaten men's freedom to have fun with the guys, or as fantasy sex objects. We would love to see further research on these kinds of ads that focus on audiences. Many people might simply dismiss the ads as meaningless, or just say that they "laugh them off." But we wonder in what ways they are consequential; after all, beer and liquor companies spend millions every year to produce, test, and run these ads under the assumption that they encourage guys to buy their product. We would be interested in other questions: How do members of the advertisers' target audience (young-to-middle-aged males) interpret the ads' gender and sexual themes? Do these ads help to shape young men's attitudes toward and relationships with other men, and with women? Do different groups of men (e.g., by race or sexual orientation) interpret these ads differently? Are these ads a part of the larger puzzle of understanding the connections between alcohol use, sports, men's insecurities, men's relationships with other men, and men's violence against women?

The historical development of modern men's sport has been closely intertwined with the consumption of alcohol and with the financial promotion and sponsorship provided by beer and liquor producers and distributors, as well as pubs and bars (Collins and Vamplew 2002). The beer and liquor industry plays a key economic role in commercialized college and professional sports (Zimbalist 1999; Sperber 2000). Liquor industry advertisements heavily influence the images of masculinity promoted in sports broadcasts and magazines (Wenner 1991). Alcohol consumption is also often a key aspect of the more dangerous and violent dynamics at the heart of male sport cultures (Curry 2000; Sabo, Gray, and Moore 2000). By itself, alcohol does not "cause" men's violence against women or against other men; however, it is commonly one of a cluster of factors that facilitate violence (Koss and Gaines 1993; Leichliter et al. 1998). In short, beer and liquor are central players in "a high holy trinity of alcohol, sports, and hegemonic masculinity" (Wenner 1998). This essay examines beer and liquor advertisements in two "mega sports media events" consumed by large numbers of boys and men—the 2002 and 2003 Super Bowls and the 2002 and 2003 *Sports Illustrated* swimsuit issues. Our goal is to illuminate tropes of masculinity that prevail in those ads. We see these ads as establishing a pedagogy of youthful masculinity that does not passively teach male consumers about the qualities of their products so much as it encourages consumers to think of their products as essential to creating a stylish and desirable lifestyle. These ads do more than just dupe consumers into product loyalty; they also work with consumers to construct a consumption-based masculine identity relevant to contemporary social conditions. Drawing on insights from feminist cultural studies (Walters 1999), we argue that these gendered tropes watched by tens of millions of boys and men offer a window through which we can broaden our understanding of contemporary continuities, shifts, and strains in the social construction of masculinities.

GENDER, MEN'S SPORTS, AND ALCOHOL ADS

Although marketing beer and liquor to men is not new, the imagery that advertisers employ to pitch their product is not static either. Our analysis of past Super Bowls and *Sports Illustrated* beer and liquor ads suggests shifting patterns in the gender themes encoded in the ads. Consistently, over time, the ads attempt not to simply "plug" a particular product but to situate products within a larger historically specific way of life. Beer and liquor advertisers normally do not create product differentiation through typical narratives of crisis and resolution in which the product is the rescuing hero. Instead, they paint a series of images that evoke feelings, moods, and ways of being. In short, beer and liquor advertising engages in "lifestyle branding." Rather than simply attaching a name to a product, the brand emanates from a series of images that construct a plausible and desirable world to consumers. Lifestyle branding—more literary and evocative than simple crisis/resolution narratives—theorizes the social location of target populations and constructs a desiring subject whose consumption patterns can be massaged in specific directions. As we shall see, the subject constructed by the beer and liquor ads that we examined is an overtly gendered subject.

Beer and alcohol advertising construct a "desirable lifestyle" in relation to contemporary social conditions, including shifts and tensions in the broader gender order. Ads from the late 1950s through the late 1960s commonly depicted young or middle-aged white heterosexual couples happily sharing a cold beer in their suburban backyards, in their homes, or in an outdoor space like a park.

In these ads, the beer is commonly displayed in a clear glass, its clean, fresh appearance perhaps intended to counter the reputation of beer as a working-class male drink. Beer in these ads symbolically unites the prosperous and happy postwar middle-class couple. By the mid-1970s, women as wives and partners largely disappeared from beer ads. Instead of showing heterosexual couples drinking in their homes or backyards, these ads began primarily to depict images of men drinking with other men in public spaces. Three studies of beer commercials of the 1970s and 1980s found that most ads pitched beer to men as a pleasurable reward for a hard day's work. These ads told men that "For all you do, this Bud's for you." Women were rarely depicted in these ads, except as occasional background props in male-dominated bars (Postman et al. 1987; Strate 1992; Wenner 1991).

The 1950s and 1960s beer ads that depicted happy married suburban couples were part of a moment in gender relations tied to postwar culture and

Figure 11.1. Schlitz Beer, "Good Living," *Sports Illustrated*, 1959.

Fordist relations of production. White, middle-class, heterosexual masculinity was defined as synonymous with the male breadwinner, in symmetrical relation to a conception of femininity grounded in the image of the suburban housewife. In the 1970s and early 1980s, the focus on men's laboring bodies, tethered to their public leisure with other men, expressed an almost atavistic view of hegemonic masculinity at a time when women were moving into public life in huge numbers and blue-collar men's jobs were being eliminated by the tens of thousands.

Both the postwar and the postindustrial ads provide a gendered pedagogy for living a masculine lifestyle in a shifting context characterized by uncertainty. In contrast to the depiction of happy white families comfortably living lives of suburban bliss, the postwar era was characterized by anxieties over the possibility of a postwar depression, nuclear annihilation, suburban social dislocation, and disorder from racial and class movements for social justice (Lipsitz 1981; May 1988; Spigel 1992). Similarly, the 1970s and 1980s beer ads came in the wake of the defeat of the United States in the Vietnam War, the 1972 gas crisis, the collapse of Fordism, and the turbulence in gender relations brought on by the women's and gay/lesbian liberation movements. All of these social ruptures contributed to produce an anxious white male subject (Connell 1995; Lipsitz 1998). Therefore, there is a sort of crisis/resolution narrative in these beer ads: the "crisis" lies broadly in the construction of white masculinities in the latter half of the twentieth century (Kimmel 1987), and the resolution lies in the construction of a lifestyle outside of immediate anxieties. The advertisements do not straightforwardly tell consumers to buy; rather, they teach consumers how to live a happy, stress-free life that includes regular (if not heavy) consumption of alcoholic beverages.

The 2002 and 2003 ads that we examine here primarily construct a white male "loser" whose life is apparently separate from paid labor. He hangs out with his male buddies, is self-mocking and ironic about his loser status, and is always at the ready to engage in voyeurism with sexy fantasy women but holds committed relationships and emotional honesty with real women in disdain. To the extent that these themes find resonance with young men of today, it is likely because they speak to basic insecurities that are grounded in a combination of historic shifts: deindustrialization, the declining real value of wages and the male breadwinner role, significant cultural shifts brought about by more than three decades of struggle by feminists and sexual minorities, and challenges to white male supremacy by people of color and by immigrants. This cluster of social changes has destabilized hegemonic masculinity and defines the context of gender relations in which today's young men have grown toward adulthood.

In theorizing how the loser motif in beer and liquor ads constructs a version of young white masculinity, we draw on Mikhail Bakhtin's (1981) concept of the chronotope. This is especially relevant in analyzing how lifestyle branding goes beyond the reiteration of a name to actually creating desirable and believable worlds in which consumers are beckoned to place themselves. The term *chronotope*—literally meaning "time-space"—describes how time and space fuse in literature to create meaningful structures separate from the text and its representations (Bakhtin 1981). The ads that we looked at consistently construct a leisure-time lifestyle of young men meeting in specific sites of sports and alcohol consumption: bars, television rooms, and stadiums. This meeting motif gives a temporal and spatial plane to male fantasy where desire can be explored and symbolic boundaries can simultaneously be transgressed and reinscribed into the social world.

TWO MEGA SPORTS MEDIA EVENTS

This essay brings focus to the commercial center of sports media by examining the gender and sexual imagery encoded in two mega sports media events: the 2002 and 2003 Super Bowls and the 2002 and 2003 *Sports Illustrated* swimsuit issues. (See the appendix for a complete list of the ads and commercials.)

Mega sports media events are mediated cultural rituals (Dayan and Katz 1988) that differ from everyday sports media events in several key ways: sports media actively build audience anticipation and excitement throughout the year for these single events; the Super Bowl and the swimsuit issue are each preceded by major pre-event promotion and hype—from the television network that will broadcast the Super Bowl to *Sports Illustrated* and myriad other print and electronic media; the Super Bowl and the swimsuit issue are used as marketing tools for selling the more general products of National Football League (NFL) games and *Sports Illustrated* magazine subscriptions; the Super Bowl and the swimsuit issue each generate significant spin-off products (e.g., videos, books, "making of" television shows, calendars, frequently visited Web pages); the Super Bowl and the swimsuit issue generate significantly larger audiences than does a weekly NFL game or a weekly edition of *Sports Illustrated*; and advertisements are usually created specifically for these mega sports media events and cost more to run than do ads in a weekly NFL game or a weekly edition of *Sports Illustrated*.

To be sure, the Super Bowl and the *Sports Illustrated* swimsuit issue are different in some fundamental ways. First, the Super Bowl is a televised event, while the swimsuit issue is a print event. Second, the Super Bowl is an actual sporting contest, while the swimsuit issue is a departure from *Sports Illustrated*'s normal coverage of sports. However, for our purposes, we see these two events as comparable, partly because they are mega sports media events but also because their ads target young males who consume sports media.

Super Bowl Ads

Since its relatively modest start in 1967, the NFL Super Bowl has mushroomed into one of the most expensive and most watched annual media events in the United States, with a growing world audience (Martin and Reeves 2001), the vast majority of whom are boys and men. Increasingly over the past decade, Super Bowl commercials have been specially created for the event. Newspapers, magazines, television news shows, and Web sites now routinely run pre–Super Bowl stories that focus specifically on the ads, and several media outlets run post–Super Bowl polls to determine which ads were the most and least favorite. Postgame lists of "winners" and "losers" focus as much on the corporate sponsors and their ads as on the two teams that—incidentally?—played a football game between the commercials.

Fifty-five commercials ran during the 2003 Super Bowl (not counting pregame and postgame shows), at an average cost of $2.1 million for each thirty-second ad. Fifteen of these commercials were beer or malt liquor ads. Twelve of these ads were run by Anheuser-Busch, whose ownership of this Super Bowl was underlined at least twenty times throughout the broadcast, when, after commercial breaks, the camera lingered on the stadium scoreboard, atop which was a huge Budweiser sign. On five other occasions, "Bud" graphics appeared on the screen after commercial breaks, as voice-overs reminded viewers that the Super Bowl was "brought to" them by Budweiser. This represented a slight increase in beer advertising since the 2002 Super Bowl, which featured thirteen beer or malt liquor commercials (eleven of them by Anheuser-Busch), at an average cost of $1.9 million per thirty-second ad. In addition to the approximately $31.5 million that the beer companies paid for the 2003 Super Bowl ad slots, they paid millions more creating and testing those commercials with focus groups. There were 137.7 million viewers watching all or part of the 2003 Super Bowl on ABC, and by far the largest demographic group watching was men, aged twenty-five to fifty-five.

Sports Illustrated *Swimsuit Issue Ads*

Sports Illustrated began in 1964 to publish an annual February issue that featured five or six pages of women modeling swimsuits, embedded in an otherwise normal sixty-four-page magazine (Davis 1997). This modest format continued until the late 1970s, when the portion of the magazine featuring swimsuit models began gradually to grow. In the 1980s, the swimsuit issue morphed into a special issue in which normal sports coverage gradually disappeared. During this decade, the issue's average length had grown to 173 pages, 20% of which were focused on swimsuit models. By the 1990s, the swimsuit issue averaged 207 pages in length, 31% of which featured swimsuit models. The magazine has continued to grow in recent years. The 2003 issue was 218 pages in length, 59% of which featured swimsuit models. The dramatic growth in the size of the swimsuit issue in the 1990s, as well as the dropping of pretence that the swimsuit issue had anything to do with normal "sports journalism," were facilitated by advertising that began cleverly to echo and spoof the often highly sexualized swimsuit imagery in the magazine. By 2000, it was more the rule than the exception when an ad in some way utilized the swimsuit theme. The gender and sexual themes of the swimsuit issue became increasingly seamless, as ads and *Sports Illustrated* text symbiotically echoed and played off of each other. The 2002 swimsuit issue included seven pages of beer ads and seven pages of liquor ads, which cost approximately $230,000 per full page to run. The 2003 swimsuit issue ran the equivalent of sixteen pages of beer ads and thirteen pages of liquor ads. The ad space for the 2003 swimsuit issue sold for $266,000 per full-page color ad.

The millions of dollars that beer and liquor companies spent to develop and buy space for these ads were aimed at the central group that reads the magazine: young and middle-aged males. *Sports Illustrated* estimates the audience size of its weekly magazine at 21.3 million readers, roughly 76% of whom are males. Nearly half of the male audience is in the coveted eighteen-to thirty-four-year-old demographic group, and three quarters of the male *Sports Illustrated* audience is between the ages of eighteen and forty-nine. A much larger number of single-copy sales gives the swimsuit issue a much larger audience, conservatively estimated at more than thirty million readers.

The Super Bowl and the *Sports Illustrated* swimsuit issue are arguably the biggest single electronic and print sports media events annually in the United States. Due to their centrality, size, and target audiences, we suggest that mega sports media events such as the Super Bowl and the swimsuit issue offer a magnified view of the dominant gender and sexual imagery emanating from the center of the sports-media-commercial complex. Our concern is not simply to describe the stereotypes of masculinity and femininity in these ads; rather, we use these ads as windows into the ways that cultural capitalism constructs gender relationally, as part of a general lifestyle. In this essay, we will employ thick description of ads to illuminate the four main gender relations themes that we saw in the 2002 and 2003 ads, and we will follow with a discussion of the process through which these themes are communicated: erotic and often humorous intertextual referencing. We will end by discussing some of the strains and tensions in the ads' major tropes of masculinity.

LOSERS AND BUDDIES, HOTTIES AND BITCHES

In the 2002 and 2003 beer and liquor ads that we examined, men's work worlds seem mostly to have disappeared. These ads are less about drinking and leisure as a reward for hard work and more about leisure as a lifestyle in and of itself. Men do not work in these ads; they recreate. And women are definitely back in the picture, but not as wives who are partners in building the good domestic life. It is these relations among men as well as relations between men and women that form the four dominant gender themes in the ads we examined. We will introduce these four themes by describing a 2003 Super Bowl commercial for Bud Lite beer.

Two young, somewhat nerdy-looking white guys are at a yoga class, sitting in the back of a room full of sexy young women. The two men have attached prosthetic legs to their bodies so that they can fake the yoga moves. With their bottles of Bud Lite close by, these voyeurs watch in delight as the female yoga teacher instructs the class to "relax and release that negative energy... inhale, arch, *thrust* your pelvis to the sky and exhale, *release* into the stretch." As the instructor uses her hands to push down on a woman's upright spread-eagled legs and says "focus, focus, focus," the camera (serving as prosthesis for male spectators at home) cuts back and forth between close-ups of the women's breasts and bottoms, while the two guys gleefully enjoy their beer and their sexual voyeurism. In the final scene the two guys are standing outside the front door of the yoga class, beer bottles in hand, and someone throws their fake legs out the door at them. As they duck to avoid being hit by the legs, one of them comments, "*She's* not very relaxed."

We begin with this ad because it contains, in various degrees, the four dominant gender themes that we found in the mega sports media events ads:

1. *Losers*: Men are often portrayed as chumps, losers. Masculinity— especially for the lone man—is precarious. Individual men are always on the cusp of being publicly humiliated, either by their own stupidity, by other men, or, worse, by a beautiful woman.
2. *Buddies*: The precariousness of individual men's masculine status is offset by the safety of the male group. The solidity and primacy— and emotional safety—of male friendships are the emotional center of many of these ads.
3. *Hotties*: When women appear in these ads, it is usually as highly sexualized fantasy objects. These beautiful women serve as potential prizes for men's victories and proper consumption choices. They sometimes serve to validate men's masculinity, but their validating power also holds the potential to humiliate male losers.
4. *Bitches*: Wives, girlfriends, or other women to whom men are emotionally committed are mostly absent from these ads. However, when they do appear, it is primarily as emotional or sexual blackmailers who threaten to undermine individual men's freedom to enjoy the erotic pleasure at the center of the male group.

To a great extent, these four gender themes are intertwined in the Super Bowl "Yoga Voyeurs" ad. First, the two guys are clearly not good-looking,

Figure 11.2. Budweiser, "Yoga Voyeurs,"Anheuser-Busch, 2003 Super Bowl on ABC.

high-status, muscular icons of masculinity. More likely they are intended to represent the "everyman" with whom many boys and men can identify. Their masquerade as sensitive men allows them to transgress the female space of the yoga class, but they cannot pull the masquerade off and are eventually "outed" as losers and rejected by the sexy women. But even if they realize that they are losers, they do not have to care because they are so happy and secure in their bond with each other. Their friendship bond is cemented in frat-boy-style hijinks that allow them to share close-up voyeurism of sexy women who, we can safely assume, are way out of these men's league. In the end, the women reject the guys as pathetic losers. But the guys do not seem too upset. They have each other and, of course, they have their beers.

Rarely did a single ad in our study contain all four of these themes. But taken together, the ads show enough consistency that we can think of these themes as intertwined threads that together make up the ideological fabric at the center of mega sports media events. Next, we will illustrate how these themes are played out in the 2002 and 2003 ads, before discussing some of the strains and tensions in the ads.

REAL FRIENDS, SCARY WOMEN

Five twenty-something white guys are sitting around a kitchen table playing poker. They are laughing, seemingly having the time of their lives, drinking Jim Beam whiskey. The caption for this ad reflects the lighthearted, youthful mood of the group: "Good Bourbon, ice cubes, and whichever glasses are clean." This ad, which appeared in the 2002 *Sports Illustrated* swimsuit issue, is one in a series of Jim Beam ads that have run for the past few years in *Sports Illustrated* and in other magazines aimed at young men. Running under the umbrella slogan of "Real Friends, Real Bourbon," these Jim Beam ads hail a white, college-age (or young college-educated) crowd of men with the appeal of playful male bonding through alcohol consumption in bars or pool halls. The main theme is the safety and primacy of the male group, but the accompanying written text sometimes suggests the presence of women. In one ad, four young white guys partying up a storm together and posing with arms intertwined are accompanied by the caption, "Unlike your girl-friend, they never ask where this relationship is going." These ads imply that women demand levels of emotional commitment and expression undesirable to men, while life with the boys (and the booze) is exciting, emotionally comfortable, and safe. The comfort that these ads suggest is that bonding and intimacy have clear (though mostly unspoken) boundaries that limit emotional expression in the male group. When drinking with the guys, a man can feel close to his friends, perhaps even drape an arm over a friend's shoulder, embrace him, or tell him that he loves him. But the context of alcohol consumption provides an escape hatch that contains and rationalizes the eruption of physical intimacy.

Although emotional closeness with and commitment to real women apparently are to be avoided, these ads also do suggest a role for women. The one ad in the Jim Beam series that includes an image of a woman depicts only a body part (*Sports Illustrated* ran this one in its 2000 swimsuit issue in 3-D). Four guys drinking together in a bar are foregrounded by a set of high-heeled legs that appear to be an exotic dancer's. The guys drink, laugh, and seem thoroughly amused with each other. "Our lives would make a great sitcom," the caption reads, and continues, "of course, it would have to run on cable." That the guys largely ignore the dancer affirms the strength and primacy of their bond with one another—they do not need her or any other women, the ad seems to say. On the other hand—and just as in the "Yoga Voyeurs" commercial—the female dancer's sexualizing of the chronotopic space affirms that the bond between the men is safely within the bounds of heterosexuality.

Although these ads advocate keeping one's emotional distance from women, a commitment to heterosexuality always carries the potential for developing actual relationships with women. The few ads that depict real women portray them consistently as signs of danger to individual men and to the male group. The ads imply that what men really want is sex (or at least titillation), a cold beer, and some laughs with the guys. Girlfriends and wives are undesirable because they push men to talk about feelings and demonstrate commitment to a relationship. In "Good Listener," a 2003 Super Bowl ad for Budweiser, a young white guy is sitting in a sports bar with his girlfriend while she complains about her best friend's "totally self-centered and insensitive boyfriend."

As he appears to listen to this obviously boring "girl talk," the camera pulls to a tight close-up on her face. She is reasonably attractive, but the viewer is not supposed to mistake her for one of the model-perfect fantasy women in other beer ads. The close-up reveals that her teeth are a bit crooked, her hair a bit stringy, and her face contorts as she says of her girlfriend that "she has these *emotional* needs he can't meet." Repelled, the guy spaces out and begins to peer over her shoulder at the television. The camera takes the guy's point of view and focuses on the football game while the speaking woman is in the fuzzy margins of his view. The girlfriend's monologue gets transposed by a football announcer describing an exciting run. She stops talking, and just in time his gaze shifts back to her eyes. She lovingly says, "You're such a great listener." With an "aw-shucks" smile, he says "thanks," and the "Budweiser TRUE" logo appears on the screen. These ads suggest that a sincere face and a bottle of beer allow a guy to escape the emotional needs of his partner while retaining regular access to sex. But the

Figure 11.3. Bud Lite, "Good Listner," Anheuser-Busch, 2003 Super Bowl on ABC.

apparent dangers of love, long-term commitment, and marriage remain. The most overtly misogynist ad in the 2003 Super Bowl broadcast was "Sarah's Mom." While talking on the phone to a friend, a young, somewhat nerdy-looking white guy prepares to meet his girlfriend's mother for the first time. His friend offers him this stern advice: "Well, get a good look at her. 'Cause in twenty years, that's what Sarah's gonna look like." The nerd expresses surprised concern, just as there is a knock on the door. Viewed through the door's peephole, the face of Sarah's mother appears as young and beautiful as Sarah's, but it turns out that Sarah's mother has grotesquely large hips, thighs, and buttocks. The commercial ends with the screen filled mostly with the hugeness of the mother's bottom, her leather pants audibly stretching as she bends to pet the dog, and Sarah shoveling chips and dip into her mouth, as she says of her mother, "Isn't she incredible?" The guy replies, with obvious skepticism, "yeah."

The message to boys and men is disturbing. If you are nerdy enough to be thinking about getting married, then you should listen to your male friends' warnings about what to watch out for and what is important. If you have got to have a wife, make sure that she is, and always will be, conventionally thin and beautiful.

In beer ads, the male group defines men's need for women as sexual, not emotional, and in so doing it constructs women as either whores or bitches and then suggests ways for men to negotiate the tension between these two narrow and stereotypical categories of women. This, we think, is a key point of tension that beer and liquor companies are attempting to exploit to their advantage. They do so by creating a curious shift away from the familiar "madonna-whore" dichotomy of which Western feminists have been so critical, where wives/mothers/girlfriends are put on a pedestal and the women one has sex with are put in the gutter. The alcohol industry would apparently prefer that young men not think of women as madonnas. After all, wives and girlfriends to whom men are committed, whom they respect and love, often do place limits on men's time spent out with the boys, as well as limits on men's consumption of alcohol. The industry seems to know this: as long as men remain distrustful of women, seeing them either as bitches who are trying to ensnare them and take away their freedom or as whores with whom they can party and have sex with no emotional commitment attached, then men remain more open to the marketing strategies of the industry.

WINNERS AND LOSERS

In the 2002 and 2003 Super Bowls, Budweiser's "How Ya Doin'?" ads featured the trope of a country bumpkin, or hick, in the big city to highlight the

Figure 11.4. Bud Lite, "Sarah's Mom," Anheuser-Busch, 2003 Super Bowl on ABC.

rejection of men who transgress the symbolic boundaries of the male peer group. These ads also illustrate the communication and emotional processes that police these boundaries. Men may ask each other "how's it goin'," but they do not want to hear how it's *really* goin'. It is these unspoken limits that make the group bond feel like an emotionally safe place: male buddies at the bar will not ask each other how the relationship is going or push each other to get in touch with their feminine sides. But men who transgress these boundaries, who do not understand the unwritten emotional rules of the male group, are suspect, are branded as losers, and are banished from the inner circle of the group.

REVENGE OF THE REGULAR GUYS

If losers are used in some of these ads to clarify the bounds of masculine normality, this is not to say that hypermasculine men are set up as the norm. To the contrary, overly masculine men, muscle men, and men with big cars who flash their money around are often portrayed as the real losers, against whom regular guys can sometimes turn the tables and win the beautiful women. In the ads we examined, however, this "regular guy wins beautiful fantasy woman" outcome was very rare. Instead, when the regular guy does manage to get the beautiful fantasy woman's attention, it is usually not in the way that he imagined or dreamed. A loser may want to win the attention of—and have sex with—beautiful women. But, ultimately, these women are unavailable to a loser; worse, they will publicly humiliate him if he tries to win their attention. But losers can always manage to have another beer.

If white-guy losers risk punishment or humiliation from beautiful women in these ads, the level of punishment faced by black men can be even more severe. Although nearly all of the television commercials and print ads that we examined depict white people, a very small number do focus centrally on African Americans. In "Pick-Up Lines," a Bud Lite ad that ran during the 2002 Super Bowl, two black males are sitting at a bar next to an attractive black female. Paul, the man in the middle, is obviously a loser; he's wearing a garish shirt, and his hair looks like an Afro gone terribly wrong. He sounds a bit whiny as he confides in his male friend, "I'm just not good with the ladies like you, Cedric." Cedric, playing Cyrano de Bergerac, whispers opening pickup lines to him. The loser turns to the woman and passes on the lines. But just then, the bartender brings another bottle of beer to Cedric, who asks the bartender, "So, how much?" Paul, thinking that this is his next pickup line, says to the woman, "So, how much?" Her smile turns to an angry frown, and she delivers a vicious kick to Paul's face, knocking him to the floor. After we see the Budweiser logo and hear the voice-over telling us that Bud Lite's great taste "will never let you down," we see a stunned Paul rising to his knees and trying to pull himself up to his bar stool, but the woman knocks him down again with a powerful backhand fist to the face.

This Bud Lite "Pick-Up Lines" ad—one of the very few ads that depict relations between black men and black women—was the only ad in which we saw a man being physically beaten by a woman. Here, the African American woman as object turns to subject, inflicting direct physical punishment on the African American man. The existence of these very few "black ads" brings into relief something that might otherwise remain hidden: most of these ads construct a youthful white masculinity that is playfully self-mocking, always a bit tenuous, but ultimately lovable. The screwups that white-guy losers make are forgivable, and we nearly always see these men, in the end, with at least a cold beer in hand. By contrast, the intersection of race, gender, and class creates cultural and institutional contexts of suspicion and punishment for African American boys and men (Ferguson 2000). In the beer ads this translates into the message that a black man's transgressions are apparently deserving of a kick to the face.

EROTIC INTERTEXTUALITY

One of the dominant strategies in beer and liquor ads is to create an (often humorous) erotic tension among members of a "threesome": the male reader/viewer, a woman depicted as a sexy fantasy object, and a bottle of cold beer. This tension is accomplished through intertextual referencing between the advertising text and the sport text. For instance, on returning to live coverage of the Super Bowl from a commercial break, the camera regularly lingered on the stadium scoreboard, above which was a huge Budweiser sign. One such occasion during the 2003 Super Bowl was particularly striking. Coors had just run its only commercial (an episode from its successful "twins" series) during this mega sports media event that seemed otherwise practically owned by Anheuser-Busch. Immediately on return from the commercial break to live action, the handheld field-level camera focused one by one on dancing cheerleaders (once coming so close that it appears that the camera bumped into one of the women's breasts), all the while keeping the Budweiser sign in focus in the background. It was almost as though the producers of the Super Bowl were intent on not allowing the Coors "twins" to upstage Anheuser-Busch's ownership of the event.

Omnipresent advertising images in recent years have continued to obliterate the already blurry distinction between advertising texts and other media texts (Goldman and Papson 1996). This is surely true in the world of sport: players' uniforms, stadium walls, the corner of one's television screen,

Figure 11.5. Bud Lite, "Pick-Up Lines," Anheuser-Busch, 2002 Super Bowl on ABC.

and even moments within telecasts are regularly branded with the Nike swoosh or some other corporate sign. Stephanie O'Donohoe argues that "popular texts have 'leaky boundaries,' flowing into each other and everyday life.... This seems especially true of advertising" (1997, 257–258). The "leakiness" of cultural signs in advertising is facilitated, O'Donohoe argues, "by increasing institutional ties between advertising, commercial media, and mass entertainment. . . . Conglomeration breeds intertextuality" (257–258). When ads appropriate or make explicit reference to other media (e.g., other ads, celebrities, movies, television shows, or popular music), they engage in what Robert Goldman and Stephen Papson call "cultural cannibalism" (1998, 10). Audiences are then invited to make the connections between the advertised product and the cultural meanings implied by the cannibalized sign; in so doing, the audience becomes "the final author, whose participation is essential" (O'Donohoe 1997, 259). As with all textual analyses that do not include an audience study, we must be cautious in inferring how differently situated audiences might variously take up, and draw meanings from, these ads. However, we suspect that experiences of "authorship" in the process of decoding and drawing intertextual connections are a major part of the pleasure of viewing mass media texts.

The 2002 and 2003 *Sports Illustrated* swimsuit issues offer vivid examples of texts that invite the reader to draw intertextual connections between erotically charged ads and other non-ad texts. Whereas in the past the *Sports Illustrated* swimsuit issue ran ads that were clearly distinct from the swimsuit text, it has recently become more common for the visual themes in the ads and the swimsuit text to be playfully intertwined, symbiotically referencing each other. A 2003 Heineken ad shows a close-up of two twenty-four-ounce "keg cans" of Heineken beer, side by side. The text above the two cans reads, "They're big. And yeah, they're real." As if the reference to swimsuit models' breast size (and questions about whether some of the models have breast implants) were perhaps too subtle, *Sports Illustrated* juxtaposed the ad with a photo of a swimsuit model, wearing a suit that liberally exposed her breasts.

For the advertisers and for *Sports Illustrated*, the payoff for this kind of intertextual coordination is probably large: for the reader, the text of the swimsuit issue becomes increasingly seamless, as ads and swimsuit text melt into each other, playfully, humorously, and erotically referencing each other. As with the Super Bowl ads, the *Sports Illustrated* swimsuit issue ads become something that viewers learn not to ignore or skip over; instead, the ads become another part of the pleasure of consuming and imagining.

In 2003, Miller Brewing Company and *Sports Illustrated* further developed the symbiotic marketing strategy that they had introduced in 2002. The 2003 swimsuit issue featured a huge Miller Lite ad that included the equivalent of fourteen full pages of ad text. Twelve of these pages were a large, pull-out

Figure 11.6. Heineken ad juxtaposed with *Sports Illustrated* swimsuit model, *Sports Illustrated* swimsuit issue, 2003.

poster, one side of which was a single photo of "Sophia," a young model wearing a bikini with the Miller Lite logo on the right breast cup. On the opposite side of the poster were four one-page photos and one two-page photo of Sophia posing in various bikinis, with Miller Lite bottles and/or logos visible in each picture.

As it did in the 2002 ad, Miller invites viewers to enter a contest to win a trip to the next *Sports Illustrated* swimsuit issue photo shoot. The site of the photo shoot fuses the text-based space of the magazine with the real space of the working models in exotic, erotic landscapes of desire that highlight the sexuality of late capitalist colonialism (Davis 1997). The accompanying text invites the reader to "visit http://www.cnnsi.com" to "check out a 360 degree view of the *Sports Illustrated* swimsuit photo shoot." And the text accompanying most of the photos of Sophia and bottles of Miller Lite teasingly encourages the reader to exercise his consumer power: "So if you had to make a choice, which one would it be?"

This expansive ad evidences a multilevel symbiosis between *Sports Illustrated* and Miller Brewing Company. The playful tease to "choose your favorite" (model, swimsuit, and/or beer) invites the reader to enter another medium—the *Sports Illustrated* swimsuit Web site, which includes access to a *Sports Illustrated* swimsuit photo shoot video sponsored by Miller. The result is a multifaceted media text that stands out as something other than mere advertisement and other than business-as-usual *Sports Illustrated* text. It has an erotic and commercial charge to it that simultaneously teases the reader as a sexual voyeur and hails him as an empowered consumer who can freely choose his own beer and whichever sexy woman he decides is his "favorite."

"LIFE IS HARSH": MALE LOSERS AND ALCOHOLIC ACCOMMODATION

In recent years, the tendency in the *Sports Illustrated* swimsuit issue to position male readers as empowered individuals who can "win" or freely choose the sexy fantasy object of their dreams has begun to shift in other directions. To put it simply, many male readers of the swimsuit issue may find the text erotically charged, but most know that these are two-dimensional images of sexy women who in real life are unavailable to them. In recent years, some swimsuit issue ads have delivered this message directly. In 1997, a two-page ad for Tequila Sauza depicted six women in short red skirts, posing flirtatiously, some of them lifting their blouses provocatively to reveal bare midriffs, or opening their blouses to reveal parts of their breasts. In small letters, across the six women's waists, stretching all the way across the two pages, the text reads, "We can say with 99.9% accuracy that there is no possible way whatsoever in

Figure 11.7. Miller Lite, "Choose Your Favorite," Anheuser-Busch, *Sports Illustrated* swimsuit issue, 2003.

this lifetime that you will ever get a date with one of these women." Then, to the side of the ad is written "LIFE IS HARSH. Your tequila shouldn't be." A similar message appears in other ads. For instance, in the 1999 swimsuit issue, a full-page photo of a Heineken bottle included the written text "The only heiny in this magazine you could actually get your hands on."

These ads play directly to the male reader as loser and invite him to accommodate to his loser status, to recognize that these sexy fantasy women, though "real," are unavailable to him, and to settle for what he can have: a good bottle of Tequila Sauza or a cold (rather than a hot) "Heiny." The Bud Lite Super Bowl commercials strike a similar chord. Many Bud Lite ads either titillate the viewer with sexy fantasy women, point to the ways that relationships with real women are to be avoided, or do both simultaneously. The break that appears near the end of each Bud Lite ad contrasts sharply with the often negative depiction of men's relations with real women in the ad's story line. The viewer sees a close-up of a bottle of Bud Lite. The bottle's cap explodes off, and beer ejaculates out, as a male voice-over proclaims what a man truly can rely on in life: "For the great taste that won't fill you up, and never lets you down...make it a Bud Lite."

REVENGE OF THE LOSERS

The accommodation theme in these ads may succeed, momentarily, in encouraging a man to shift his feelings of being a sexual loser toward manly feelings of empowerment through the consumption of brand-name beers and liquor. If the women in the ads are responsible for heightening tensions that result in some men's sense of themselves as losers, one possible outcome beyond simply drinking a large amount of alcohol (or one that accompanies the consumption of alcohol) is to express anger toward women and even to take revenge against them. This is precisely a direction that some of the recent ads have taken.

A full-page ad in the 2002 swimsuit issue showed a large photo of a bottle of Maker's Mark Whiskey. The bottle's reflection on the shiny table on which it sits is distorted in a way that suggests an hourglass-shaped female torso. The text next to the bottle reads, "'Your bourbon has a great body and fine character. I WISH the same could be said for my girlfriend.' D. T., Birmingham, AL." This one-page ad is juxtaposed with a full-page photo of a *Sports Illustrated* model, provocatively using her thumb to begin to pull down the right side of her bikini bottom.

Together, the ad text and *Sports Illustrated* text angrily express the bitch-whore dichotomy that we discussed above. D. T.'s girlfriend is not pictured, but the description of her clearly indicates that not only does she lack a beautiful

Figure 11.8. "Great Body," *Sports Illustrated* swimsuit model juxtaposed with Maker's Mark Whiskey ad, *Sports Illustrated*, swimsuit issue, 2002.

body; worse, she's a bitch. While D. T.'s girlfriend symbolizes the real woman whom each guy tolerates, and to whom he avoids committing, the juxtaposed *Sports Illustrated* model is the beautiful and sexy fantasy woman. She is unavailable to the male reader in real life; her presence as fantasy image highlights that the reader, like D. T., is stuck, apparently, with his bitchy girlfriend. But at least he can enjoy a moment of pseudo-empowerment by consuming a Maker's Mark whiskey and by insulting his girlfriend's body and character. Together, the Maker's Mark ad and the juxtaposed *Sports Illustrated* model provide a context for the reader to feel hostility toward the real women in his life.

This kind of symbolic male revenge toward women is expressed in a different way in a four-page Captain Morgan rum ad that appeared in the 2003 *Sports Illustrated* swimsuit issue. On the first page, we see only the hands of the cartoon character "Captain Morgan" holding a fire hose spraying water into the air over what appears to be a tropical beach. When one turns the page, a three-page foldout ad reveals that "the Captain" is spraying what appears to be a *Sports Illustrated* swimsuit issue photo shoot. Six young women in tiny bikinis are laughing, perhaps screaming, and running for cover (five of them are huddled under an umbrella with a grinning male character who looks suspiciously like Captain Morgan). The spray from the fire hose causes the women's bathing suits to melt right off their bodies. The readers do not know if the swimsuits are painted on or are made of meltable candy or if perhaps Captain Morgan's ejaculate is just that powerfully corrosive. One way or the other, the image suggests that Captain Morgan is doing a service to the millions of boys and men who read this magazine. Written across a fleeing woman's thigh, below her melting bikini bottom, the text reads "Can you say birthday suit issue?"

Two men—apparently photographers—stand to the right of the photo, arms raised to the heavens (with their clothing fully intact). The men in the picture seem ecstatic with religious fervor. The male reader is perhaps invited to identify with these regular guys: like them, he is always good enough to look at these beautiful women in their swimsuits but never good enough to get them to take it off for him. But here, "the Captain" was clever enough to strip the women naked so that he and all of his male buddies could enjoy a vengeful moment of voyeurism. The relational gender and sexual dynamics of this ad—presented here without overt anger and with cartoonish humor—allegorize the common dynamics of group sexual assaults (Beneke 1982). These sexy women have teased men enough, the ad suggests. First they arouse men, and then they inevitably make them feel like losers. They deserve to be stripped naked against their will. As in many male rape fantasies, the ad suggests that women ultimately find that they like it. And all of this action is facilitated by a bottle of rum, the Captain's magical essence.

Figure 11.9. Captain Morgan Rum, "Can you say birthday suit issue?" *Sports Illustrated* swimsuit issue, 2003.

TENSION, STABILIZATION, AND MASCULINE CONSUMPTION

We argued in our introduction that contemporary social changes have destabilized hegemonic masculinity. Examining beer and liquor ads in mega sports media events gives us a window into the ways that commercial forces have seized on these destabilizing tendencies, constructing pedagogical fantasy narratives that aim to appeal to a very large group—eighteen- to thirty-four-year-old men. They do so by appealing to a broad zeitgeist among young (especially white, heterosexual) men that is grounded in widespread tensions in the contemporary gender order. The sexual and gender themes of the beer and liquor ads that we examine in this chapter do not stand alone; rather they reflect, and in turn contribute to, broader trends in popular culture and marketing to young white males. Television shows like *The Man Show*, new soft-core porn magazines like *Maxim* and *FHM*, and radio talk shows like the syndicated "Tom Leykus Show" share similar themes and are targeted to similar audiences of young males. Indeed, radio talk show hosts like Leykus didactically instruct young men to avoid "girlie" things, to eschew emotional commitment, and to think of women primarily as sexual partners (Messner 2002, 107–108). The chronotope of these magazines and television and radio shows constructs young male lifestyles saturated with sexy images of nearly naked, surgically enhanced women; unabashed and unapologetic sexual voyeurism shared by groups of laughing men; and explicit talk of sexual exploits with "hotties" or "juggies." A range of consumer products that includes—often centrally, as in *The Man Show*—consumption of beer as part of the young male lifestyle stitches together this erotic bonding among men. Meanwhile, real women are either absent from these media or they are disparaged as gold diggers (yes, this term has been resuscitated) who use sex to get men to spend money on them and trick them into marriage. The domesticated man is viewed as a wimpy victim who has subordinated his own pleasures (and surrendered his paychecks) to a woman. Within this framework, a young man should have sex with as many women as he can while avoiding (or at least delaying) emotional commitments to any one woman. Freedom from emotional commitment grants 100% control over disposable income for monadic consumption and care of self. And that is ultimately what these shows are about: constructing a young male consumer characterized by personal and emotional freedom who can attain a hip lifestyle by purchasing an ever-expanding range of automobile-related products, snack foods, clothes, toiletries, and, of course, beer and liquor.

At first glance, these new media aimed at young men seem to resuscitate a 1950s "*Playboy* philosophy" of men's consumption, sexuality, and gender relations (Ehrenreich 1983). Indeed, these new media strongly reiterate the dichotomous bitch–whore view of women that was such a lynch-pin of Hugh Hefner's "philosophy." But today's tropes of masculinity do not simply reiterate the past; rather, they give a postfeminist twist to the *Playboy* philosophy. A half-century ago, Hefner's pitch to men to recapture the indoors by creating (purchasing) one's own erotic "bachelor pad" in which to have sex with women (and then send them home) read as a straightforwardly masculine project. By contrast, today's sexual and gender pitch to young men is delivered with an ironic, self-mocking wink that operates, we think, on two levels.

First, it appears to acknowledge that most young men are neither the heroes of the indoors (as Hefner would have it) nor of the outdoors (as the 1970s and 1980s beer ads suggested). Instead, the ads seem to recognize that young white men's unstable status leaves them always on the verge of being revealed as losers. The ads plant seeds of insecurity on this fertile landscape, with the goal of creating a white guy who is a consistent and enthusiastic consumer of alcoholic beverages. The irony works on a second level as well: the throwback sexual and gender imagery—especially the bitch-whore dichotomization of women—is clearly a defensively misogynistic backlash against feminism and women's increasing autonomy and social power. The wink and self-mocking irony allow men to have it both ways: they can engage in humorous misogynist banter and claim simultaneously that it is all in play. They do not take themselves seriously, so anyone who takes their misogyny as anything but boys having good fun just has no sense of humor. The humorous irony works, then, to deflect charges of sexism away from white males, allowing them to define themselves as victims, as members of an endangered species. We suspect, too, that this is a key part of the process that constructs the whiteness in current reconstructions of hegemonic masculinity. As we have suggested, humorous "boys-will-be-boys" misogyny is unlikely to be taken ironically and lightly when delivered by men of color.

The white-guy-as-loser trope, though fairly new to beer and liquor ads, is certainly not new to U.S. media. Part of the irony of this character is not that he is a loser in every sense; rather he signifies the typical everyman who is only a loser in comparison to versions of masculinity more typical to beer and liquor ads past—that is, the rugged guys who regularly get the model-beautiful women. Caught between the excesses of a hypermasculinity that is often discredited and caricatured in popular culture and the increasing empowerment of women, people of color, and homosexuals, while simultaneously being undercut by the postindustrial economy, the "Average Joe" is positioned as the ironic, vulnerable but lovable hero of beer and liquor ads. It is striking that the loser is not, or is rarely, your "Jose Mediano," especially if we understand the construction as a way to unite diverse eighteen- to thirty-four-year-old men. This is to say that the loser motif constructs the universal subject as implicitly white, and as a reaction against challenges to hegemonic masculinity it represents an ongoing possessive investment in whiteness (Lipsitz 1998).

Our analysis suggests that the fact that male viewers today are being hailed as losers and are being asked to identify with—even revel in—their loser status has its limits. The beer and liquor industry dangles images of sexy women in front of men's noses. Indeed, the ads imply that men will go out of their way to put themselves in position to be voyeurs, be it with a television remote control, at a yoga class, in a bar, or on the *Sports Illustrated* Miller

Beer swimsuit photo shoot Web site. But, ultimately, men know (and are increasingly being told in the advertisements themselves) that these sexy women are not available to them. Worse, if men get too close to these women, these women will most likely humiliate them. By contrast, real women—women who are not model-beautiful fantasy objects—are likely to attempt to ensnare men into a commitment, push them to have or express feelings that make them uncomfortable, and limit their freedom to have fun watching sports or playing cards or pool with their friends. So, in the end, men have only the safe haven of their male friends and the bottle.

This individual sense of victimization may feed young men's insecurities while giving them convenient scapegoats on which to project anger at their victim status. The cultural construction of white males as losers, then, is tethered to men's anger at and desire for revenge against women. Indeed, we have observed that revenge-against-women themes are evident in some of the most recent beer and liquor ads. And it is here that our analysis comes full circle. For, as we suggested in the introduction, the cultural imagery in ads aimed at young men does not simply come from images "out there." Instead, this imagery is linked to the ways that real people live their lives. It is the task of future research—including audience research—to investigate and flesh out the specific links between young men's consumption of commercial images, their consumption of beer and liquor, their attitudes toward and relationships with women, and their tendencies to drink and engage in violence against women.

Appendix Commercials and Advertisements in the Sample

2002 Super Bowl: Michelob Lite, "Free to Be" Budweiser, "Robobash" Budweiser, "Pick-Up Lines" Bud Lite, "Hawk" Budweiser, "Clydesdales" Bud Lite, "Greeting Cards" Budweiser, "How Ya Doin'?" Bud Lite, "Black Teddy" Budweiser, "Meet the Parents" Budweiser, "History of Budweiser" Budweiser, "Designated Driver" Smirnoff Ice

2003 Super Bowl: Budweiser, "Zebras" Bud Lite, "Refrigerator" Bud Lite, "Clown" Bud Lite, "Rasta Dog" Bud Lite, "Conch" Bud Lite, "Date Us Both" Smirnoff Lite, "Blind Date" Bud Lite, "Sarah's Mom" Bud Lite, "Three Arms" Coors, "Twins" Budweiser, "Good Listener" Budweiser, "'How Ya Doin'?' Redux" Michelob Ultra, "Low-Carb Bodies" Bud Lite, "Yoga Voyeurs"

2002 *Sports Illustrated* swimsuit issue (no. of pages): Miller Lite (2), Jim Beam (1), Miller Genuine Draft (2, plus card insert), Heineken (1), Budweiser (1), Captain Morgan Rum (1), Martell (1), Sam Adams Utopia (1), Maker's Mark Whiskey (1), Bicardi Rum (1.25), Jose Cuervo Tequila (1), Crown Royal (1), Chivas (1)

2003 *Sports Illustrated* swimsuit issue (no. of pages): Budweiser (1), Jose Cuervo Tequila (1), Smirnoff Vodka (1), Captain Morgan Rum (4), Seagrams (1), Miller Lite (11, including poster pullout), Crown Royal (1), Heineken (1), Skyy Vodka (1), Knob Whiskey (1), Chivas (1)

Bibliography

Acker, Joan. 1990. "Hierarchies, Jobs, Bodies: A Theory of Gendered Organizations." *Gender and Society* 4:139–158.

Adler, Patricia A., and Peter Adler. 1998. *Peer Power: Preadolescent Culture and Identity*. New Brunswick, NJ: Rutgers University Press.

Alt, John. 1983. "Sport and Cultural Reification: From Ritual to Mass Consumption." *Theory Culture and Society* 13:93–107.

Amateur Athletic Foundation of Los Angeles. 1999. *Children and Sports Media*. Los Angeles: Author.

Anderson, Elijah. 1990. *Streetwise: Race, Class, and Change in an Urban Community*. Chicago: University of Chicago Press.

Attfield, Judy. 1996. Barbie and Action Man: Adult Toys for Girls and Boys, 1959–93. Pp. 80–89 in *The Gendered Object*, edited by Pat Kirkham. Manchester, UK, and New York: Manchester University Press.

Atyeo, Don. 1979. *Blood and Guts: Violence in Sports*. New York: Paddington Press.

Baca Zinn, Maxine. 1982. "Chicano Men and Masculinity." *Journal of Ethnic Studies* 10:29–44.

Baca Zinn, Maxine, and Bonnie Dill Thornton. 1996. "Theorizing Difference from Multiracial Feminism." *Feminist Studies* 22 (2):321–331.

Baca Zinn, Maxine, Lynn Weber Canon, Elizabeth Higginbotham, and Bonnie Dill Thornton, 1986. "The Cost of Exclusionary Practices in Women's Studies." *Signs: Journal of Women in Culture and Society* 11:290–303.

Bagdikian, Ben H. 1990. *The Media Monopoly*. 3rd ed. Boston: Beacon Press.

Bakhtin, Mikhail. 1981. "Forms of Time and the Chronotope in the Novel." Pp 84–258 in *The Dialogic Imagination: Four Essays*, trans. Caryl Emerson and Michael Holmquist. Austin: University of Texas Press.

Banet-Weiser, Sarah. 1999. *The Most Beautiful Girl in the World: Beauty Pageants and National Identity*. Berkeley: University of California Press.

Banner, Louis W. 1983. *American Beauty*. Chicago: University of Chicago Press.

Beck, B. A. 1980. The Future of Women's Sport: Issues, Insights, and Struggle. Pp. 299–314 in *Jock: Sports and Male Identity*, edited by Don Sabo and Ross Runfola. Englewood Cliffs, NJ: Prentice-Hall.

Benedict, Jeffrey. 1998. *Athletes and Acquaintance Rape*. Thousand Oaks, CA: Sage Publications.

Benedict, Jeffrey, and Alan Klein 1997. "Arrest and Conviction Rates for Athletes Accused of Sexual Assault." *Sociology of Sport Journal* 14:73–85.

Beneke, Timothy. 1982. *Men on Rape*. New York: St. Martin's.

Benjamin, Jessica. 1988. *The Bonds of Love: Psychoanalysis, Feminism, and the Problem of Domination*. New York: Pantheon.

Bennett, Roberta S., K. Gail Whitaker, Nina Jo Wooley Smith, and Anne Sablove. 1987. "Changing the Rules of the Game: Reflections Towards a Feminist Analysis of Sport." *Women's Studies International Forum* 10(4).

Berghorn, Forrest J., Norman Yetman, and William Hanna. 1988. " Racial Participation and Integration in Men's and Women's Intercollegiate Basketball: Continuity and Change, 1958–1985." *Sociology of Sport Journal* 5:107–124.

Bianchi, Eugene C. 1980: "The Super Bowl Culture of Male Violence." Pp. 117–130 in *Jock: Sports and Male Identity*, edited by Don Sabo and Ross Runfola. Englewood Cliffs, NJ: Prentice-Hall.

Birrell, Susan. 1984. Studying Gender in Sport: A Feminist Perspective. Pp. 125–135 in *Sport and the Sociological Imagination*, edited by Nancy Theberge and Patricia Donnelly. Fort Worth: Texas Christian University Press.

———. 1989. "Racial Relations and Sport: Suggestions for a More Critical Analysis." *Sociology of Sport Journal* 6: 212–227.

———. 1990. Women of Color, Critical Autobiography, and Sport. Pp. 185–189 in *Sport, Men and the Gender Order: Critical Feminist Perspectives*, edited by Michael A. Messner and Don F. Sabo. Champaign, IL: Human Kinetics.

Biskind, Peter, and Barbara Ehrenreich. 1980: "Machismo and Hollywood's Working Class." *Socialist Review* 10 (2/3).

Boeringer, Scot B. 1996. "Influences of Fraternity Membership, Athletics and Male Living Arrangements on Sexual Aggression." *Violence Against Women* 2: 134–147.

Boswell, A. Ayres, and Joan Z. Spade. 1996. "Fraternities and Collegiate Gang Rape: Why Some Fraternities Are More Dangerous Places for Women," *Gender and Society* 10: 133–147.

Boutilier, Mary A., and Lucinda L. San Giovanni. 1983. *The Sporting Woman.* Champaign, IL: Human Kinetics.

Boyle, Maree, and Jim McKay. 1995. "'You Leave Your Troubles at the Gate': A Case Study of the Exploitation of Older Women's Labor and 'Leisure' in Sport." *Gender and Society* 9:556–576.

Bradbard, Marilyn. 1985. "Sex Differences in Adults' Gifts and Children's Toy Requests." *Journal of Genetic Psychology* 145: 283–284.

Bredemeier, Brenda J. 1983: Athletic Aggression: A Moral Concern. Pp. 47–82 in *Sports Violence* edited by Jeffrey H. Goldstein. New York: Springer-Verlag.

Bredemeier, Brenda J., and David L. Shields. 1986: "Athletic Aggression: An Issue of Contextual Morality." *Sociology of Sport Journal* 3: 15–28.

Brod, Harry. 1983–1984. "Work Clothes and Leisure Suits: The Class Basis and Bias of the Men's Movement." *M: Gentle Men for Gender Justice* 11: 10–12, 38–40.

———, ed. 1987. *The Making of Masculinities: The New Men's Studies.* Boston: Allen and Unwin.

Brohm, Jean M. 1978. *Sport: A Prison of Measured Time.* London: Ink Links.

Brown, Sandra A., M. S. Goldman, A. Inn, and L. R. Anderson. 1980. "Expectations of Reinforcement from Alcohol: Their Domain and Relation to Drinking Patterns." *Journal Consulting and Clinical Psychology* 48: 419–426.

Brownmiller, Susan. 1975. *Against Our Will: Men, Women and Rape.* New York: Simon and Schuster.

———. 1984. *Femininity.* New York: Fawcett Columbine.

Bryant, J. 1980. "A Two-Year Investigation of the Female in Sport as Reported in the Paper Media." *Arena Review* 4: 32–44.

Bryson, L. 1987. "Sport and the Maintenance of Masculine Hegemony." *Women's Studies International Forum* 10, 349–360.

Butler, Judith. 1990. *Gender Trouble: Feminism and the Subversion of Identity.* New York and London: Routledge.

Cahn, Susan K. 1994. *Coming on Strong: Gender and Sexuality in Twentieth Century Women's Sport.* New York: Free Press.

Calahan, Don. 1970. *Problem Drinkers: A National Survey.* San Francisco: Jossey-Bass.

Campenni, C. Estelle. 1999. "Gender Stereotyping of Children's Toys: A Comparison of Parents and Nonparents." *Sex Roles* 40:121–138.

Canada, Jeffrey. 1995. *Fist Stick Knife Gun: A Personal History of Violence in America.* Boston: Beacon Press.

Carpenter, Linda J. 1993. Letters Home: My Life with Title IX. Pp. 79–94 in *Women in Sport: Issues and Controversies*, edited by Greta L. Cohen. Newbury Park, CA: Sage.

Carrigan, Tim, Bob Connell, and John Lee. 1987. Toward a New Sociology of Masculinity. In *The Making of Masculinities: The New Men's Studies*, pp. 63–100, edited by Harry Brod. Boston: Allen and Unwin.

Cayleff, Susan E. 1995. *Babe: The Life and Legend of Babe Didrikson Zaharias.* Urbana: University of Illinois Press.

Chalip, Laurence. 1990. "Rethinking the Applied Social Sciences of Sport: Observations on the Emerging Debate." *Sociology of Sport Journal* 7:172–178.

Chodorow, Nancy J. 1978. *The Reproduction of Mothering.* Berkeley: University of California Press.

———. 1999. *The Power of Feelings: Personal Meanings in Psychoanalysis, Gender, and Culture.* New Haven, and London: Yale University Press.

Clarke, Alan, and John Clarke. 1982. Highlights and Action Replays: Ideology, Sport, and the Media. Pp. 62–87 in *Sport, Culture, and Ideology*, edited by J. Hargreaves. London: Routledge and Kegan Paul.

Clarke, Stuart A. 1991. "Fear of a Black Planet." *Socialist Review* 21:37–59. July–December.

Coakley, Jay. 1978. *Sport in Society: Issues and Controversies.* St. Louis: Mosby.

Cole, CL 1994. Resisting the Canon: Feminist Cultural Studies, Sport, and Technologies of the Body. Pp. 5–29 in *Women, Sport, and Culture*, edited by S. Birrell and CL Cole. Champaign, IL: Human Kinetics.

Cole, CL, and Amy Hribar. 1995. "Celebrity Feminism: Nike Style, Post Fordism, Transcendence, and Consumer Power." *Sociology of Sport Journal* 12:347–369.

Coleman, D., and Murray A. Straus. 1983. Alcohol Abuse and Family Violence. Pp. 104–124 in *Alcohol, Drug Abuse and Aggression*, edited by E. Gottheil, K. A. Druley, T. E. Koloda, and H. M. Waxman. Springfield, IL: Charles C Thomas.

Collins, Patricia Hill. 1990. *Black Feminist Thought: Knowledge, Consciousness, and the Politics of Empowerment*. Boston: Unwin Hyman.

Collins, Tony, and Wray Vamplew. 2002. *Mud, Sweat, and Beers: A Cultural History of Sport and Alcohol*. New York: Berg.

Connell, R. W. 1985: Masculinity, Violence and War. In *War/Masculinity*, edited by P. Patton and R. Poole. Sydney: Intervention Pub.

———. 1987. *Gender and Power*. Stanford: Stanford University Press.

———. 1989. "Cool Guys, Swots and Wimps: The Interplay of Masculinity and Education." *Oxford Review of Education* 15:291–303.

———. 1990. An Iron Man: The Body and Some Contradictions of Hegemonic Masculinity. Pp. 83–96. In *Sport, Men and the Gender Order: Critical Feminist Perspectives*, edited by M. A. Messner and D. F. Sabo. Champaign, IL: Human Kinetics.

———. 1995. *Masculinities*. Berkeley: University of California Press.

Critcher, Chas. 1986. "Radical Theorists of Sport: The State of Play." *Sociology of Sport Journal* 3:333–343.

Crittenden, Ann. 1979. Closing the Muscle Gap. Pp. 5–10 in *Out of the Bleachers: Writings on Women and Sport*, edited by S. L. Twin. Old Westbury, NY: Feminist Press.

Crosset, Todd W. 1990. Masculinity, Sexuality and the Development of Early Modern Sport. Pp. 45–54 in *Sport, Men and the Gender Order: Critical Feminist Perspectives*, edited by M. A. Messner and D. F. Sabo. Champaign, IL: Human Kinetics.

———. 2000. Athletic Affiliation and Violence Against Women: Toward a Structural Prevention Project. Pp. 147–161 in *Masculinities, Gender*

Relations, and Sport, edited by J. McKay, D. F. Sabo, and M. A. Messner. Thousand Oaks, CA: Sage Publications.

Crosset, Todd W., Jeffrey R. Benedict, and Mark McDonald. 1995. "Male Student Athletes Reported for Sexual Assault: A Survey of Campus Police Departments and Judicial Affairs Offices." *Journal of Sport and Social Issues* 19:126–140.

Crosset, Todd W., J. Ptacek, Mary MacDonald, and Jeffrey R. Benedict. 1996. "Male Student Athletes and Violence Against Women: A Survey of Campus Judicial Affairs Offices." *Violence Against Women* 2:163–179.

Curry, Timothy J. 1991. "Fraternal Bonding in the Locker room: A Profeminist Analysis of Talk about Competition and Women." *Sociology of Sport Journal* 8:119–135.

———. 2000. Booze and Bar Fights: A Journey to the Dark Side of College Athletics. Pp. 162–175 in *Masculinities, Gender Relations, and Sport*, edited by J. McKay, D. F. Sabo, and M. A. Messner. Thousand Oaks, CA: Sage.

Davis, Angela. 1981. *Women, Race and Class*. New York: Vintage Books.

Davis, Laurel L. 1997. *The Swimsuit Issue and Sport: Hegemonic Masculinity in Sports Illustrated*. Albany: State University of New York Press.

Dayan, Daniel, and Elihu Katz. 1988. Articulating Consensus: The Ritual and Rhetoric of Media Events. Pp. 161–186 in *Durkheimian Sociology: Cultural Studies*, edited by J. C. Alexander. Cambridge: Cambridge University Press.

Dobash, R. Emerson, Russell P. Dobash, Margo Wilson, and Martin Daly.1992. "The Myth of Sexual Symmetry in Marital Violence." *Social Problems* 39:71–91.

Donohew, Lewis, David Helm, and John Haas. 1989. Drugs and Len Bias on the Sports Page. Pp. 225–239 in *Media, Sports, and Society*, edited by L. A. Wenner. Newbury Park, CA: Sage.

Dreier, Peter. 1982. "The Position of the Press in the U.S. Power Structure." *Social Problems* 29:298–310.

Dubbert, Joe L. 1979. *A Man's Place: Masculinity in Transition*. Englewood Cliffs, NJ: Prentice-Hall.

DuCille, Anne. 1994. "Dyes and Dolls: Multicultural Barbie and the Merchandising of Difference." *Differences: A Journal of Cultural Studies* 6:46–68.

Duncan, Margaret C. 1990. "Sports Photographs and Sexual Difference: Images of Women and Men in the 1984 and 1988 Olympic Games." *Sociology of Sport Journal* 7:22–43.

Duncan, Margaret C., and Cynthia A. Hasbrook. 1988. "Denial of Power in Televised Women's Sports." *Sociology of Sport Journal* 5:1–21.

Duncan, Margaret C., and Michael A. Messner. 1998. The Media Image of Sport and Gender. Pp. 170–195 in *MediaSport*, edited by L. A. Wenner. New York: Routledge.

Duncan, Margaret C., and Amoun Sayaovong. 1990. "Photographic Images and Gender in *Sports Illustrated for Kids.*" *Play and Culture* 3:91–116.

Duncan, Margaret C., Michael A. Messner, and Linda Williams. 1991, January. *Coverage of Women's Sports in Four Daily Newspapers*. Research Report. Los Angeles: Amateur Athletic Foundation of Los Angeles.

Dunkle, M. 1985. "Minority and Low-Income Girls and Young Women in Athletics." *Equal Play* 5 (Spring–Summer):12–13.

Dunn, Robert. 1986. "Television, Consumption, and the Commodity Form." *Theory Culture and Society* 3(1):49–64.

Dunning, Eric. 1986. Sport as a Male Preserve: Notes on the Social Sources of Masculine Identity and its Transformations." Pp. 79–90 in *Quest for Excitement: Sport and Leisure in the Civilizing Process*, edited by N. Elias and E. Dunning. Oxford: Basil Blackwell.

Duquin, Mary E. 1984. "Power and Authority: Moral Consensus and Conformity in Sport." *International Review for Sociology of Sport* 19: 295–304.

Dworkin, Shari L., and Michael A. Messner. 1999. Just Do...what?: Sport, Bodies, Gender. Pp. 341–361 in *Revisioning Gender*, edited by M. Marx Ferree, J. Lorber, and B. B. Hess. Thousand Oaks, CA: Sage.

Dyer, Ken. 1983. *Challenging the Men: The Social Biology of Female Span Achievement*. St. Lucia: University of Queensland Press.

"Editorial." 1986, September. *Muscle and Beauty*, pp. 5–6.

Edwards, Harry. 1971. "The Myth of the Racially Superior Athlete." *The Black Scholar* 3 November.

———. 1973. *The Sociology of Sport*. Homewood, IL: Dorsey.

———. 1984. "The Collegiate Athletic Arms Race: Origins and Implications of the 'Rule 48' Controversy." *Journal of Sport and Social Issues* 8:4–22.

Ehrenreich, Barbara. 1983. *The Hearts of Men: American Dreams and the Flight from Commitment.* New York: Anchor Doubleday.

Eitzen, D. Stanley, and Dean A. Purdy. 1986. "The Academic Preparation and Achievement of Black and White College Athletes." *Journal of Sport and Social Issues* 10:15–29.

Eitzen, D. Stanly. and Norman R. Yetman. 1977. "Immune from Racism?" *Civil Rights Digest* 9:3–13.

Etaugh, C., and M. B. Liss. 1992. "Home, School, and Playroom: Training Grounds for Adult Gender Roles." *Sex Roles* 26:129–147.

Ewing, Wayne. 1982. "The Civic Advocacy of Violence." *M: Gentle Men for Gender Justice* 8, Spring.

Farr, Kathryn A. 1988. "Dominance Bonding Through the Good Old Boys Sociability Group." *Sex Roles* 18:259–277.

Fausto-Sterling, Ann. 1985. *Myths of Gender: Biological Theories About Women and Men.* New York: Basic Books.

Ferguson, Ann Arnett. 2000. *Bad Boys: Public Schools in the Making of Black Masculinity.* Ann Arbor: University of Michigan Press.

Ferris, Elizabeth. 1978. *Sportswomen and Medicine.* Report of the First International Conference on Women and Sport.

Filene, Peter G. 1975. *Him/Her/Self: Sex Roles in Modern America.* New York: Harcourt Brace Jovanovich.

Fine, Gary Alan. 1987. *With the Boys: Little League Baseball and Preadolescent Culture.* Chicago: University of Chicago Press.

Fleck, Joseph H., 1982: *The Myth of Masculinity.* Cambridge: MIT Press.

Foley, Douglas E. 1990. "The Great American Football Ritual: Reproducing Race, Class, and Gender Inequality." *Sociology of Sport Journal* 7:111–135.

Foucault, Michel. 1978. *The History of Sexuality: Volume I, An Introduction.* New York: Pantheon.

Frankenberg, Ruth. 1993. *White Women, Race Matters: The Social Construction of Whiteness.* Minneapolis: University of Minnesota Press.

Franklin, Clyde W. 1984. *The Changing Definition of Masculinity.* New York: Plenum.

———. 1986. Surviving the Institutional Decimation of Black Males: Causes, Consequences, and Intervention. Pp. 155–70 in *The Making of*

Masculinities: The New Men's Studies, edited by H. Brod. Winchester, MA: Alien and Unwin.

Fritner, M. P., and L. Rubinson. 1993. "Acquaintance Rape: The Influence of Alcohol, Fraternity Membership and Sports Team Membership." *Journal of Sex Education and Therapy* 19:272–284.

Gamson, Josh. 1995. "Must Identity Movements Self-Destruct?: A Queer Dilemma." *Social Problems* 42:390–407.

Gamson, William A., and Andre Modigliani. 1989. "Media Discourse and Public Opinion on Nuclear Power: A Constructionist Approach." *American Journal of Sociology* 95:1–37.

Gibbs, Jewelle T., ed. 1988. *Young, Black, and Male in America: An Endangered Species.* Dover, MA: Auburn House.

Gilligan, Carol. 1982. *In a Different Voice: Psychological Theory and Women's Development.* Cambridge: Harvard University Press.

Gitlin, Todd. 1979. "News as Ideology and Contested area: Toward a Theory of Hegemony, Crisis, and Opposition." *Socialist Review* 9:11–14.

———. 1980. *The Whole World Is Watching: Mass Media in the Making and Unmaking of the New Left.* Berkeley: University of California Press.

Goffman, Erving. 1974. *Frame Analysis.* New York: Harper and Row.

Goldman, Robert. 1983/1984, Winter. "We Make Weekends: Leisure and the Commodity Form." *Social Text* 8:84–103.

Goldman, Robert, and Stephen Papson. 1996. *Sign Wars: The Cluttered Landscape of Advertising.* New York: Guilford.

———. 1998. *Nike Culture: The Sign of the Swoosh.* Thousand Oaks, CA: Sage.

Goldstein, J. H., ed. 1983. Sports Violence. New York: Springer-Verlag.

———. 1984. Sports Violence. In *Sport in Contemporary Society,* edited by D. S. Eitzen. 2nd ed. New York: St. Martin's Press.

Gorn, Elliott J. 1986. *The Manly Art: Bare-Knuckle Prize Fighting in America.* Ithaca, NY: Cornell University Press.

Graydon, Jan. 1983, February. "'But It's More Than a Game. It's an Institution.' Feminist Perspectives on Sport." *Feminist Review* 13:5–16.

Gruneau, Richard. 1983. *Class, Sports, and Social Development.* Amherst: University of Massachusetts Press.

Gruneau, Richard, and David Whitson. 1994. *Hockey Night in Canada: Sport, Identities, and Cultural Politics.* Toronto: Garamond Press.

Hall, M. Ann. 1984. Toward a Feminist Analysis of Gender Inequality in Sport. Pp. 82–103 in *Sport and the Sociological Imagination*, edited by N. Theberge and P. Donnelly. Fort Worth: Texas Christian University Press.

———, ed. 1987. "The Gendering of Sport, Leisure, and Physical Education." *Women's Studies International Forum* 10:361–474.

Halley, Janet E. 1993. The Construction of Heterosexuality. Pp. 82–102 in *Fear of a Queer Planet: Queer Politics and Social Theory*, edited by M. Warner. Minneapolis: University of Minnesota Press.

Hansen, Karen V. 1992. 'Our Eyes Behold Each Other': Masculinity and Intimate Friendship in Antebellum New England. Pp. 35–58 in *Men's Friendships*, edited by P. M. Nardi. Newbury Park, CA: Sage Publications.

Hantover, Jeffrey. 1978. "The Boy Scouts and the Validation of Masculinity." *Journal of Social Issues* 341:184–195.

Hare, Nathan, and Julia Hare. 1984. *The Endangered Black Family: Coping with the Unisexualization and Coming Extinction of the Black Race.* San Francisco: Black Think Tank.

Hargreaves, Jennifer, ed. 1982. *Sport, Culture, and Ideology.* London: Routledge and Kegan Paul.

———. 1986. "Where's the Virtue? Where's the Grace? A Discussion of the Social Production of Gender through Sport." *Theory Culture and Society* 31:109–122.

Hargreaves, John 1986. *Sport, Power and Culture: A Social and Historical Analysis of Sports in Britain.* New York: St. Martin's Press.

Harris, D. S., and D. Stanley Eitzen. 1978. "The Consequences of Failure in Sport." *Urban Life* 7:177–188.

Hart, M. Marie. 1979. On Being Female in Sport. Pp. 24–34 in *Out of the Bleachers: Writings on Women and Sport*, edited by S. L. Twin. Old Westbury, NY: Feminist Press.

Hartmann, Heidi. 1976. "Capitalism, Patriarchy, and Job Segregation." *Signs* 13:366–394.

Haug, Frigga. 1987. *Female Sexualization: A Collective Work of Memory.* London: Verso.

Heywood, Leslie, and Jennifer Drake, Eds. 1997. *Third Wave Agenda: Being Feminist, Doing Feminism*. Minneapolis: University of Minnesota Press.

Hill, P., and B. Lowe. 1978. "The Inevitable Metathesis of the Retiring Athlete." *International Review of Sport Sociology* 9:5–29.

Hoch, Paul. 1972. *Rip Off the Big Game*. Garden City, NY: Doubleday.

———. 1979. *White Hero Black Beast: Racism, Sexism and the Mask of Masculinity*. London: Pluto Press.

Hochschild, Arlie Russell. 1994. "The Commercial Spirit of Intimate Life and the Abduction of Feminism: Signs from Women's Advice Books." *Theory, Culture and Society* 11:1–24.

Hogan, Candace L. 1979. Shedding Light on Title IX. Pp. 173–181 in *Out of the Bleachers: Writings on Women and Sport*, edited by S. L. Twin. Old Westbury, NY: Feminist Press.

———. 1982. "Revolutionizing School and Sports: Ten Years of Title IX. *Ms.*, May, pp. 25–29.

hooks, bell. 1984. *Feminist Theory: From Margin to Center*. Boston: South End Press.

———. 1990. Black Women and Men: Partnership in the 1990's. Pp. 203–214 in *Yearning: Race, Gender, and Cultural Politics*, edited by b. hooks. Boston: South End Press.

———. 1992. Reconstructing Black Masculinity. Pp. 87–114 in *Black Looks: Race and Representation*, edited by b. hooks. Boston: South End Press.

Horsefall, J. 1991. *The Presence of the Past: Male Violence in the Family*. Sydney, Australia: Allen and Unwin.

Hotaling, Gerald T., and David B. Sugarman. 1986. "An Analysis of Risk Markers in Husband to Wife Violence: The Current State of Knowledge." *Violence and Victims* 1:101–124.

Humphreys, Laud. 1971. *Tea Room Trade*. London: Duckworth.

Hunt, Darnell. 1999. *O. J. Simpson Facts and Fictions*. New York: Cambridge University Press.

Ingham, Alan G., and Peter Donnelly. 1990. "Whose Knowledge Counts? The Production of Knowledge and Issues of Application in the Sociology of Sport." *Sociology of Sport Journal* 7:58–65.

Ingraham, Chrys. 1994. "The Heterosexual Imaginary: Feminist Sociology and Theories of Gender." *Sociological Theory* 12:203–219.

Jacoby, Russell. 1987. *The Last Intellectuals: American Culture in the Age of Academe*. New York: Basic Books.

Jansen, Sue C., and Donald Sabo. 1994. "The Sport/War Metaphor: Hegemonic Masculinity, the Persian Gulf War, and the New World Order." *Sociology of Sport Journal* 11:1–17.

Jhally, Sut. 1984. "The Spectacle of Accumulation: Material and Cultural Factors in the Evolution of the Sports/Media Complex." *Insurgent Sociologist* 123:41–52.

Jordan, Ellen, and Angela Cowan. 1995. "Warrior Narratives in the Kindergarten Classroom: Renegotiating the Social Contract?" *Gender and Society* 9:727–743.

Kane, Mary Jo. 1995. "Resistance/Transformation of the Oppositional Binary: Exposing Sport as a Continuum." *Sociology of Sport Journal* 19:191.

Kane, Mary Jo, and Lisa J. Disch. 1993. "Sexual Violence and the Reproduction of Male Power in the Locker Room: The 'Lisa Olsen Incident'." *Sociology of Sport Journal* 10: 331–352.

Kane, Mary Jo, and Lenskyj, H. J. 1998. Media Treatment of Female Athletes: Issues of Gender and Sexualities. Pp. 186–201 in *MediaSport*, edited by L. A. Wenner. New York: Routledge.

Kantor, Glenda, and Murray A. Straus. 1987. "The 'Drunken Bum' Theory of Wife Beating." *Social Problems* 34:213–230.

Katz, Jonathan N. 1995. *The Invention of Heterosexuality*. New York: Button.

Kaufman, Michael. 1987. The Construction of Masculinity and the Triad of Men's Violence. Pp. 1–29 in *Beyond Patriarchy: Essays by Men on Pleasure, Power, and Change*, edited by M. Kaufman. Toronto: Oxford University Press.

Kessler, Suzanne J., and Wendy McKenna. 1978. *Gender: An Ethnomethodological Approach*. New York: John Wiley.

Kidd, Bruce. 1987. Sports and Masculinity. Pp. 250–265 in *Beyond Patriarchy: Essays by Men on Pleasure, Power, and Change*, edited by M. Kaufman. Toronto: Oxford University Press.

———. 1990. The Men's Cultural Centre: Sports and the Dynamic of Women's Oppression/Men's Repression. Pp. 31–42 in *Sport, Men and the Gender Order: Critical Feminist Perspectives*, edited by Michael A. Messner and Don F. Sabo. Champaign, IL: Human Kinetics.

Kimmel, Michael S. 1986. "Toward Men's Studies." *American Behavioral Scientist* 295:517–530.

———. 1987. "Men's Responses to Feminism at the Turn of the Century." *Gender and Society* 13:261–283.

———. 1995. *Manhood in America: A Cultural History.* New York: Free Press.

Klein, Melissa. 1997. Duality and Redefinition: Young Feminism and the Alternative Music Community. Pp. 207–225 in *Third Wave Agenda: Being Feminist, Doing Feminism*, edited by L. Heywood and J. Drake. Minneapolis: University of Minnesota Press.

Kolnes, Liv-Jorunn. 1995. "Heterosexuality as an Organizing Principle in Women's Sports." *International Review for the Sociology of Sport* 30:61–80.

Komisar, Lucy. 1980: "Violence and the Masculine Mystique." in *Jock*, edited by D. Sabo and R. Runfola. Englewood Cliffs, NJ: Prentice-Hall.

Koppett, Leonard. 1981. *Sports Illusion, Sports Reality.* Boston: Houghton Mifflin.

Koss, Mary P., and Thomas E. Dinero. 1988. "Predictors of Sexual Aggression among a National Sample of Male College Students." *Human Sexual Aggression: Current Perspectives. Annals of the New York Academy of Sciences* 528:133–146.

Koss, Mary, and John A. Gaines. 1993. "The Prediction of Sexual Aggression by Alcohol Use, Athletic Participation, and Fraternity Affiliation." *Journal of Interpersonal Violence* 81:94–108.

Kurz, Dorothy E. 1989. "Social Science Perspectives on Wife Abuse: Current Debates and Future Directions." *Gender and Society* 3:489–505.

Lakoff, Robin T., and Raquel L. Scherr. 1984. *Face Value: The Politics of Beauty.* Boston: Routledge and Kegan Paul.

Lasch, Christopher. 1979. *The Culture of Narcissism.* New York: Warner.

Lederman, Doug. 1992. "Blacks Make Up Large Proportion of Scholarship Athletes, Yet Their Overall Enrollment Lags at Division I Colleges." *Chronicle of Higher Education*, XXXVIII, A1. No. 41, June 17.

Lefkowitz, Bernard. 1997. *Our Guys.* New York: Vintage Books.

Lefkowitz-Horowitz, Helen. 1986, April. *Before Title IX.* Presented at Stanford Humanities Center Sport and Culture Meetings.

Leichliter, Jami S., Philip W. Meilman, Cheryl A. Presley, and Jeffrey R. Cashin. 1998. "Alcohol Use and Related Consequences among Students with Varying Levels of Involvement in College Athletics." *Journal of American College Health* 466:257–262.

Lemert, Charles. 1994. "Subjectivity's Limit: The Unsolved Riddle of the Standpoint." *Sociological Theory* 10:63–72.

Lenskyj, Helen. 1986. *Out of Bounds: Women, Sport, and Sexuality.* Toronto: Women's Press.

Leonard, W. M. II, and J. M. Reyman, 1988. "The Odds of Attaining Professional Athlete Status: Refining the Computations." *Sociology of Sport Journal* 5:162–169.

Lever, Janet. 1976. "Sex Differences in the Games Children Play." *Social Problems* 23:478–487.

Levinson, Daniel J. 1978. *The Seasons of a Man's Life.* New York: Ballantine.

Lipsitz, George. 1981. *Class and Culture in Cold War America: "A Rainbow at Midnight."* New York: Praeger.

———. 1998. *The Possessive Investment in Whiteness: How White People Profit from Identity Politics.* Philadelphia: Temple University Press.

Lopiano, Donna. 1992. "Quick Fix or Radical Surgery: Reform in College Athletics." Keynote address to the North American Society for the Sociology of Sport Meetings, Toledo, Ohio, November 5.

Lorber, Judith. 1994. *Paradoxes of Gender.* New Haven, and London: Yale University Press.

Lorenz, Konrad. 1966: *On Aggression.* New York: Harcourt Brace Jovanovich.

Lyman, Peter 1987. The Fraternal Bond as a Joking Relationship: A Case Study of Sexist Jokes in Male Group Bonding. Pp. 148–163 in *Changing Men: New Directions in Research on Men and Masculinity,* edited by M. S. Kimmel. Newbury Park, CA: Sage Publications.

Majors, Richard. 1986. "Cool Pose: The Proud Signature of Black Survival." *Changing Men: Issues in Gender, Sex, and Politics* 17:5–6.

———. 1990. "Cool Pose: Black Masculinity in Sports." In *Sport, Men, and the Gender Order: Critical Feminist Perspectives,* edited by M. A. Messner and D. S. Sabo. Champaign, IL: Human Kinetics.

Marcuse, Herbert. 1955. *Eros and Civilization: A Philosophical Inquiry into Freud.* Boston: Beacon Press.

Martin, Christopher R., and Jimmie L. Reeves. 2001. "The Whole World Isn't Watching but We Thought They Were: The Super Bowl and U.S. Solipsism." *Culture, Sport, and Society* 42:213–254.

May, Elaine Tyler. 1988. *Homeward Bound: American Families in the Cold War Era.* New York: Basic Books.

Mazur, A. 1984. "The Journalists and Technology: Reporting about Love Canal and Three Mile Island." *Minerva,* XXII:45–66.

McClelland, David C., William N. Davis, R. Kalin, and E. Wanner. 1972. *The Drinking Man.* New York: Free Press.

McCormack, Thelma. 1984: "Hollywood's Prizefight Films: Violence or 'Jock Appeal'?" *Journal of Sport and Social Issues*: 19–29.

McGuffy, C. Shawn, and B. Lindsay Rich. 1999. "Playing in the Gender Transgression Zone: Race, Class and Hegemonic Masculinity in Middle Childhood." *Gender and Society* 13:608–627.

McKay, Jim. 1986. "Marxism as a Way of Seeing: Beyond the Limits of Current 'Critical' Approaches to Sport." *Sociology of Sport Journal* 3:261–272.

Melnick, Merrill. 1992. "Male Athletes and Sexual Assault." *Journal of Physical Education, Recreation, and Dance* 635:32–35.

Messner, Michael A. 1985. "The Changing Meaning of Male Identity in the Lifecourse of the Athlete." *Arena Review,* 92, 31–60.

———. 1987a. The Life of a Man's Seasons: Male Identity in the Lifecourse of the Jock. Pp. 53–67 in *Changing Men: New Directions in Research on Men and Masculinity,* edited by M. S. Kimmel. Newbury Park, CA: Sage.

———. 1987b. The Meaning of Success: The Athletic Experience and the Development of Male Identity. Pp 193–209 in *The Making of Masculinities: The New Men's Studies,* edited by H. Brod. Boston: Allen and Unwin.

———. 1988. "Sports and Male Domination: The Female Athlete as Contested Ideological Terrain." *Sociology of Sport Journal* 5:197–121.

———. 1989: "Masculinities and Athletic Careers." *Gender and Society* 3:71–88.

———. 1992. *Power at Play: Sports and the Problem of Masculinity.* Boston: Beacon Press.

————. 1993. "'Changing Men' and Feminist Politics in the United States." *Theory and Society*, 22.

————. 1990. "When Bodies Are Weapons: Masculinity and Violence in Sport." *International Review for the Sociology of Sport* 90:203–220.

————. 1994. Gay Athletes and the Gay Games: An Interview with Tom Waddell. Pp. 113–119 in *Sex, Violence, and Power in Sports: Rethinking Masculinity*, edited by M. A. Messner and D. F. Sabo. Freedom: Crossing Press.

————. 2002. *Taking the Field: Women, Men, and Sports*. Minneapolis: University of Minnesota Press.

Messner, Michael A., Margaret C. Duncan, and Kerry Jensen. 1993. "Separating the Men from the Girls: The Gendered Language of Televised Sports." *Gender and Society* 7:121–137.

Messner, Michael A., and Donald Sabo, eds. 1990. *Sport, Men, and the Gender Order: Critical Feminist Perspectives*. Champaign, IL: Human Kinetics.

Messner, Michael A., and William S. Solomon. 1993. "Outside the Frame: Newspaper Coverage of the Sugar Ray Leonard Wife Abuse Story." *Sociology of Sport Journal* 10:119–134.

Miller, R., and S. Smith. 1992. "Up Against the Wall." *Sports Illustrated*, October 19, pp. 44–53.

Mills, Kay. 1988. *A Place in the News: From Women's Pages to the Front Page*. New York: Columbia University Press.

Mishkind, Mark E., J. Rodin, L. R. Silberstein, and R. H. Striegel-Moore. 1986. "The Embodiment of Masculinity: Cultural, Psychological, and Behavioral Dimensions." *American Behavioral Scientist* 29(5), May/June:531–540.

Molotch, Harvey, and Marilyn Lester. 1974. "News as Purposive Behavior: On the Strategic Use Routine Events, Accidents, and Scandals." *American Sociological Review* 39(1):101–112.

Moore, Robert A. 1966. *Sports and Mental Health*. Springfield, IL: Charles C Thomas.

Moraga, Cherrie, and Gloria Anzaldua. 1982. *This Bridge Called My Back*. New York: Persephone Press.

Morse, Margaret. 1983: Sport on Television: Replay and Display." Pp. 44–66 in *Regarding Television: Critical Approaches*, edited by E. A. Kaplan. Los Angeles: University Publications of America.

Naison, Mark. 1980. Sports, Women, and the Ideology of Domination. Pp. 30–36 in *Jock: Sports and Male Identity*, edited by D. Sabo and R. Runfola. Englewood Cliffs, NJ: Prentice-Hall.

Nelson, Mariah Burton. 1991. *Are We Winning Yet? How Women Are Changing Sports and Sports Are Changing Women*. New York: Random House.

———. 1995, October. "Breaking the Rules." *Women's Review of Books* XIII, 10.

Nixon, Howard L., II. 1997. "Gender, Sport, and Aggressive Behavior Outside Sport." *Journal of Sport and Social Issues* 21:379–391.

O'Donohoe, Stephanie. 1997. Leaky Boundaries: Intertextuality and Young Adult Experiences of Advertising. Pp. 257–275 in *Buy This Book: Studies in Advertising and Consumption*, edited by M. Nava, A. Blake, I. McRury, and B. Richards. London: Routledge.

Oriard, Michael. 1981. "Professional Football as Cultural Myth." *Journal of American Culture*, 4(3):27–41.

Peña, Manuel. 1991. "Class, Gender and Machismo: The 'Treacherous Woman' Folklore of Mexican Male Workers." *Gender and Society* 5:30–46.

Piaget, Jean. 1965. *The Moral Judgment of the Child*. New York: Free Press.

Pleck, Joseph H. 1982. *The Myth of Masculinity*. Cambridge: MIT Press.

Plummer, Kenneth. 1995. *Telling Sexual Stories: Power, Change and Social Worlds*. London and New York: Routledge.

Pope, Harrison G., Jr., Roberto Olivarda, Amanda Gruber, and John Borowiecki. 1999. "Evolving Ideals of Male Body Image as Seen through Action Toys." *International Journal of Eating Disorders* 26:65–72.

Postman, Neil, Christine Nystrom, Lance Strate, and Charlie Weingartner. 1987. *Myths, Men, and Beer: An Analysis of Beer Commercials on Broadcast Television, 1987*. Washington, DC: AAA Foundation for Traffic Safety.

Pronger, Brian. 1990a. *The Arena of Masculinity: Sports, Homosexuality, and the Meaning of Sex*. New York: St. Martin's Press.

———. 1990b. Gay Jocks: A Phenomenology of Gay Men in Athletics. Pp. 141–152 in *Sport, Men and the Gender Order: Critical Feminist Perspectives*, edited by M. A. Messner and D. F. Sabo. Champaign, IL: Human Kinetics.

————. 1994, November. *Body, Territory: Sport and the Art of Non–Fascist Living.* Paper delivered to the North American Society for the Sociology of Sport annual meeting in Savannah, Georgia.

Raag, Tarja, and Christine L. Rackliff. 1998. "Preschoolers' Awareness of Social Expectations of Gender: Relationships to Toy Choices." *Sex Roles* 38:685–700.

Rand, Erica. 1998. Older Heads on Younger Bodies. Pp. 382–393 in *The Children's Culture Reader*, edited by H. Jenkins. New York: New York University Press.

Reich, Wilhelm. 1972. *Sex-Pol Essays, 1929–1934.* New York: Vintage Books.

Reynaud, Emmanuel. 1981. *Holy Virility: The Social Construction of Masculinity.* London: Pluto Press.

Rich, Adrienne. 1980. "Compulsory Heterosexuality and the Lesbian Existence." *Signs: Journal of Women in Culture and Society* 54:631–661.

Rigauer, Bero. 1981. *Sport and Work.* New York: Columbia University Press.

Rinehart, Robert. 1998. "Inside of the Outside: Pecking Orders within Alternative Sport at ESPN's 1995 'The eXtreme Games.'" *Journal of Sport and Social Issues* 22:398–415.

Rintala, Jan, and Susan Birrell. 1984. "Fair Treatment for the Active Female: A Content Analysis of *Young Athlete* Magazine." *Sociology of Sport Journal* 1:231–250.

Risman, Barbara. 1998. *Gender Vertigo: American Families in Transition.* New Haven and London: Yale University Press.

Robinson, C. C., and J. T. Morris. 1986. "The Gender-Stereotyped Nature of Christmas Toys Received by 36-, 48-, and 60-Month-Old Children: A Comparison Between Nonrequested vs. Requested Toys." *Sex Roles* 15:21–32.

Rochlin, Martin. 1995. The Heterosexual Questionnaire. P. 405 in *Men's Lives*, edited by M. S. Kimmel and M. A. Messner. Boston: Allyn and Bacon.

Rogers, Mary F. 1999. *Barbie Culture.* Thousand Oaks, CA: Sage.

Rohrbaugh, JoAnna B. 1979, August. "Femininity on the Line." *Psychology Today*, pp. 31–33.

Rubin, Lillian B. 1982. *Intimate Strangers: Men and Women Together.* New York: Harper and Row.

————. 1985. *Just Friends: The Role of Friendship in Our Lives*. New York: Harper and Row.

Rudman, W. J. 1986. "The Sport Mystique in Black Culture." *Sociology of Sport Journal* 3:305–319.

Sabo, Donald F. 1985. "Sport, Patriarchy, and Male Identity: New Questions about Men and Sport." *Arena Review* 9:1–30.

————. 1986. "Pigskin, Patriarchy and Pain." *Changing Men: Issues in Gender, Sex and Politics* 16:24–25.

————. 1994. The Myth of the Sexual Athlete. Pp. 36–41 in *Sex, Violence and Power in Sport: Rethinking Masculinity*, edited by M. A. Messner and D. F. Sabo. Freedom, CA: Crossing Press.

Sabo, Donald F, Phil Gray, and Linda Moore. 2000. Domestic Violence and Televised Athletic Events: 'It's a man thing.' Pp. 127–146 in *Masculinities, Gender Relations, and Sport*, edited by J. McKay, D. Sabo, and M. A. Messner. Thousand Oaks, CA: Sage.

Sabo, Donald F., and Sue C. Jansen. 1992. Images of Men in Sport Media: The Social Reproduction of Masculinity. Pp. 169–184 in *Men, Masculinity, and the Media*, edited by S. Craig. Newbury Park, CA: Sage.

————. 1994. Seen but Not Heard: Images of Black Men in Sports Media. Pp. 150–160 in *Sex, Violence and Power in Sport: Rethinking Masculinity*, edited by M. A. Messner and D. F. Sabo. Freedom, CA: Crossing Press.

Sabo, Donald F., and Joe Panepinto. 1990. Football Ritual and the Social Production of Masculinity. Pp. 115–126 in *Sport, Men, and the Gender Order: Critical Feminist Perspectives*, edited by M. A. Messner and D. S. Sabo. Champaign, IL: Human Kinetics.

Sabo, Donald F., and Ross Runfola, eds. 1980. *Jock: Sports and Male Identity*. Englewood Cliffs, NJ: Prentice-Hall.

Saltzman Chafetz, Janet, and Joseph A. Kotarba. 1999. Little League Mothers and the Reproduction of Gender. Pp. 46–54 in *Inside Sports*, edited by J. Coakley and P. Donnelly. London and New York: Routledge.

Sanday, Peggy 1981. *Female Power and Male Dominance: On the Origins of Sexual Inequality*. New York: Cambridge University Press.

————. 1990. *Fraternity Gang Rape: Sex, Brotherhood and Privilege on Campus*. New York: New York University Press.

Schafer, W. E. 1975. "Sport and Male Sex Role Socialization." *Sport Sociology Bulletin* 4:47–54.

Scher, M., and Stevens, M. 1987. "Men and Violence." *Journal of Counseling and Development* 6:351–355.

Schneider, John, and Stanley D. Eitzen. 1983. "The Structure of Sport and Participant Violence." *Arena Review* 7(3):1–16.

Sedgewick, Eve K. 1990. *Epistemology of the Closet*. Berkeley: University of California Press.

Segal, Lynne. 1994. *Straight Sex: Rethinking the Politics of Pleasure*. Berkeley: University of California.

Seidman, Steven. 1993. Identity and Politics in a 'Postmodern' Gay Culture: Some Historical and Conceptual Notes. Pp. 105–142 in *Fear of a Queer Planet: Queer Politics and Social Theory*, edited by M. Warner. Minneapolis: University of Minnesota Press.

Seiter, Ellen. 1995. *Sold Separately: Parents and Children in Consumer Culture*. New Brunswick, NJ: Rutgers University Press.

Smith, Michael D. 1974: "Significant Other Influence on the Assaultive Behavior of Young Hockey Players." *International Review of Sport Sociology* 3(4):45–56.

———. 1986 "Reaction to 'Athletic Aggression: An Issue of Contextual Morality' by Bredemeier and Shields." Sociology of Sport Journal 3:62–64.

Smith, Robert A. 1970. "The Rise of Basketball for Women in Colleges." *Canadian Journal of History of Sport and Physical Education*, 1:21–23.

Smith, Yvonne R. 1992. "Women of Color in Society and Sport." *Quest*, 44:228–250.

Solomon, William S. 1992. "News Frames and Media Packages: Covering El Salvador." *Critical Studies in Mass Communication*, 9:56–74.

Sperber, Murray. 2000. *Beer and Circus: How Big-Time College Sports Is Crippling Undergraduate Education*. New York: Henry Holt.

Spigel, Lynn. 1992. *Make Room for TV: Television and the Family Ideal in Postwar America*. Chicago: University of Chicago Press.

———. 2001. Barbies without Ken: Femininity, Feminism, and the Art-Culture System. In *Welcome to the Dreamhouse: Popular Media and*

Postwar Suburbs, edited by L. Spigel. Durham, NC: Duke University Press.

Stacey, Judy, and Barrie Thorne. 1985. "The Missing Feminist Revolution in Sociology." *Social Problems*, 32(4):301–316.

Staples, Robert. 1982. *Black Masculinity*. San Francisco: Black Scholar Press.

———. 1992. Stereotypes of Black Masculinity: The Facts behind the Myths. Pp. 432–438 in *Men's Lives*, 2nd Ed., edited by M. S. Kimmel and M. A. Messner. New York: Macmillan.

Stein, Arlene, and Kenneth Plummer. 1994. "'I Can't Even Think Straight': Queer Theory and the Missing Sexual Revolution in Sociology." *Sociological Theory*, 12:178–187.

Stevens, Mark. 1993. College Men and Sexual Violation: Counseling Process and Programming Considerations. Pp. 239–258 in *Campus Violence: Kinds, Causes, and Cures*, edited by L. Whitaker and J. Pollard. Binghamton, NY: Haworth.

Strate, Lance. 1992. Beer Commercials: A Manual on Masculinity. Pp. 78–92 in *Men, Masculinity, and the Media*, edited by S. Craig. Newbury Park, CA: Sage.

Stuck, M. F. 1988. "Editor's Comment: Drugs and Sport." *Arena Review*, 12:i–iii.

Theberge, Nancy. 1987. "Sport and Women's Empowerment." *Women's Studies International Forum* 10:387–93.

———. 1989. "A Feminist Analysis of Responses to Sports Violence: Media Coverage of the 1989 World Junior Hockey Championship." *Sociology of Sport Journal*, 6(3):247–256.

Theberge, Nancy, and Alan Cronk. 1986. "Work Routines in Newspaper Sports Departments and the Coverage of Women's Sports." *Sociology of Sport Journal*, 3:195–203.

Thomas, David J. 1995. "The 'Q' Word." *Socialist Review*, 25(1):69–93.

Thorne, Barrie. 1993. *Gender Play: Girls and Boys in School*. New Brunswick, NJ: Rutgers University Press.

Tolson, Andrew. 1977. *The Limits of Masculinity: Male Identity and Women's Liberation*. New York: Harper and Row.

Trujillo, Nick. 1991. "Hegemonic Masculinity on the Mound: Media Representations of Nolan Ryan and American Sports Culture." *Critical Studies in Mass Communication*, 8:290–308.

———. 1995. "Machines, Missiles, and Men: Images of the Male Body on ABC's *Monday Night Football*." *Sociology of Sport Journal*, 12:403–423.

Twin, Stephanie L. 1979. *Out of the Bleachers: Writings on Women and Sport*. Old Westbury, NY: Feminist Press.

Underwood, John. 1979. *The Death of an American Game*. Boston: Little, Brown.

Vaz, Edmund W. 1980. The Culture of Young Hockey Players: Some Initial Observations. Pp. 142–157 in *Jock: Sports and Male Identity*, edited by D. F. Sabo and R. Runfola. Englewood Cliffs, NJ: Prentice-Hall.

Wallace, Maurice. 1978. *Black Macho and the Myth of the Super-Woman*. New York: Warner Books.

Walters, Suzanna Danuta. 1999. Sex, Text, and Context: In Between Feminism and Cultural Studies. Pp. 222–257 in *Revisioning Gender*, edited by M. Marx Ferree, J. Lorber, and B. B. Hess. Thousand Oaks, CA: Sage.

———. 2001. *All the Rage: The Story of Gay Visibility in America*. Chicago: University of Chicago Press.

Ward, Steven. 1995. "The Revenge of the Humanities: Reality, Rhetoric, and the Politics of Postmodernism." *Sociological Perspectives*, 38(2):109–128.

Warner, Michael, ed. 1993. *Fear of a Queer Planet: Queer Politics and Social Theory*. Minneapolis: University of Minnesota Press.

Warshaw, Robin. 1988. *I Never Called It Rape*. New York: Harper and Row.

Wellman, David. 1986. "The New Political Linguistics of Race." *Socialist Review* 87/88:43–62.

Wenner, Lawrence A. 1991. One Part Alcohol, One Part Sport, One Part Dirt, Stir Gently: Beer Commercials and Television Sports. Pp. 388–407 in *Television Criticism: Approaches and Applications*, edited by L. R. Vande Berg and L. A. Wenner. New York: Longman.

———. 1998. In Search of the Sports Bar: Masculinity, Alcohol, Sports, and the Mediation of Public Space. Pp. 303–32 in *Sport and Postmodern Times*, edited by G. Rail. Albany: State University of New York Press.

West, Candace, and Don Zimmerman. 1987. "Doing Gender." *Gender and Society* 1:125–151.

Weston, Kath. 1991. *Families We Choose: Lesbians, Gays, Kinship.* New York: Columbia University Press.

Whannel, Gary. 1998. Reading the Sports Media Audience. Pp. 221–232 in *MediaSport*, edited by L. A. Wenner. New York: Routledge.

Wheaton, Belinda, and Alan Tomlinson. 1998. "The Changing Gender Order in Sport? The Case of Windsurfing Subcultures." *Journal of Sport and Social Issues*, 22:252–274.

Whitson, D. 1990. Sport and the Social Construction of Masculinity. Pp. 19–30 in *Sport, Men and the Gender Order: Critical Feminist Perspectives*, edited by M. A. Messner and D. F. Sabo. Champaign, IL: Human Kinetics.

Wilkinson, Rupert. 1984. *American Tough: The Tough Guy Tradition in American Character.* New York: Harper and Row.

Williams, Christine. 1993. Psychoanalytic Theory and the Sociology of Gender. Pp. 131–49 in *Theory on Gender, Gender on Theory*, edited by Paula England. New York: Aldine.

Willis, Paul. 1982. Women in Sport in Ideology. Pp. 117–135 in *Sport, Culture, and Ideology*, edited by J. Hargreaves. London: Routledge and Kegan Paul.

Wilson, William J. 1987. *The Truly Disadvantaged.* Chicago: University of Chicago Press.

Wilson, William J., and Kathryn M. Neckerman. 1986. Poverty and Family Structure: The Widening Gap Between Evidence and Public Policy Issues. Pp. 232–259 in *Fighting Poverty*, edited by S. H. Danzinger and D. H. Weinberg. Cambridge: Harvard University Press.

Wittig, Monique. 1992. *The Straight Mind: And Other Essays.* Boston: Beacon Press.

Wojciechowski, G., and C. Dufresne. 1988: "Football Career Is Taking Its Toll on NFL's Players." *Los Angeles Times* June 26. Section lll, pp. 1, 12–13.

Wood, Julian 1984. Groping Toward Sexism: Boys' Sex Talk. Pp. 54–84 in *Gender and Generation*, edited by A. McRobbie and M. Nava. London: Macmillan.

Woodward, S. 1985, November 5. "Women Alter Outlook on Sports: Attitude Is Positive in Survey." *USA Today*, p. 1A.

Yiannakis, Andrew. 1989. "Toward an Applied Sociology of Sport: The Next Generation." *Sociology of Sport Journal*, 6:1–16.

Young, Kevin, and Philip White. 2000. "Researching Sports Injury: Reconstructing Dangerous Masculinities." In *Masculinities and Sport: Difference, Discontinuity, and Disruption*, edited by J. McKay, D. F. Sabo, and M. A. Messner. Thousand Oaks: Sage Publications.

Zaretsky, Eli. 1973. *Capitalism, the Family, and Personal Life*. New York: Harper Colophon Books.

Zimbalist, Andrew. 1999. *Unpaid Professionals: Commercialism and Conflict in Big-Time College Sports*. Princeton: Princeton University Press.

Index

7731

Ralph C. Wilcox, David L. Andrews, Robert Pitter, and Richard L. Irwin (eds.), *Sporting Dystopias: The Making and Meanings of Urban Sport Cultures.*

Robert E. Rinehart and Synthia Sydnor (eds.), *To the Extreme: Alternative Sports, Inside and Out.*

Eric Anderson, *In the Game: Gay Athletes and the Cult of Masculinity.*

Pirkko Markula (ed.), *Feminist Sport Studies: Sharing Experiences of Joy and Pain.*

Murray G. Phillips (ed.), *Deconstructing Sport History: A Postmodern Analysis.*

Alan Tomlinson and Christopher Young (eds.), *National Identity and Global Sports Events: Culture, Politics, and Spectacle in the Olympics and the Football World Cup.*

Caroline Joan S. Picart, *From Ballroom to DanceSport.*